THE MURDER OF HERODES

KATHLEEN FREEMAN received MA and D. Litt degrees from University College, Cardiff, Wales, and was for many years lecturer in Greek there.

She published a dozen studies in Greek history and literature, some thirty novels and detective stories, several children's books, and many other volumes.

# THE
# MURDER *of* HERODES

### AND
### OTHER TRIALS FROM THE
### ATHENIAN LAW COURTS

*by*

# KATHLEEN FREEMAN

Hackett Publishing Company, Inc.
Indianapolis/Cambridge

Copyright © 1963 by W. W. Norton & Company, Inc.
Copyright renewed 1991 by Liliane Clopet

All rights reserved
Printed in the United States of America

00  99  98  97  96  95  94        1  2  3  4  5  6  7

For further information, please address

Hackett Publishing Company, Inc.
P.O. Box 44937
Indianapolis, Indiana 46244-0937

Cover design adapted from original
design by Robert Hagenhofer


ISBN 0-87220-306-9 paperbound
ISBN 0-87220-307-7 clothbound
Library of Congress Catalog Card Number: 94-072804


The paper used in this publication meets the minimum requirements of
American National Standard for Information Sciences—Permanence of
Paper for Printed Library Materials, ANSI Z39.48-1984.

# CONTENTS

# CONTENTS

# I

## INTRODUCTORY

EVERY trial is a drama. No matter who are the persons involved, whether important or obscure; no matter what is at stake, whether a man's life or merely the possession of a plot of land or a sum of money: there is a struggle which is of absorbing interest to the actors, and a decision to be taken which closely affects them. In the law-courts of any country and any age, human nature as it really is, not as we would like it to be, is clearly and minutely revealed: the passions of men, their hopes, desires and fears, their baseness and occasionally their nobility. Selfishness, cruelty, avarice, lust, darken the picture; but to cheer us we have the gleam of courage, and above all the presiding genius of Justice, the desire to live and make others live harmoniously together; and Law, the instrument by which all social progress is achieved.

It is therefore no mere interest in a dead past that makes us turn to a study of any nation's law-courts and the business that came before them. It is essential to our understanding of that people and that society, and will add something to our knowledge of human nature as a whole. In studying these trials from the law-courts of ancient Athens, we find several additional appeals to our interest. Foremost should be placed the brilliancy of the period itself: this little City-State, which produced so many of civilization's highest gifts in politics, poetry, science, history, architecture and the whole art of living, rose to the height of its prosperity, and fell into dependence, during the period that is covered by the lives of the speakers represented in this book. But apart from this general consideration, there are at least two others which give these trials a special value, and claim for them a wider attention than that of scholars only.

In the first place, they are a corrective to the sentimental idea that everybody in ancient Hellas was absorbed in the quest for Truth and Beauty. Athens had no newspaper reports. These speeches, embodying true stories from the lives of ordinary men and women, give us a background to which we can relate the

9

achievement of the great poets, Aeschylus, Sophocles, Euripides ; the great statesmen, Aristeides and Pericles ; the great thinkers, Socrates, Plato and Aristotle ; through a knowledge of this background we can better understand the material with which the statesmen had to deal, the audiences for which the dramatists wrote, the society about which the philosophers generalized and which they wished to reform ; and so we can better assess the amazing quality of their work. More people would be drawn to the study of the classics, with the greatest pleasure and profit to themselves, if they realized that the average Athenian was not a superman with his eyes turned all day long to the Parthenon and his mind to Absolute Goodness, but a busy citizen, concerned with running his household, controlling his wife and children, making money, exercising his vote, insisting on his legal rights, and other mundane matters. They were an energetic, lively, quarrelsome little community, not demigods but flesh and blood like ourselves.

Incidentally, when the truth is revealed about them we may lose something of the ideal quality of the more sentimental picture, but we can take to ourselves a little credit for a progress which modern historians tell us has not been made in the intervening centuries. However far from perfect the world may be today, the fact is that in ancient Athens, that is, in the highest civilization achieved in the ancient world, there were practices tolerated, accepted as a matter of course, and even legalized, which are not permitted either by law or by public opinion in the most highly civilized states today. These practices do occur, as we know to our cost ; but—and this is the point—they are no longer universally defended in principle, nor allowed to be openly practised, nor left unpunished in the end. This represents a progress, slow historically, but as far as can be seen, definite, in the social conscience of the world's intellectual vanguard ; and sooner or later the rest must follow. I refer in particular, not only to the institution of slavery, but to such legal provisions as the regular torturing of slaves for evidence in cases in which their owners were involved ; and the legal right of an injured husband to kill the adulterer caught in the act.

In the second place, the forensic speeches which have come down to us not only embody true stories and actual characters ; they happen to be works of art. This has come about owing to that provision in the Athenian legal code by which in any law-suit the principals were obliged to deliver their speeches to the jury in person; no hiring of an advocate to speak for one was permitted. The result of this stipulation was that men who lacked self-confidence or experience or the ability to compose a speech were driven to getting an expert to do this for them; and so the profession of Logographos, Speechwriter, grew up in Athens in the fifth century B.C. Men who seldom or never appeared on a public platform made fortunes by writing speeches for clients, and running schools where the arts of composition and delivery were taught; and so it came about that elegant phrases and subtle arguments dropped from the lips of farmers and business men who were rich enough to buy these goods from men cleverer than themselves. The best speechwriters considered the character of the client when composing the speech for him to deliver; and the result is a dramatic monologue in the first person. In particular, there is a section of every speech called the Narrative, in which the speaker puts the facts of the case before the jury. Some of these are models in the art of story-telling: the tale of the seduction of Euphiletus's wife, for instance, and the tale of Lysias's escape from his captors, are among the world's best short stories; but because they occur as part of a forensic speech, they have not been recognized as early examples of this art—an art of which the Greeks were as much masters as they were of the lyric, the epic and the drama.

The law-suits chosen have been divided according to the nature of the cause being tried. There are four cases of MURDER, and three cases of VIOLENCE. Under the heading of PROPERTY have been grouped four diverse cases, concerning legacies, a claim for damages, and a contested right to a State pension. The Athenian law-courts were not troubled with divorce-suits: no legal process was necessary for a divorce, whether sought by the husband or the wife. If the husband wished to get rid of his wife, he sent her back to her own family, having declared his decision before witnesses; if a wife was dissatisfied with her husband, she left him and returned to the custody of her own nearest male relative. In certain circumstances, divorce was compulsory, being prescribed by law. Disputes, however, might arise in connection with the wife's maintenance, the disposal of any property, or the legality of the marriage itself, which involved the legitimacy of children; the case given under the heading MARRIAGE belongs to the last kind.

The Athenians had one very important class of trial which we are happily without : the indictment for sacrilege. This was a very serious matter : it could involve the death penalty, or banishment with confiscation of property. It was often used for political reasons, to rouse the passions of the mob against a person of whom some party or clique wished to get rid. The scientist Anaxagoras was indicted for having taught that the sun and moon are not deities but a red-hot mass and a stone respectively; but the real reason for the attack was that he was the friend and *protégé* of the prime minister Pericles. Fortunately his powerful patron shipped him away before the trial could take place. Socrates was indicted for teaching strange religious doctrines and corrupting the young men; he not only refused to avoid trial by going into exile as his friends would have wished, but he also insisted on accepting the death sentence pronounced by the jury, although his escape could easily have been arranged. His Defence, written by Plato, is one of the most moving documents in the world; but it is not included here because it is not the actual speech delivered at the trial. Socrates employed no speechwriter, but relied on himself, and enjoyed the opportunity of giving the jury a plain statement of his views. His Defence is therefore a version of the speech he made, but not a verbatim version : it was written up afterwards by Socrates's most brilliant disciple and admirer. The speech given under the heading RELIGION in this book deals with the more banal but still poignant defence of a farmer against a charge of having uprooted a sacred olive-tree.

The last speech, under the heading SLANDER, was written for delivery not before a law-court but before a private gathering; but since it is connected with a law-suit, it has been included because of its interest.

The fifteen cases in this book have been chosen for their human interest and the skill of their presentation, not for their historical or political importance; hence the preponderance of the speeches of Lysias over those of Demosthenes. It has always seemed to the present writer a pity that the exquisite art of Lysias should be so little known, except among classical scholars. His genius was appreciated in antiquity, even by the Romans, who might have been expected to admire Demosthenes' force and his concern with matters of high moment to the exclusion of Lysias' subtlety and charm. Even among students of Greek, in schools and universities, the speeches of Lysias are not read often enough, with the exception of the great speech against Eratosthenes; but the speeches written for lesser causes are gems of their kind, and unlike the public orations of Demosthenes, do not need an acquaintance with the somewhat tedious intricacies of Athenian politics for their understanding and appreciation.

One admission must be made: in none of the trials that follow is the verdict known, and in only one or two of them can it be even guessed at. This is tantalizing; and since we have in each case the speech of one side only, defence or prosecution, all speculation on the result is inconclusive. The reader can, however, generally deduce from the speech of the prosecution what is likely to be argued by the defence; and from the speech of the defence, what has been alleged by the prosecution. There are also indications, which a knowledge of the methods of these speechwriters soon makes easy to detect, pointing to a weak or a strong case. By following these, some idea of the actual merits of the case can be arrived at; but no man, even with the whole of the depositions before him, could ever have predicted which way the Athenian jury-court would go; nor can one guess today at their decision. The answer to every one of these burning problems is lost; and with that we must remain satisfied, or dissatisfied.

# II

## LEGAL CODE AND PROCEDURE

THE legal code of Athens, very complicated and exact in historical times, had its origin in a remote past of custom and tradition. In the days of monarchy, the king was supreme judge in peace and war; but when the government passed from the hands of a hereditary monarchy into those of the nobles, the king's power of jurisdiction passed with all his other powers to the supreme Council of State, which met on the low rocky hill called the Areopagus. Some of the powers of jurisdiction were vested in magistrates, who all had to be of the noble class; and the law they administered was the old law of custom (the Greek word for 'law', *nomos*, means 'custom') which had grown up with the community and had been altered and added to as circumstances required, but which had never been fixed or codified or written down or even published. Knowledge of it was believed to belong by divine dispensation first to the king, and then to the aristocracy of birth, the heads of the chief families. Such a law, devised and administered by the ruling class, was bound to be one-sided; and when in addition the common people did not know exactly what the laws were except by tradition and observation, there was bound to be great hardship and injustice.

In the seventh century B.C., economic distress in Athens and the neighbourhood brought popular discontent to a climax. A great increase in commerce brought greater prosperity to the already wealthy and powerful, and greater poverty to the poor. The inequality between the classes became glaring; and in particular it was seen how severely the administration of the law bore upon the common people. Their discontent gave an ambitious adventurer his chance. In 630 B.C. a nobleman named Cylon, who had married the daughter of a neighbouring ruler, endeavoured to establish himself as dictator in Athens. He actually seized the Acropolis with the help of foreign troops sent by his father-in-law; but the time was not ripe. The people, especially the farmers, would not rise against the governing class, and the attempt was a failure.

Cylon himself escaped; but his supporters were starved out and eventually slaughtered in cold blood by the authorities. However, the nobles were alarmed; and in 621 B.C. they made a great concession: they appointed one of their own class to draw up for the first time a written code of the existing law.

This was the famous code of DRACON. The Athenians had a saying that the laws of Dracon were written not in ink but in blood. It was found that the penalty for almost all offences was death, no distinction being made between those who stole fruit or vegetables, and those who robbed a temple or murdered a man. The adjective 'Draconian' is still used of harsh and cruel laws; but this is unfair to Dracon. He did not invent these laws; he merely collected and recorded the current practice. However, once the laws were written down, it could no longer be denied how harsh they were, and reform could not long be delayed.

The man chosen for the work of revision was SOLON, one of the greatest law-givers of all time. He was appointed in 594 B.C., as Chief Magistrate with extraordinary powers, for one year only, and was asked to reform the whole constitution of Athens, including the administration of justice and the legal code. He was a man of aristocratic family, who had travelled and had also engaged in commerce; by great good fortune he was the very man they needed, for he was born with the principle of Justice in his soul. He carried out his work with commendable fairness and thoroughness, and fully earned the title of Mediator which was bestowed upon him. His new constitution, intended to give a fair share of power to all classes, did not survive and did not end class warfare; but he cured the worst of the people's troubles by abolishing all debts contracted on the security of personal freedom and so saving many from enslavement and exile; he also restored all mortgaged land. His greatest and most enduring gift to the Athenian people was his new legal code and new law-courts. This was the system, with certain necessary changes, which was used throughout the whole of the three succeeding centuries; under it Athens grew to be an imperial power, and the Romans themselves, when compiling their own legal code, the Twelve Tables, sent a commission to Athens in 454 B.C. to examine the laws of Solon.

This, then, was the system in force at the time when our law-suits were heard. What were the courts before which these trials came ? Solon retained the old Court of the Areopagus, now denuded of almost all political power, as a law-court; he continued to allow it and its subdivisions to try cases of bloodshed. But it ceased to be recruited from the aristocracy. Under his constitutional reforms, it was recruited from ex-magistrates, and as he decreed that the qualification for all offices of state should be annual income, not birth, it was virtually open to all citizens. In time, when the property-qualification also was swept away, the Court of the Areopagus became, like all the other government institutions, a purely democratic body; so that by the time our speeches were delivered, the jurisdiction in cases of homicide, like everything else, had passed into the hands of the people. The Court of the Areopagus, meeting in the open air on the same hillside, always retained the right to try cases of alleged intentional homicide, intentional wounding, or arson, in accordance with the law. Subdivisions of this court, meeting elsewhere, tried other cases of bloodshed, as in ancient times. When trying cases of alleged involuntary homicide, the court met in a building called the Palladion. If there was a plea of justification, another building, the Delphinion, was used. In certain rare cases, when a man who had been found guilty of manslaughter and punished with exile was later accused of another murder, the court met on the seashore at a spot called Phreatto ; the defendant was not allowed to land on his native soil, but the court, it is said, heard him pleading from a boat. There was an even more remarkable survival from antiquity : when an animal or an inanimate object such as a tile or a weapon was said to have caused the death of a man, a special trial was held in the Prytaneion or City Hall, and the creature or object, if found guilty, was condemned and taken away to be flung over the borders of Attica. These are all archaic survivals ; their source is the belief that the man or object which sheds human blood is polluted, and will bring, by contact, actual pollution on the rest of the community. This was why the Court of the Areopagus met in the open air : so that members of the Court, and the prosecutors, should not run the risk of being under the same roof with one guilty of homicide, even involuntary ; for blood-pollution, according to orthodox belief, was as dangerous as a contagious disease and could have most serious consequences to persons and States. In fact, even if acquired only by contact, it had to be purged by elaborate ritual exercises, as a disease is expelled from the body by medicine.

Apart from homicide and allied causes, the bulk of the work of jurisdiction came before the popular jury-courts. Solon was the first to institute a jury-court, called the Heliaea; this was open to all citizens, and was chosen by lot from the citizen-body. He intended it to hear appeals against the sentences pronounced by magistrates; but it very rapidly developed into the supreme judicial power in the State, and all cases except those of bloodshed and arson came before it. By the time that our speeches were delivered—two centuries later, more or less—the immense panel of jurymen (six thousand) was divided into bodies of different sizes according to the particular cases with which they had to deal. Their size is one of the most remarkable features about them: an Athenian jury for an important case would number five hundred and one members, and could be as many as two thousand. In the fifth and fourth centuries before Christ, they were not only chosen by lot from the whole body of adult male citizens: they were paid. Their verdict was given by a majority-vote. It was usual to arrange that an odd number should be present; but if by chance the voting was equal, the defendant was acquitted. The verdict of the jury's vote was final: there was no appeal from it to a higher court. A magistrate or some official presided; but he had no power to direct the jury or to pronounce judgment. In most cases the penalty was prescribed by law; but if there was any choice of alternatives, the prosecution could propose one penalty, and the defendant another; the result was again decided by taking a vote of the jury. This happened in the trial of Socrates. After he had been voted guilty, the question of the penalty arose. The prosecution proposed death. Socrates, when asked for his suggestion, amazed the jury, who were used to appeals for mercy, by saying that his true reward would be maintenance in the City Hall, because he was a benefactor and a poor man who needed leisure to carry on his work; but if they did not see eye to eye with him, he did not mind paying a small sum of money, which, as he could not afford it himself, would be contributed by his friends. The jury voted for the death-penalty; and so with a few final words to them on the nature of death and the reasons why men should not fear it, Socrates went his way, remarking: " Which of us, you or I, is going to the better fate, is unknown to all except God."

The Athenian jury-court, therefore, owing to its composition, its size, and its manner of functioning, was not, like our own jury, a handful of men ignorant of the law, presided over by an expert, addressed by experts, and with its powers strictly circumscribed. To come before it was like addressing a public meeting; and feeling very often ran high. In the speeches that have come down to us, it is common to find the litigant appealing to the jury "not to raise a din," or "not to shout me down." The art of playing on the jury's feelings of pity and vanity by every possible means was taught in the schools of rhetoric. It was customary for defendants to bring their small children into court and to shed tears; the best people considered this to be shameful and undignified, but it was often done, so that it must have been effective. The jurymen took a solemn oath, said to have been instituted by Solon, that they would hear both sides impartially; but the atmosphere did not conduce to judicial calm; and it was also possible to use bribery. This abuse reached such proportions that at the end of the fifth century B.C. elaborate arrangements were made to prevent jurors from knowing to which court they would be allotted on any given day until just before the trial opened. Intimidation was also practised; and the new arrangements included a complicated scheme for ensuring the secrecy of the ballot, which was done by placing pebbles or other tokens into urns. The ordinary courts met in buildings which were mostly in or near the Agora or market-place. The buildings have perished without leaving a trace, but some of the names of the courts have come down to us: the Middle Court, the Greater Court, the Red Court, the Green Court, and others. The atmosphere of the Areopagus Court was calmer and more dignified than that of the ordinary courts, and the oath its members swore was more solemn, invoking destruction on them and theirs if they did not judge fairly.

The legal code administered in all courts was the code of Solon, together with such alterations and additions as time had made necessary and the supreme Assembly of the People decreed. The Athenians were chary of altering their laws; it had been one of Solon's principles that the law should remain unaltered, so that the whole structure should not be weakened or brought into contempt. When new legislation was proposed, a State official was appointed to defend the existing law; and there were severe

18

penalties for proposing laws which were contrary to the existing code. Alterations did of course occur; ambiguities arose with the passage of time, for instance in Solon's testamentary law, which was giving much work to the jury-courts two and a half centuries later, in Aristotle's day; and several times a complete revision was made. But on the whole the great code stood firm; its archaic wording was appealed to and quoted and argued upon in the courts, and its provisions always remained the basis of all legal administration in the Athenian State.

This brings us to the actual laws. In this chapter I shall set forth only those of which a knowledge is necessary for the understanding of the cases that follow. One or two general principles must first be stated.

To begin with, there was no public prosecutor. The State took no cognizance of any crimes, not even murder, unless committed against itself: that is to say, the State did not prosecute for offences now commonly regarded as committed against the community, but only for offences against the actual administration, such as treason or cheating the public treasury. Until Solon's day, prosecution was allowed only to the person injured or his next of kin; under Solon's reforms, any citizen who wished could bring an indictment against another, except in cases of homicide, where the right of prosecution was left as before in the hands of the relatives of the deceased. The penalty imposed was, however, executed by the State, which had its prisons under the administration of annually-chosen officers called The Eleven; these officials also supervised the infliction of the death-penalty, usually the merciful method of giving the condemned man a fatal dose of hemlock. The State also watched over the rights of certain unprotected persons, the care of whom was allotted to certain magistrates, as for instance, wards unjustly treated by their guardians; and the Court of the Areopagus was supposed to exercise a general supervision over public morals.

Another point to remember is that only free male citizens of full Athenian parentage on both sides could address the courts; women could not plead, and had to be represented by their guardian —husband, father, eldest son or other male relative. A slave, though he could not plead, could not be put to death by his master without a decree of a jury-court. There were special courts for foreigners.

Thirdly, one must always bear in mind that the litigants had each to conduct his own case : no hired lawyer was allowed in court or at the preliminary inquiries. Since, however, cross-examination of witnesses was not allowed in court, this stipulation was not such a hardship as at first appears. Each side had merely to make a speech, and bring forward his own witnesses to support him at the relevant points.

### HOMICIDE

The following is a statement of the laws on bloodshed, laws retained by Solon from Dracon's code :

The intentional murder, or wounding with intent to kill, of a citizen, was tried before the Court of the Areopagus. Wilful murder was punished by death, which however could be avoided if the defendant chose to take flight rather than continue the case after the first day. Wounding with intent to kill was punished by banishment and confiscation of property.

Unintentional homicide could be punished by temporary banishment. The offender might return earlier than the prescribed date if he could propitiate the relatives, or when there were no relatives, the clansmen of the deceased. These cases came before the Court of the Palladion.

Intentional homicide with plea of justification came before the Court of the Delphinion. The law allowed the slaughter of an adulterer caught in the act, or of a night robber.

Cases of assault, where no intention to kill was alleged, came before the ordinary courts.

### TESTAMENTARY LAW

The testamentary law was in broad outline as follows :

If a man had legitimate male issue, his property on his death passed automatically to them and was divided equally between them, the eldest having priority of choice though not a larger share. It was the duty of the sons to maintain the widow, and to provide suitable dowries for the daughters, if any.

If there were no sons, the testator was allowed to choose his heir. This was one of Solon's innovations ; previously the property, in default of male children, passed to the next of kin. However, the freedom of the testator was restricted; the object of the law was not to give him liberty to indulge in a personal fancy, but to ensure that the property was kept whenever possible " in the household." The testator therefore chose an heir; but he was obliged to adopt this man as his son, and the adopted son was obliged to marry one of the daughters, if any. This couple then raised up children to continue the testator's line. The adopted son counted as the legal descendant of the testator, and lost all rights of inheritance or bequest in his own family; he could not bequeath, either, the property which he had acquired by marrying the testator's daughter, but merely held it in trust for their children. As for the daughter, she did not even hold it in trust: she "went with" the property, as the law phrases it; a woman could not own property in Athens. A woman in this position, that is, the daughter of a man who owned property but who died without male issue, was called *Epikléros*, a word usually translated " heiress ", but actually meaning " appendage to property." The person chosen to marry her was generally a near relative. Such adoption of an heir, in default of male issue, was the only form of will permitted, apart from personal wishes expressed by the deceased regarding the way in which the property was to be divided among the recognized heirs, and so on.

If the deceased died without male issue and without adopting a son and heir, the property passed to the next of kin according to recognized principles. If he left daughters, it was the right of the nearest male relative or relatives to marry them and so acquire the dowry. If there was no property or only a small one, the nearest male relative was obliged to marry the portionless girl, being permitted to divorce his own wife if he had one; the only alternative was to provide her with a dowry out of his own means. The so-called " heiresses " were the special wards of the Chief Magistrate or Archon Eponymus. The law laid down by Solon contained many obscurities and gave rise to much litigation, as when there was a large property and no " will " had been made—that is, no heir had been adopted—the right to marry the daughter or daughters and acquire the property that went with them was sometimes contested by several claimants.

The right to a share in the property was often contested on the score of the claimant's illegitimacy. To prove his legitimacy, he had to prove that his father and mother were full Athenians by birth. Marriage of an Athenian to a foreigner was illegal and the children were illegitimate, under a law proposed by Pericles: by "foreigner" was meant any non-Athenian, even if Greek. Pericles himself lived with Aspasia, who was not only Greek and highly-cultivated, but came from Miletus, an old colony of Athens; yet by Pericles' own proposal she ranked as a foreigner and could not be his legal wife. To live with a foreign woman and pretend that she was one's legal wife was a punishable offence; there was, however, no penalty for mere cohabitation, though it might render a man ineligible for certain offices. A marriage had to have been properly conducted before witnesses; it was useful if one could produce witnesses who had been present at the festivities. A child had to have been formally accepted by the father at birth if it was to be accepted by the State as legitimate; and about seven days after the birth, a ceremony took place called *Amphidromia* (Running round), when the baby was carried by the father or nurse round the family altar, and received its name. Finally, the child had to be registered: its name was early entered as a member of its father's clan, and a boy in his eighteenth year was enrolled as a member of his father's locality or deme, as these divisions of Attica were called. The full designation of an Athenian citizen was therefore his own name, his father's name, and the name of his deme, the place on whose roll he was registered; these were his titles to legitimacy. Sometimes, even if these titles could be shown, it was alleged that there had been tampering with the registers—that some local official had been bribed to insert the name of a person of partly foreign birth, whose children were really illegitimate. This would be for a court of law to decide after a careful investigation of the evidence.

On all these grounds, legacies could be contested. There was even a clause in Solon's law decreeing that the testator without male issue could adopt a male heir " unless by reason of attacks of madness, or old age, or disease, or under the influence of a woman, he be out of his mind, or be under constraint of violence or bondage." These words afforded endless opportunity for litigation; indeed, at one time, under the brief rule of the Thirty Tyrants, they were repealed, but came into force again after the overthrow of that short-lived government and the restoration of the full democracy.

If the children of the deceased were under age at the time of their father's death, their care and the care of their inheritance passed to the nearest male relative, such as a brother of the deceased. Sometimes these guardians used the opportunity to embezzle the money of their wards, so that the legacy had evaporated before the children were entitled to enter into possession. This happened to Demosthenes himself: his guardians squandered the handsome property left to him by his father, and ignored the wishes of the deceased. When Demosthenes came of age, his first act was to bring an action against the fraudulent guardians; but though he won his case, the property was lost, so that he was obliged to take up work as a professional speechwriter in order to make money. Thus began the career of this great orator.

## MARRIAGE

Marriage was permitted between closer degrees of kin than with us; for instance, an uncle could marry a niece, and a half-brother his half-sister if the parent they had in common was the father; half-brothers and half-sisters by the same mother could not marry.

Marriage was carefully protected against adultery. A woman found guilty of adultery had to be divorced by her husband, and the adulterer could be killed if caught with the wife. Adultery by a husband, though unaccompanied by cruelty, was regarded as a sufficient reason for his wife's leaving him if she wished to do so. These regulations protected the legitimacy of children and the descent of property within the family; the Chief Archon kept a record of divorces. Prostitution in itself was not penalized; but the procuring of a free youth or woman was visited with severe penalties, and serious irregularity of life could mean loss of citizenship. The law recognized concubinage: the children of a concubine were not legitimate, but if she herself and the father were Athenians and free, the children of the union were free also. The violation of a free Athenian woman was punishable by a fine of one hundred drachmas (about £20); but as she never left the house except on certain specified occasions, and when at home lived in her own quarters and never met any males except her husband and her relatives, custom protected her even more powerfully than the law. On the occasions when she could leave the house, for instance in order to attend certain religious ceremonies, or a performance of the tragic drama at the theatre, she was always in company with others. Shopping, except in poor families, was done by servants and slaves. Under Solon's law, a virgin caught in unchastity could be sold by her nearest male relatives, father or brothers; and an adulteress was forbidden to wear ornaments, or to appear at religious ceremonies, on pain of being publicly dishonoured; any treatment short of mutilation or death could be inflicted on her. The seclusion in which a free Athenian woman lived, whether married or unmarried, is well illustrated in the following trials; for example, there is the difficulty experienced by the seducer in getting into touch with the wife of Euphiletus; and the diffidence felt by a mother at having to state her grievances before a gathering of men, even though they were her relatives. There is also the little picture of a mother and her daughters " whose lives are so respectable that they shrink from being seen even by the other members of the household ", and of the extreme outrage to their feelings when a drunken man burst in upon them in their own quarters.

## SLANDER AND ORAL ABUSE

The gossip complained of by the young man before a private gathering of his friends was not actionable. Under Solon's code, abuse of a person in any public place was forbidden on pain of a fine. The penalty for insulting a magistrate in his place of session was loss of citizenship. Abuse of a magistrate to his face was also an offence, but apparently the words had to be spoken in his actual presence, and it was a valid defence to plead that the slander had been spoken to others. To apply certain epithets to any person in public, whether in his presence or not, was also an offence : these epithets, called " the banned words ", were Murderer, Father-beater or Mother-beater, Deserter, Bandit or Kidnapper. Beyond this, the law does not seem to have protected the private citizen against defamation of character. One of the most famous of Solon's laws prohibited speaking ill of the dead in any place and under any provocation.

## STATE MAINTENANCE

Under Solon's code, a soldier maimed in war was entitled to maintenance at the expense of the State. Some say Solon extended this maintenance to the children of men slain in war. Under the

completed democracy, pensions were granted to all who were
"unfit", that is, all who in military service or civil life had
been so severely injured as to be unable to work. From time
to time, the lists of those in receipt of State relief came up for
scrutiny; the pensioner's right to receive his pension might be
challenged by any citizen, and he would then have to defend
it before the body which dealt with all financial matters, the
Council of Five Hundred, which was chosen by lot from all the
citizens and which prepared all business for the Assembly of the
People.

The above extracts from the legal code of Athens will suffice to
make the cases that follow intelligible. It remains to say a few
words about procedure. The procedure in cases of homicide or
wounding with homicidal intent has been discussed : the right of
prosecution was in the hands of the relatives, and the case came before
the Court of the Areopagus or before a jury sitting in one of the
special courts such as the Palladion or Delphinion. In other cases
there was often a choice of procedure ; and there was a distinction
drawn between Public and Private suits, which however was not
the same as that between our criminal and civil cases. The chief
difference was that a public action usually came at once before a
jury, when the preliminary investigation had been completed ;
whereas a private suit was taken in the first place to an arbitrator
and was often settled without coming before a jury-court. Any
Athenian citizen could begin a public action ; but a private action
had to be brought by the person directly interested, or if this was
a woman, a minor, or a resident alien, by his or her legal guardian.
In a public action, the penalty exacted was regarded as paid to the
State, and the prosecutor seldom received any share of a fine
inflicted ; in a private action, however, the object of the claim, or
the damages, went to the plaintiff. In a public action, the prosecutor
had to obtain a fifth of the votes, or pay a fine of one thousand
drachmas (£200) and forfeit his right to bring a similar action in
future. In private actions, if they came into court and the plaintiff
failed to obtain one-fifth of the jury's votes, a penalty was exacted
as in a public suit, but it was paid to the defendant, not to the State,
and the amount was usually fixed at one-sixth of the sum at issue
in the case.

The choice between a public or a private suit often lay with the prosecutor. Sometimes it was open to him to arrest the defendant himself and convey him to the prison officials, the Eleven; this was permitted in cases of alleged theft, house-breaking, kidnapping and similar offences. Sometimes he could lay his complaint directly before a magistrate. The regular procedure, however, was to catch one's opponent in some public place, and summon him, orally in the presence of at least two witnesses, to appear before the appropriate magistrate at a given date and time. The magistrate examined the complaint, which was made by the prosecutor in writing, and appointed a time for a preliminary hearing. At this hearing, the defendant put in a written answer to the charge. If he claimed that the action had been brought in the wrong form, this objection had to be taken first, and came before a jury-court as a separate case: such complaints were commonly used as delaying tactics. If the defendant put in a denial of the charge, the magistrate proceeded to collect all the evidence, documentary proofs and depositions of witnesses. Everything had to be produced in writing: the witnesses were not bound to appear in person before the magistrate, though they had to appear at the actual trial when their depositions were read out. Nothing could be produced at the trial which had not already been produced before the magistrate. Any citizen was bound to give evidence on request, unless he was prepared to swear a public oath that he knew nothing of the matter; if he refused, he was fined one thousand drachmas (£200). The two principals could question each other, and their answers were taken down, to be used at the trial.

When each side had completed their case, the magistrate took over all the documents and kept them in a sealed box called a " hedgehog ", which was not opened till the trial. At the trial, the magistrate presided. The Clerk of the Court read out the prosecutor's charge and the defendant's reply; then each party was called upon to address the jury, first the prosecutor, then the defendant. Either side could call upon a friend or relative to speak in his support; but apart from this, no outside help was allowed. A time-limit was fixed for the speeches; this varied according to the nature and importance of the case. The speaker, at necessary points, appealed to his evidence, which was read out by the Clerk of the Court. Time was measured by the water-clock, an instrument in which a given amount of water dripped from one chamber to another, like sand in an hour-glass. During the reading of any documents, the water-clock was stopped. Witnesses who had given evidence were called upon to appear and vouch for the genuineness of the evidence read out, but they could not be cross-examined. The two principals, however, could question each other as at the preliminary hearing. In some cases, each side spoke twice. When the speakers had finished, the voting was taken, the verdict was announced, and the penalty, if necessary, was decided by a further vote.

One more feature of the Athenian legal system must be mentioned : it occurs constantly in the trials that follow. This is the provision that the evidence of slaves can in general be admitted only if given under torture. This was defended by the orators, when it suited them, on the ground that the slave will not speak the truth except under the influence of fear. When, however, it is in a litigant's interest to maintain the contrary, he will assert that a slave who has given evidence in favour of his opponent has lied to escape from torment, or to gain his freedom. In the following trials it will be found that the same speechwriter will put forward both points of view on different occasions. A litigant could challenge his opponent to allow him to examine his opponent's slaves under torture ; if the opponent refused, his refusal would be used in court against him. A litigant would sometimes offer his own slaves to his opponent for torture, and later he would plead that this offer was evidence of his own strong case. The point of view of the slave was not considered : he was merely a piece of property. Refusals to allow the torture of slaves proceeded from the owner's disinclination to have a valuable instrument spoiled or destroyed, not from any humane considerations. Male and female slaves were equally liable to this infliction. No free Athenian citizen could be tortured.

The business that came before the courts was very great for such a small community, in spite of the existence of arbitration. The population of Attica in the latter half of the fifth century B.C. has been estimated at about 45,000 men, that is, about 30,000 male citizens and about 15,000 resident aliens. There is no means of computing the number of women and children, but a rough guess sets the whole free population of Attica at about 200,000. The number of slaves may have been anything from

200,000 to 400,000; but they play no part in the political life of the community, and can be discounted. Thus, for a population of 200,000 we have a panel of 6,000 jurors; and the courts were apparently working all the time. The Athenians enjoyed litigation : it appealed to their unfailing dramatic sense. They enjoyed watching other people's quarrels, and it became a real passion with some of them to sit on the jury. The comic playwright Aristophanes draws a picture of an elderly man who was to be found in the market-place before daybreak, waiting for the court to open so that he could get a good seat on the jurors' benches, and whose son had to lock him up to keep him at home. This love of litigation was partly an inborn trait, and partly the fruit of leisure : all but the poorest citizens were freed from menial work by their slaves. This applies to the townsmen, the inhabitants of Athens itself, not to the farmers of the surrounding countryside, who had plenty of work to do and who were no match for the sharper-witted town-dwellers.

The magistrates of Athens, who presided over the courts, were elected annually by lot from the body of free Athenian citizens. Fifty names were put forward from each of the ten administrative divisions of Attica, which were called Tribes. From these five hundred men, nine were chosen as Chief Magistrates : they were called the Nine Archons. Of these, the head was called the Eponymous Archon, because his name was given to his year of office; events were said to have taken place " in the archonship of So-and-so " at Athens. Judicially, he had special charge of cases concerning married women, wards and " heiresses ", that is, the family. Next in importance was the Archon Polemarchus, that is, Field-Marshal Archon, who had once been supreme commander in war, but who now was a magistrate whose special charge was cases concerning aliens. Next came the Archon Basileus or King-Archon, a relic of monarchy, who under the democracy had charge of State sacrifices, and who dealt with cases in which religion was concerned : this included homicide, because of the religious importance of blood-pollution. The six other members of the board of magistrates were called Thesmothetae, " Legislators "; they shared out the less important work between them. In some cases the magistrates had summary jurisdiction; but their chief function was to preside, first over the preliminary investigation, and then over the trial before the jury-court. Each was allowed two assessors to help him. The democratic State, while making use of the lot as a means of choice, protected itself from the holding of office by unworthy persons : any man so selected had to pass an examination of his character, or scrutiny, before entering upon office ; and also to submit to a review of his conduct during office at the end of the year when he retired. There were special rules for the King-Archon, whose duties concerned religion : his wife, to whom certain functions of this office were assigned, had to have been a virgin before marriage. The magistrates had no powers of jurisdiction when sitting with a jury-court; the verdict of the jury was supreme.

In legislation, the Assembly of the People (*Ecclesia*) consisting of all male citizens over thirty years of age, was supreme. Business was prepared for the Assembly, and resolutions framed, by the Council of Five Hundred, consisting of five hundred citizens chosen by lot, fifty from each of the ten administrative divisions or Tribes. The councillors sat in committees of fifty members, each committee in turn for one-tenth of the year ; a different member, chosen by lot, presided each day. The periods of session of these committees were called " the first Presidency," " the second Presidency ", and so on, dividing the official year into ten : the order of session was also decided by lot. They had no power to legislate, but they had charge of the State finances, and could even sit as a court of justice in certain cases, such as those which concerned the Treasury.

Throughout the period covered by the following trials, jurymen were paid a sum of three obols (about two shillings) a day, so that even the poorest could afford to sit when chosen. The use of the lot as the method of choice for jurymen, councillors, and all officials except the ten chief Generals, arose out of a primitive belief that though such means look like chance, the divine will is given an opportunity of expressing itself through them ; nevertheless, common sense demanded that a close watch should be kept on those thus chosen, by means of the scrutiny of incoming councillors and magistrates. The fact that offices were open to all citizens might seem to open the door to a flood of incompetents ; but actually, the average free Athenian managed such official duties quite easily, as he was used from boyhood to taking an interest in public life, and expected to have his share of public activities. Also, in such a small community it was easy for every man to be well-informed, when he could meet his friends every morning in the market-place and discuss the latest news. Thus the system, though it had obvious faults and made glaring mistakes, was nevertheless a remarkably intricate and effective piece of machinery, the like of which the world had never seen, for the dispensation of justice equally to all.

It was typical of all Hellenic thought, as opposed to oriental ideas of absolute obedience to a personal ruler, that in every rightly-constituted State the Law must stand above human caprice and ambition. " The people must fight to defend their laws as they would their fortifications ", says Heracleitus. In the Athenian democracy, the constitution was designed to ensure that supreme power remained in the hands of the People, whose duty it was to defend the Law : no single person or group of persons must ever rise so far above his fellows as to be out of control by the People, and above the Law.

# III

## RHETORIC AND THE ORATORS

THE art of persuasion is as old as human speech itself; but the systematic study of this art, and its application to public life, which the Greeks called Rhetoric, first emerges into the light of history in Sicily in the fifth century B.C., when CORAX, a citizen of the Greek colony of Syracuse, first wrote a Handbook on Rhetoric for the ordinary citizen, to help him to speak before a court of law. In this handbook, which he called *The Technique of Speaking*, Corax divided the model speech into five parts: the Proem or Introduction; the Narrative; the Arguments; Subsidiary Matters; and Epilogue, that is, Conclusion or Peroration. This basic scheme was accepted by all who came after him; and it can be traced in all the speeches that have come down to us.

Corax also analysed and illustrated a subject which all Greek forensic writers and orators carefully studied and employed: the subject of Probability. He showed how arguments from probability could be used to convince a jury, and how they could be devised and employed in both of two contradictory situations. For instance, a man is accused of murder. He may say: "I was the first person to notify the disappearance of the missing man: is it *probable* that I would have done this if I had been guilty of his murder?" The prosecution, however, can argue: "You first notified his disappearance; but in doing this, you were attempting to divert suspicion from yourself, and therefore it is *probable* that you are the guilty man." Many instances of this kind of reasoning will be found in the speeches that follow; to be able to invent arguments from probability was part of any speaker's stock-in-trade. It quickly developed into an instrument for using fallacious arguments without being detected, and helped to make Rhetoric the art not only of Persuasion but of Deception. This tendency caused Rhetoric to become the *bête noire* of the philosophers, as the enemy of truth, logic and morals; but while society remains what it is, the art of putting a convincing case must always remain very necessary, for self-protection if not for self-advancement.

31

TEISIAS, a pupil of Corax, also wrote a book on Rhetoric, in which he further developed the theme of Probability. He is said to have been the teacher of Lysias when the latter was living at Thourioi, the Greek colony on the south coast of Italy, and also to have travelled to Athens and given instruction there.

These two Sicilian Greeks, then, by their writings and oral teaching, first systematized the study of Rhetoric. At Athens, where a knowledge of public speaking was essential to success, schools of rhetoric began to spring up. The subject formed part of the advanced education of all young men who wished to play a part in public life. Athens had many excellent speakers, both gifted and highly-trained; a dignified manner, a good voice, clear arrangement, and restrained style, were preferred. Nevertheless, when another Sicilian with a natural gift for extempore oratory visited their city in 427 B.C., they were carried away by the flow of his eloquence, and for a time his more florid style, full of antitheses and poetical diction, became the fashion. This visitor was GORGIAS of Leontini in eastern Sicily, twenty-two miles north of Syracuse; he came to Athens on an embassy, to ask for aid for his native city against Syracuse. He impressed the Athenians with displays of impromptu speaking, and used to offer to answer any question put to him by an audience. He travelled about Greece, delivering public orations on great occasions such as the Olympic Games; and his pupils included princes. He also wrote model speeches for the benefit of his pupils; some of these have survived, and though their sentiments are not profound, they are clever in manner. It is said that he used to make his pupils learn these speeches by heart; this method was criticized by Aristotle, who said that it was like teaching the craft of the cobbler by giving the apprentice a great number of different sorts of shoes, instead of explaining the rules of the craft.

Other teachers arose, men of wide culture and general interests, who earned their living and sometimes made huge fortunes, by teaching rhetoric. These were all non-Athenian Greeks, but they visited Athens, the intellectual metropolis, and stayed for periods, teaching and meeting the intelligentsia. There was PROTAGORAS, a fellow townsman of Democritus the inventor of the Atomic Theory, and himself a philosopher. There was PRODICUS, possessed of a mighty booming voice, whose special subject was synonyms and the meaning of words. There was HIPPIAS, who invented a mnemonic scheme, and claimed that he could remember fifty names at one hearing; he boasted that he had learnt archaeology as a preparation for a visit to Sparta, having gathered that this was what they would best like to hear about. These men, who are grouped together under the general name of the SOPHISTS, contributed no work of oratorical genius; but they improved the standard of oratory by their studies, and increased the interest of the Athenians in a subject in which they were themselves naturally gifted.

The first Athenian, however, to take up rhetoric as a profession was ANTIPHON, two of whose speeches are given in this book. Antiphon was born in 480 B.C., and throughout the century until his death in 411 B.C., he was a power behind the scenes in Athenian politics. But he rarely appeared in public, and was known as a teacher of rhetoric—the best-known in Athens—and a writer of speeches for others. He was the first Athenian to take up the profession of Logographos. He wrote speeches for the Assembly of the People as well as for the law-courts; but his special study was homicide. He was not a supporter of the democratic government; he is said to have been the prime mover in the anti-democratic revolution of 411 B.C. This enterprise cost him his life. When the temporary Government of Four Hundred fell and the full democracy was restored, Antiphon was impeached. He defended himself in a speech which is said by Thucydides to have been the greatest defence made by any man on trial for his life in the memory of that age. Nevertheless it was unsuccessful. Party feeling ran high; Antiphon was personally unpopular, because he " laboured under the popular suspiciousness of his brilliance," Thucydides says; and he was condemned and executed.

Thucydides in his History pays Antiphon a splendid tribute : he says that Antiphon was second to none among the Athenians of his day in virtue, and was a proved master of argument and expression : he was the man who above all others had the greatest ability to assist those fighting a cause either in the law-court or the Assembly. It is said that after his condemnation, his speech was praised by his friend Agathon the tragic dramatist; Antiphon replied : " A high-minded man is bound to care more for the opinion of one man who counts rather than that of many nobodies."

Fifteen of his compositions survive. Twelve of these, in groups of four, are imaginary speeches written for the instruction of pupils.

The other three were written for clients : two of them, *On the Murder of Herodes*, and *Against a Step-Mother*, on a charge of *Poisoning*, are given in this book. All deal with cases of homicide ; and all except the speech *Against a Step-Mother* are for the defence. The style inclines to stiffness and an over-elaborate balancing of phrases ; but the argumentation is brilliant, and the language, always subtle, sometimes rises to a kind of austere poetry, in the best Attic manner. It must be remembered that he was usually writing for delivery before the Court of the Areopagus, a task for which his gifts best suited him.

LYSIAS was not an Athenian. His father Cephalus came from Syracuse, and took up residence in Athens, on the invitation of Pericles. The family was wealthy ; they ran a shield-factory, and had several houses, in Athens and down at the Peiraeus. One of their houses at Peiraeus was the scene of the conversation supposed to have taken place in Plato's *Republic*, and the brothers Lysias and Polemarchus were well-known to the best Athenian society, mixing, in spite of their non-Athenian parentage, on an equality with all.

At the age of fifteen, Lysias went with his brother to Thourioi in south Italy. Here he was educated, taking lessons in rhetoric from Teisias of Syracuse. In 412 B.C. the brothers were expelled with three hundred others, by an anti-Athenian party. They returned to Athens, and lived prosperously on the proceeds of the business ; it was war-time, and the shield-factory was flourishing. Though they were prominent in social life, their Sicilian birth prevented their entrance into politics, and they remained non-citizens, or *Metoikoi* as the resident aliens were called, with restricted privileges and no part in the city's public affairs. They were on good terms with everybody ; and like their father, they had never been engaged in litigation with anyone, a notable achievement in the Athens of their day. Then came disaster.

In 404 B.C., after the end of the long and unsuccessful war which Athens was waging with Sparta, the democratic government was again temporarily overthrown, as it had been before in 411 B.C. This time, power was seized by a few determined men who formed a cabal of thirty, known as the Thirty Tyrants, and who proceeded to consolidate their position by getting rid of their enemies. The seven months that followed left an indelible mark on the memory of the Athenians, and are always described as a reign of terror. Men were arrested, put to death without trial, and their property seized; no man was safe, especially if he were known to have strong democratic sympathies or considerable wealth. Among the victims was the harmless Polemarchus, Lysias' elder brother; and Lysias himself would also have perished if he had not managed to escape.

The Thirty Tyrants came into power in April, 404 B.C. They were overthrown in the following December, and the democratic constitution was restored, to remain unshaken until the loss of Athenian independence in 338 B.C. Lysias, in exile, did all he could to help the democratic party. On his return, his first act was to bring a charge of murder against the man who had arrested his brother. This man was one of the Thirty Tyrants, called Eratosthenes. The speech of Lysias on that occasion—his first, and the only speech he is known to have delivered himself,—is given in part in this book. Whether he was successful or not—and it is unlikely that he secured a verdict—the family property had been confiscated and could not be recovered. Lysias therefore devoted himself to the career of Logographos to restore his fortunes, and between 403 and 380 B.C., wrote not less than two hundred speeches for clients. He became rich and famous, and delivered at least one speech at Olympia, an honour reserved for distinguished speakers. He probably died in 380 B.C., aged about eighty.

Twenty-three entire speeches by Lysias have survived; of the rest, many fragments, some of considerable length, remain. The complete speeches are all forensic; they include both public and private suits. The public suits concern offences of officials, such as treason, embezzlement, taking bribes; unconstitutional procedure; State claims for money; military offences; murder or intent to murder; and impiety. The private suits that survive are four in number: for the plaintiff in a case of defamation of character; for a ward, against a guardian; and two cases of disputed claims to property. Of Lysias' speeches, eight are given in the following chapters, as well as the address to a private gathering on a complaint of slander.

Appreciation of Lysias is easy. He is the master of the " plain " style, and of the art that conceals art. He was original, in that he forsook the somewhat artificial rhetoric of the schools and wrote his speeches dramatically, in such style as would best suit the person delivering them, yet without any sacrifice of distinction. His diction is the purest Attic; there is no trace of his Sicilian origin, nor of his long sojourn in Italy. His arrangement is simple : proem, narrative, argument, epilogue. His sense of character was most acute ; so too his sense of humour. Above all, he possessed the indefinable quality of charm, apparent in everything he wrote. The only orator of whom he falls short is Demosthenes, and that only in one sphere—vigour and fire. Writing as he did for others, he never used commonplace or false ornament ; his subject-matter rarely gave him scope for flights of impassioned oratory. His style at least was appreciated by Plato, who hated all rhetoricians; and Aristotle in his book on Rhetoric mentions the famous ending of the speech against Eratosthenes, though unfortunately mis-quoting it. Many famous orators took Lysias as their model. Cicero appraised his merits at length, saying that he had the essentially Attic quality of "nothing unsuitable or inept", and calling him "*almost* another Demosthenes," though Cicero thought that Lysias could not have risen to Demosthenes' heights. Quintilian, the Roman literary critic, praises Lysias for plain elegance of language and mastery of exposition, remarking : "If exposition is sufficient for an orator, you will nowhere find greater perfection than Lysias " ; but he places Demosthenes a long way first, for in his view Lysias lacked the power of moving his audiences as Demosthenes did. But Quintilian is speaking not as a hearer but as a reader of Greek oratory, and he forgets that Demosthenes' great speeches were delivered by himself before public assemblies in causes about which he felt deeply, whereas Lysias' task was to prepare a suitable speech for another to deliver in a court of law.

The best appreciation of Lysias ever written is that of Dionysius of Halicarnassus, a literary critic, Greek by birth, who lived in Rome in the time of the Emperor Augustus. He wrote a series of essays on the Attic orators ; of these, the essays on Lysias, Isocrates and Isaeus survive, as well as part of that on Demosthenes. He sums up the genius of Lysias in the following piece of advice to students : "To those wishing to discover the nature of his charm, I would advise long-continued and diligent study—the assimilation, by means of the non-rational *feeling* faculty, of what is a non-rational percept." He adds that when puzzled as to the authenticity of any speech attributed to Lysias. he falls back on the test : "Does it exhibit the Lysian grace or charm ? " Two more points noted by Dionysius bring out Lysias' quality : contrasting him with the testamentary lawyer Isaeus, he remarks : "Isaeus sticks at no scurrility in his attack on the opponent, but Lysias is never found using any trick unworthy of a gentleman." And in analysing the famous charm, he says that it appears most strongly in the proem and narrative, grows weaker at the third stage, the argument, and in the epilogue it dies away. That is to say, Lysias is most effective where simplicity and vividness are required, less effective in controversy, and least effective where most orators indulge in an emotional appeal or peroration. His endings have their own quality, the indefinable Attic power of getting an effect by saying less than the situation calls for. The classic example of this is the ending of the speech against Eratosthenes, the only one in which Lysias' own feelings were engaged : " I shall finish speaking. You have heard, you have seen, you have suffered. The power is yours. Deliver your verdict."

ISAEUS lived from about 420 to 350 B.C. He was a strictly professional writer of speeches, and confined himself to one special branch of law—property claims and legacies. Thus he took no part in public life, and almost nothing is known of him outside his work. He was a pupil of Isocrates, the great essayist and educationist, for a time ; but his career proved to be of the kind most despised by Isocrates, who though he himself had begun with forensic speeches written for others, later conveniently forgot this period of his activity and spoke with contempt of those who wrote for the law-courts. There is nothing to show that Isaeus himself ever spoke in a court of law ; all his extant speeches are written for clients and deal with property claims. Like Antiphon, he was a specialist ; but unlike Antiphon, he never became involved in politics. He was accredited with over sixty speeches, eleven of which survive entire. These all deal with private causes, and all concern, directly or indirectly, bequests. They are the oldest documents in the world which exhibit in detail the workings of a testamentary law.

Isaeus had a " lawyer's reputation " for cleverness in devising arguments to support a weaker cause ; and it is suggested that he went to greater lengths in his attacks on opponents. One of his speeches is given in this book. Isaeus had a complete mastery of that clarity without which the details of the case he was expounding would have become confusing and tedious ; such is his power that we follow the fortunes of the property in dispute through all its vicissitudes without any slackening of interest. He had great dramatic and descriptive skill. He is said to have taken Lysias as his model, and to have made a careful study of his works.

DEMOSTHENES is too well-known to need lengthy description here. He is accepted as the greatest orator the world has ever known, combining the gifts of clarity, subtlety, humour and psychological penetration with the power to move and sway his audiences by his own impassioned belief in his cause. He was born in 384 B.C., and owing to the fraudulent conduct of his guardians, lost his patrimony. For a time he was obliged to write speeches for others, in order to repair his loss, as Lysias had done ; but his real interest was in the politics, home and foreign, of Athens ; and by a series of speeches in public causes, some delivered by himself, some written for others, he made himself the most persuasive speaker of his day. He early foresaw the danger to Athenian independence which was growing up in Macedon, ruled by King Philip II ; and in spite of opposition at home, he used his great gifts in persuading Athens, as well as other Greek States, to put up an uncompromising resistance to Philip, even when Philip offered friendship. In 338 B.C., Philip gained the mastery of Greece, at the battle of Chaeronea ; but in 336 he was assassinated. He was succeeded by his son Alexander the Great, whose generals managed to hold Philip's conquests in Greece although their master was absent on his victorious campaigns in Asia ; but Demosthenes' views remained unchanged : he knew that the domination of Macedon meant the end of freedom for the Greek City-States, including Athens. For the next twelve years, with a Macedonian garrison in Athens, Demosthenes' position was precarious. He suffered a period of exile ; but in 323 B.C. came the news of Alexander's death in Babylon. Again the great orator prepared to organize resistance. A rebellion was attempted, but was soon quelled. The surrender of Demosthenes was demanded by the Macedonian general ; but Demosthenes fled from Athens, and in 322 B.C. took poison rather than fall into the hands of the Macedonian pursuers.

Two specimens of his art are here given : the minor forensic speeches *Against Conon*, on a charge of assault, and *Against Callicles*, a claim for damage to property. The speech *Against Neaera*, by an unknown author, was attributed to Demosthenes, but falsely. The examples given do not show Demosthenes at his greatest— only the political speeches can do that—but they exhibit a playful skill and a power of depicting character and situation that remind one of Lysias, and they are gems of their kind. He is said to have associated with and received help from Isaeus. His success was not won easily : he had natural disadvantages, including a stammer and a weak voice ; but he cured these defects by walking along the sea shore reciting poetry against the sound of the waves, and practising elocution with a pebble in his mouth. He combined with natural genius an immense belief in hard work : he is said once to have shaved off half his beard only, so that he would be forced to stay indoors and study.

*FOUR*

*TRIALS*

*FOR*

*MURDER*

# IV

## ON THE KILLING OF ERATOSTHENES THE SEDUCER

Speech written for the defendant, by LYSIAS. Exact date unknown: some time between 400 and 380 B.C.

The defendant's name is Euphiletus. The dead man's name is Eratosthenes. Eratosthenes had seduced the wife of Euphiletus, and Euphiletus had finally caught them together. Euphiletus had availed himself of his legal right to kill the adulterer; his act was justifiable homicide, and not punishable unless it could be proved that he had some other motive for the slaughter. However, the relatives of the dead man brought the killer to trial on the ground that the whole situation leading to the slaughter had been planned by Euphiletus; they therefore charged him with murder. Euphiletus denied the charge and affirmed that his sole motive was to exact vengeance on the adulterer, as was allowed by law.

The case came before a court sitting at the Delphinion. The penalty was death, or if the accused felt that the case was going against him, he could leave after the first day: he would then suffer exile and confiscation of his property. After the prosecution have stated their case, Euphiletus speaks:

### THE PROEM

I WOULD give a great deal, members of the jury, to find you, as judges of this case, taking the same attitude towards me as you would adopt towards your own behaviour in similar circumstances. I am sure that if you felt about others in the same way as you did about yourselves, not one of you would fail to be angered by these deeds, and all of you would consider the punishment a small one for those guilty of such conduct.

Moreover, the same opinion would be found prevailing not only among you, but everywhere throughout Greece. This is the one crime for which, under any government, democratic or exclusive, equal satisfaction is granted to the meanest against the mightiest, so that the least of them receives the same justice as the

43

most exalted. Such is the detestation, members of the jury, in which this outrage is held by all mankind.

Concerning the severity of the penalty, therefore, you are, I imagine, all of the same opinion : not one of you is so easy-going as to believe that those guilty of such great offences should obtain pardon, or are deserving of a light penalty. What I have to prove, I take it, is just this : that Eratosthenes seduced my wife, and that in corrupting her he brought shame upon my children and outrage upon me, by entering my home ; that there was no other enmity between him and me except this ; and that I did not commit this act for the sake of money, in order to rise from poverty to wealth, nor for any other advantage except the satisfaction allowed by law.

I shall expound my case to you in full from the beginning, omitting nothing and telling the truth. In this alone lies my salvation, I imagine—if I can explain to you everything that happened.

## THE NARRATIVE

Members of the jury : when I decided to marry and had brought a wife home, at first my attitude towards her was this : I did not wish to annoy her, but neither was she to have too much of her own way. I watched her as well as I could, and kept an eye on her as was proper. But later, after my child had been born, I came to trust her, and I handed all my possessions over to her, believing that this was the greatest possible proof of affection.

Well, members of the jury, in the beginning she was the best of women. She was a clever housewife, economical and exact in her management of everything. But then, my mother died ; and her death has proved to be the source of all my troubles, because it was when my wife went to the funeral that this man Eratosthenes saw her ; and as time went on, he was able to seduce her. He kept a look out for our maid who goes to market ; and approaching her with his suggestions, he succeeded in corrupting her mistress.

Now first of all, gentlemen, I must explain that I have a small house which is divided into two—the men's quarters and the women's—each having the same space, the women upstairs and the men downstairs.

After the birth of my child, his mother nursed him ; but I did not want her to run the risk of going downstairs every time she had to give him a bath, so I myself took over the upper storey, and let the women have the ground floor. And so it came about that by this time it was quite customary for my wife often to go downstairs and sleep with the child, so that she could give him the breast and stop him from crying.

This went on for a long while, and I had not the slightest suspicion. On the contrary, I was in such a fool's paradise that I believed my wife to be the chastest woman in all the city.

Time passed, gentlemen. One day, when I had come home unexpectedly from the country, after dinner, the child began crying and complaining. Actually it was the maid who was pinching him on purpose to make him behave so, because—as I found out later—this man was in the house.

Well, I told my wife to go and feed the child, to stop his crying. But at first she refused, pretending that she was so glad to see me back after my long absence. At last I began to get annoyed, and I insisted on her going.

" Oh, yes! " she said. " To leave *you* alone with the maid up here! You mauled her about before, when you were drunk! "

I laughed. She got up, went out, closed the door—pretending that it was a joke—and locked it. As for me, I thought no harm of all this, and I had not the slightest suspicion. I went to sleep, glad to do so after my journey from the country.

Towards morning, she returned and unlocked the door.

I asked her why the doors had been creaking during the night. She explained that the lamp beside the baby had gone out, and that she had then gone to get a light from the neighbours.

I said no more. I thought it really was so. But it did seem to me, members of the jury, that she had done up her face with cosmetics, in spite of the fact that her brother had died only a month before. Still, even so, I said nothing about it. I just went off, without a word.

After this, members of the jury, an interval elapsed, during which my injuries had progressed, leaving me far behind. Then, one day, I was approached by an old hag. She had been sent by a woman—Eratosthenes' previous mistress, as I found out later. This woman, furious because he no longer came to see her as before, had been on the look-out until she had discovered the reason. The old crone, therefore, had come and was lying in wait for me near my house.

45

"Euphiletus," she said, "please don't think that my approaching you is in any way due to a wish to interfere. The fact is, the man who is wronging you and your wife is an enemy of ours. Now if you catch the woman who does your shopping and works for you, and put her through an examination, you will discover all. The culprit," she added, "is Eratosthenes from Oea. Your wife is not the only one he has seduced—there are plenty of others. It's his profession."

With these words, members of the jury, she went off.

At once I was overwhelmed. Everything rushed into my mind, and I was filled with suspicion. I reflected how I had been locked into the bedroom. I remembered how on that night the middle and outer doors had creaked, a thing that had never happened before ; and how I had had the idea that my wife's face was rouged. All these things rushed into my mind, and I was filled with suspicion.

I went back home, and told the servant to come with me to market. I took her instead to the house of one of my friends ; and there I informed her that I had discovered all that was going on in my house.

"As for you," I said, "two courses are open to you : either to be flogged and sent to the tread-mill, and never be released from a life of utter misery ; or to confess the whole truth and suffer no punishment, but win pardon from me for your wrong-doing. Tell me no lies. Speak the whole truth."

At first she tried denial, and told me that I could do as I pleased —she knew nothing. But when I named Eratosthenes to her face, and said that he was the man who had been visiting my wife, she was dumbfounded, thinking that I had found out everything exactly. And then at last, falling at my feet and exacting a promise from me that no harm should be done to her, she denounced the villain. She described how he had first approached her after the funeral, and then how in the end she had passed the message on, and in course of time my wife had been over-persuaded. She explained the way in which he had contrived to get into the house, and how when I was in the country my wife had gone to a religious service with this man's mother, and everything else that had happened. She recounted it all exactly.

When she had told all, I said :

"See to it that nobody gets to know of this ; otherwise the promise I made you will not hold good. And furthermore, I expect you to show me this actually happening. I have no use for words. I want the *fact* to be exhibited, if it really is so."

She agreed to do this.

Four or five days then elapsed, as I shall prove to you by important evidence. But before I do so, I wish to narrate the events of the last day.

I had a friend and relative named Sôstratus. He was coming home from the country after sunset when I met him. I knew that as he had got back so late, he would not find any of his own people at home; so I asked him to dine with me. We went home to my place, and going upstairs to the upper storey, we had dinner there. When he felt restored, he went off; and I went to bed.

Then, members of the jury, Eratosthenes made his entry; and the maid wakened me and told me that he was in the house.

I told her to watch the door; and going downstairs, I slipped out noiselessly.

I went to the houses of one man after another. Some I found at home; others, I was told, were out of town. So collecting as many as I could of those who were there, I went back. We procured torches from the shop near by, and entered my house. The door had been left open by arrangement with the maid.

We forced the bedroom door. The first of us to enter saw him still lying beside my wife. Those who followed saw him standing naked on the bed.

I knocked him down, members of the jury, with one blow. I then twisted his hands behind his back and tied them. And then I asked him why he was committing this crime against me, of breaking into my house.

He answered that he admitted his guilt; but he begged and besought me not to kill him—to accept a money-payment instead.

But I replied:

"It is not I who shall be killing you, but the law of the State, which you, in transgressing, have valued less highly than your own pleasures. You have preferred to commit this great crime against my wife and my children, rather than to obey the law and be of decent behaviour."

Thus, members of the jury, this man met the fate which the laws prescribe for wrong-doers of his kind.

Eratosthenes was not seized in the street and carried off, nor had he taken refuge at the altar, as the prosecution alleges. The facts do not admit of it : he was struck in the bedroom, he fell at once, and I bound his hands behind his back. There were so many present that he could not possibly escape through their midst, since he had neither steel nor wood nor any other weapon with which he could have defended himself against all those who had entered the room.

No, members of the jury : you know as well as I do how wrong-doers will not admit that their adversaries are speaking the truth, and attempt by lies and trickery of other kinds to excite the anger of the hearers against those whose acts are in accordance with Justice.

*(To the Clerk of the Court):*

Read the Law.

*(The Law of Solon is read, that an adulterer may be put to death by the man who catches him.)*

He made no denial, members of the jury. He admitted his guilt, and begged and implored that he should not be put to death, offering to pay compensation. But I would not accept his estimate. I preferred to accord a higher authority to the law of the State, and I took that satisfaction which you, because you thought it the most just, have decreed for those who commit such offences.
Witnesses to the preceding, kindly step up.

*(The witnesses come to the front of the Court, and the Clerk reads their depositions. When the Clerk has finished reading, and the witnesses have agreed that the depositions are correct, the defendant again addresses the Clerk) :*

Now please read this further law from the pillar of the Court of the Areopagus :

*(The Clerk reads another version of Solon's law, as recorded on the pillar of the Areopagus Court.)*

You hear, members of the jury, how it is expressly decreed by the Court of the Areopagus itself, which both traditionally and in

48

your own day has been granted the right to try cases of murder, that no person shall be found guilty of murder who catches an adulterer with his wife and inflicts this punishment. The Lawgiver was so strongly convinced of the justice of these provisions in the case of married women, that he applied them also to concubines, who are of less importance. Yet obviously, if he had known of any greater punishment than this for cases where married women are concerned, he would have provided it. But in fact, as it was impossible for him to invent any more severe penalty for corruption of wives, he decided to provide the same punishment as in the case of concubines.

*(To the Clerk of the Court)*:

Please read me this Law also.

*(The Clerk reads out further clauses from Solon's laws on rape.)*

You hear, members of the jury, how the Lawgiver ordains that if anyone debauch by force a free man or boy, the fine shall be double that decreed in the case of a slave. If anyone debauch a woman—in which case it is *permitted* to kill him—he shall be liable to the same fine. Thus, members of the jury, the Lawgiver considered violators deserving of a lesser penalty than seducers: for the latter he provided the death-penalty; for the former, the doubled fine. His idea was that those who use force are loathed by the persons violated, whereas those who have got their way by persuasion corrupt women's minds, in such a way as to make other men's wives more attached to themselves than to their husbands, so that the whole house is in their power, and it is uncertain who is the children's father, the husband or the lover. These considerations caused the Lawgiver to affix death as the penalty for seduction.

And so, members of the jury, in my case the laws not only hold me innocent, but actually order me to take this satisfaction; but it depends on you whether they are to be effective or of no moment. The reason, in my opinion, why all States lay down laws is in order that, whenever we are in doubt on any point, we can refer to these laws and find out our duty. And therefore it is the laws which in such cases enjoin upon the injured party to exact this penalty. I exhort you to show yourselves in agreement with them; otherwise you will be granting such impunity to adulterers that

49

you will encourage even burglars to declare themselves adulterers, in the knowledge that if they allege this reason for their action and plead that this was their purpose in entering other men's houses, no one will lay a finger on them. They will all realize that they need not bother about the law on adultery, but need only fear your verdict, since this is the supreme authority in the State.

Consider, members of the jury, their accusation that it was I who on that day told the maid to fetch the young man. In my opinion, gentlemen, I should have been justified in using any means to catch the seducer of my wife. If there had been only words spoken and no actual offence, I should have been doing wrong; but when by that time they had gone to all lengths and he had often gained entry into my house, I consider that I should have been within my rights whatever means I employ to catch him. But observe that this allegation of the prosecution is also false. You can easily convince yourselves by considering the following :

I have already told you how Sôstratus, an intimate friend of mine, met me coming in from the country around sunset, and dined with me, and when he felt refreshed, went off. Now in the first place, gentlemen, ask yourselves whether, if on that night I had had designs on Eratosthenes, it would have been better for me that Sôstratus should dine elsewhere, or that I should take a guest home with me to dinner. Surely in the latter circumstances Eratosthenes would have been less inclined to venture into the house. Further, does it seem to you probable that I would have let my guest go, and been left alone, without company ? Would I not rather have urged him to stay, so that he could help me to punish the adulterer ?

Again, gentlemen, does it not seem to you probable that I would have passed the word round among my friends during the daytime, and told them to assemble at the house of one of my friends who lived nearest, rather than have started to run round at night, as soon as I found out, without knowing whom I should find at home and whom away ? Actually, I called for Harmodius and certain others who were out of town—I did not know it—and others, I found, were not at home, so I went along taking with me whomever I could. But if I had known beforehand, does it not seem to you probable that I would have arranged for servants and passed the word round to my friends, so that I myself could go in with the maximum of safety—for how did I know whether he too might not have had a dagger or something?—and also in order that I might exact the penalty in the presence of the greatest number of witnesses? But in fact, since I knew nothing of what was going to happen on that night, I took with me whomever I could get.

Witnesses to the preceding, please step up.

*(Further witnesses come forward, and confirm their evidence as read out by the Clerk.)*

You have heard the witnesses, members of the jury. Now consider the case further in your own minds, inquiring whether there had ever existed between Eratosthenes and myself any other enmity but this. You will find none. He never brought any malicious charge against me, nor tried to secure my banishment, nor prosecuted me in any private suit. Neither had he knowledge of any crime of which I feared the revelation, so that I desired to kill him; nor by carrying out this act did I hope to gain money. So far from ever having had any dispute with him, or drunken brawl, or any other quarrel, I had never even set eyes on the man before that night. What possible object could I have had, therefore, in running so great a risk, except that I had suffered the greatest of all injuries at his hands? Again, would I myself have called in witnesses to my crime, when it was possible for me, if I desired to murder him without justification, to have had no confidants?

THE EPILOGUE

It is my belief, members of the jury, that this punishment was inflicted not in my own interests, but in those of the whole community. Such villains, seeing the rewards which await their crimes, will be less ready to commit offences against others if they see that you too hold the same opinion of them. Otherwise it would be far better to wipe out the existing laws and make different ones, which will penalise those who keep guard over their own wives, and grant full immunity to those who criminally pursue them. This would be a far more just procedure than to set a trap for citizens by means of the laws, which urge the man who catches an adulterer to do with him whatever he will, and yet allow the injured party to undergo a trial far more perilous than that which faces the law-breaker who seduces other men's wives. Of this, I am an example—I, who now stand in danger of losing life, property, everything, because I have obeyed the laws of the State.

.　　　.　　　.　　　.　　　.

This speech is an excellent example of advocacy and of Lysias' particular skill. The defence rests confidently on the law of Solon permitting the slaughter of an adulterer caught in the act, and on the inability of the prosecution to prove a different motive. The advocate feels in a sufficiently strong position to let his client say that he was not merely acting in accordance with the laws, but obeying their definite instructions in slaying the adulterer. This of course is untrue: the law allowed, but did not insist upon this revenge; and it is clear that a money-payment could be offered and accepted. As no other case of the slaughter of an adulterer is recorded, we can assume that the money-compensation was usual.

The real skill of the advocate, however, is devoted to building up a character and a situation. The Proem is brief, and sketches the general detestation in which adultery is held. The Narrative is long, vivid and detailed: its purpose is to show a normal husband, kindly, trusting but not foolish, grossly deceived in his own home over a long period by a habitual seducer, so that by the time the defendant reaches the actual deed of blood, the jury will be in sympathy with him and will not be disgusted at the thought of a helpless unarmed man butchered in the presence of so many other men in spite of his plea for mercy.

The Argumentation, based mostly on probability, aims at showing that the deed was a direct punishment for the offence, and not premeditated and prearranged. The Epilogue, also short, suggests to the jury that in acquitting the defendant they will be acting in the public interest, and striking a blow for the sanctity of the home.

An outstanding feature is the passivity of the wife, or rather, the unimportance of her attitude. She was " approached " through her maid, on one of the few occasions when an Athenian woman could appear in public—at a funeral. She is described as having been " corrupted " and " seduced ", though it is clear that she was an active conspirator. Her husband does not refer to her guilt, which is ascribed to the persuasion of the seducer. The religious festival which she attended with the mother of her lover was callèd the Thesmophoria, and was a yearly celebration in honour of the goddess Demeter, attended by women only. Her adultery having been proved, she would be automatically divorced; but beyond that, we cannot guess at her fate.

The maid cannot be very much blamed for her betrayal of her mistress.

Her fate was in the hands of her master, and the " examination " suggested by the aged crone included, if he wished, physical torture. Short of putting her to death, he could do anything he liked with her.

The Narrative contains the best existing description of an ordinary Athenian house. The stairs to which the husband refers were a mere ladder: hence the danger in going up and down them, especially for a woman carrying a baby.

Though the verdict is not known, it is fairly safe to assume that the defendant was successful. Adultery was very seriously regarded in Athens, because of the importance of the blood-tie in determining inheritance, and the duty of the sons to look after the ancestral tombs and perform the rites to the dead. Every possible means were taken to ensure the chastity of free-born women, hence the harem-like seclusion of their lives. The breaking-through of the barriers round the home would arouse the strongest resentment in the jury; and though they might not fully approve of Euphiletus' savage act, they would probably feel him to be justified, and give him their votes.

# V

## ON THE EXECUTION WITHOUT TRIAL OF POLEMARCHUS

Speech for the prosecution, written and delivered by LYSIAS. Date 403 B.C.

The prosecutor is Lysias himself: this was his first and only personal appearance in a law-suit. The defendant is Eratosthenes, not the seducer of the previous trial, but a politician, a member of the short-lived government of the Thirty Tyrants, which seized power in April, 404 B.C., and fell in December of the same year. The speech was delivered in 403 B.C. when Lysias returned from exile.

The case came, not before the Court of the Areopagus, but before an ordinary jury-court. The charge was not one of actual bloodshed, but of responsibility for a judicial murder. The defendant is accused of having, during his period of office, illegally arrested the prosecutor's elder brother Polemarchus, and caused him to be put to death without trial. The defendant's answer to the charge is that he was acting under government orders and through fear.

Only the Proem, Narrative, beginning of the Argument, and Epilogue are given here. The greater part of the speech is a general attack on the late illegal and dictatorial government, and is irrelevant to the immediate charge against Eratosthenes, except as showing the whole policy of the cabal of which he was a member.

．　　　．　　　．　　　．　　　．

### THE PROEM

I FEEL no difficulty, members of the jury, in beginning my accusation. The difficulty will be in bringing my speech to an end. Such is the enormity, and so great the number of my opponent's crimes, that it would be impossible, even if one lied, to make the accusations worse than the facts, and although one wishes to speak the truth, one cannot tell all : either the accuser must tire or the time must fail.

Our position, it seems to me, is the reverse of what it was in the past. Formerly the prosecution had to explain the nature of their quarrel with the defendants ; but nowadays one has to ask the defendants what quarrel they had with their country that they were nerved to commit such crimes against her. I speak, however, not as one who has no private quarrel and injury, but at a time when there is ample cause for all men to feel indignation either on private or on public grounds.

And so I, members of the jury, a man who has never before engaged in litigation either for myself or for others, am now driven by events to bring this charge against the defendant, with the result that I have often fallen into deep despondency, fearing that my inexperience may cause me to conduct my accusation in an unskilful manner, unworthy of my brother and myself. Still, I shall try to put the facts before you from the beginning, in the fewest possible words, as best I can.

## THE NARRATIVE

My father Cephalus came to this country at the request of Pericles. Moreover, he lived here for thirty years, and on no occasion were we or he involved in any law-suit, either as prosecutors or as defendants. We conducted ourselves as citizens under a democratic *régime* in such a way as neither to commit any offence against our fellow-citizens, nor to suffer any wrong at their hands.

But when the Thirty, by means of corruption and denunciation, had won their way to power, they alleged that it was necessary to purge the State of criminal elements, and lead the citizens back to the path of virtue and righteousness. Such were their professions. The deeds they went so far as to carry out were very different, as I shall try to recall to your memories, speaking of my own experience in the first instance, and then of yours.

Well, then: Theognis and Peison (*members of the government of Thirty*) made speeches before their colleagues on the question of the resident aliens. They said that certain of them were hostile to the existing government, and that therefore this was an excellent excuse for appearing to punish them, while actually making money. In any case, they said, the State was impoverished, and the government was in need of funds.

They had no difficulty in persuading their hearers, who cared nothing at all about taking men's lives, but a great deal about acquiring their property. It was therefore resolved to arrest ten men, two of whom should be poor, so that they could avail themselves of the defence that these acts were not done for the sake of money, but in support of the constitution . . .

And so, having parcelled out the different houses among themselves, they went off.

They found me entertaining guests. These they drove out, and handed me over to Peison. The others, going to the workshop, made a list of the hands.

Meanwhile, I was asking Peison if he was willing to give me my freedom in return for a sum of money. He said yes, if it were a large sum. I said, therefore, that I was prepared to give a talent of silver (£1,200) ; and he agreed to do as I asked.

Now I knew that he believed in neither God nor man. Nevertheless, as matters stood, it seemed to me absolutely essential that I should exact a pledge from him. So he swore an oath, invoking destruction on himself and his children, that on receipt of this money he would let me escape ; and then I went into the bedroom and opened up the money-chest.

Peison, seeing this, came in. When he saw what the chest contained, he called two of his attendants and gave the order to seize the contents.

Since he now possessed, not what I had agreed to, members of the jury, but *three* talents of silver (£3,600), and five hundred gold coins, as well as four silver goblets, I requested him to let me have the fare for my journey. But he answered that I should be lucky to escape with my life.

As Peison and I were leaving, we were met by the two who were coming from the work-shop. They caught us at the very door, and asked where we were going. Peison answered that we were going to my brother's place, to inspect the contents of his house as well. They ordered him to proceed, and me to accompany them to their destination, which was the house of Damnippus. Peison came up to me and urged me to say nothing, and not to be afraid, as he would follow me there.

On our arrival, we found Theognis guarding other prisoners. They handed me to him, and went off again.

Now it seemed to me that my position was so desperate that I must take a risk : death, nothing less, was staring me in the face. So I called Damnippus, and said to him :

" You are a near connection of mine. Here I am in your house. I have done no wrong. I am being destroyed for the sake of my money. But you—since I am in this trouble, you must put your resources at my disposal, and help me to escape."

He promised to do so; but he thought that the best thing was to mention the matter to Theognis, who, he was convinced, would do anything for a bribe.

While he was parleying with Theognis, I decided that I would make a bid for escape another way. As it happened, I was familiar with the house, and I knew that it had two entrances. I thought to myself, 'If I can slip off unseen, well and good—I shall have escaped; and if I'm caught—well,' I thought, 'if Damnippus has persuaded Theognis to accept a bribe, I shall be set free none the less; and if he has not, I shall be put to death just the same.'

On the strength of this reasoning, I made a dash for it, while my captors were keeping guard at the front entrance. There were three doors through which I had to pass—and all happened to be open!

I reached the house of Archeneos the sea-captain, and sent him up to the town to find out about my brother. On his return he told me that my brother had been arrested in the street and taken off to prison, by the defendant Eratosthenes. And so, as the news was so bad, that same night I myself took ship and crossed to Megara.

But my brother Polemarchus had received from the Thirty their customary order—to drink hemlock. This was before they had stated any reason for which he had to die—so far was he from having a trial and a chance to defend himself.

When he was carried out dead from the prison, they refused to allow his funeral to take place from any of our houses, although we had three. Instead, they hired a hut, and had him laid out there. And although we had so many cloaks, they refused our request to let us have one of them for his burial. Our friends came to our aid, one contributing a cloak, another a pillow, another whatever he happened to have, towards my dear brother's burial.

They had confiscated, of our property, seven hundred shields. They held vast sums of silver and gold, bronze and jewellery and furniture and women's clothes, in such quantities as they never had hoped to obtain. They had also taken one hundred and twenty slaves, out of whom they kept the best and sold the remainder for the benefit of the Treasury. And yet listen to what a pitch of voracity and cupidity they had come—what a proof of their characters they afforded ! Polemarchus' wife was wearing, as it happened, gold ear-rings when one of them first entered the house : these they took out from her ears! In no least fraction of our possessions did they show us any mercy ; their crimes against us because of our wealth were such as others might commit under the influence of anger inspired by mighty injuries. Yet we had deserved better of the State. We had produced the required dramas at the public festivals. We had paid many contributions to the Treasury. We had conformed to law and order, and had done every duty imposed upon us. We had made not a single enemy, and had ransomed many Athenian prisoners of war. And this was our reward from them!—though we had conducted ourselves far better as aliens in this country than they had as natives. *They* had driven many of their fellow-countrymen over to the enemy. They had put to death many without cause and had denied them a grave, and many who were about to give their daughters in marriage they had prevented.

### THE ARGUMENTS

And now they have reached such a pitch of audacity that they have come forward to defend themselves and to declare that they have done nothing either wrong or disgraceful! I wish that they were speaking the truth, for then I too would have had no small share in this benefit. But in fact they can make no such claim, either to the State or to me, for I have lost my brother—put to death, as I have already told you, by the action of Eratosthenes, although he himself had suffered no private injury and had not seen my brother committing any crime against the State, but was gladly giving rein to his own love of lawless behaviour.

I should like him to step forward and let me ask him a few questions, members of the jury. What I feel is this : if it were a question of helping him, I would count it a sin even to talk about him to another person ; but in the hope of punishing him I count it holy and righteous to address even the man himself.

(*He turns to the defendant Eratosthenes.*)

Step up here, please, and answer the questions I ask you.

(*Eratosthenes comes up and stands on the dais.*)

LYSIAS : Did you, or did you not, arrest Polemarchus ?

ERATOSTHENES : I was acting under orders from the government, through fear.

LYSIAS : Were you in the Council Chamber when the discussion about us took place ?

ERATOSTHENES : I was.

LYSIAS : Did you side with those who were urging our death, or did you speak in opposition ?

ERATOSTHENES : I spoke in opposition.

LYSIAS : To prevent our being put to death ?

ERATOSTHENES : To prevent your being put to death.

LYSIAS : Because you thought we were suffering injustice, or justice ?

ERATOSTHENES : Injustice.

LYSIAS : Then, you unspeakable villain, you opposed the motion in order to save our lives, and then made the arrest in order to take them ?  And when our salvation depended upon the majority vote of your Council, you say you spoke in opposition to those who wished for our death, and yet when it depended on you alone either to save Polemarchus or not, you haled him off to prison ?  Then, according to your statement, when your opposition was useless, you claim credit for it ; and yet since you arrested him and put him to death, do you not expect to pay the penalty to me and to this Court ?

(*Eratosthenes leaves the platform. Lysias turns again to the jury.*)

But even if he is speaking the truth when he says that he opposed the motion, please observe that there is no reason for believing the further statement that he was acting under orders. His colleagues would not have chosen the case of the resident aliens as a test of his loyalty. To whom was it less likely that they would have given the order than to the very man who had opposed the motion and made a display of his sympathies ? Who was less likely to obey such orders than the man who had spoken in opposition to the policy they were set upon ? Again, for any other Athenian it seems to me a sufficient excuse for anything that happened to put the blame on the Government of the Thirty ; but how can you reasonably accept the plea of members of the Thirty themselves when they refer the blame to one another ? If there had been any other government in the State more powerful than theirs, which had ordered him to destroy human beings in defiance of justice, perhaps you might reasonably have pardoned him ; but as things are, from whom are you ever going to obtain satisfaction, if it is to be allowed to the Thirty to plead that they were carrying out the orders of the Thirty ?

Besides, it was not in my brother's house, but in the street— where he could have let him escape to safety without transgressing the decree of his government—that he arrested him and haled him away. You all feel indignation against those who entered your houses to make a search there either for yourselves or some member of your family. Yet these men are more deserving of your pardon, if one must pardon those who destroyed others to save themselves, for there was danger in not going if they were sent, and danger in denying that they had found their victim. But Eratosthenes could have said that he had not come across my brother, or had not noticed him. Such a statement admitted of no disproof or examination, so that not even his enemies could have rebutted it if they had wished.

*(He turns to the defendant.)*

Your duty, Eratosthenes, if you were a man of good will, was much rather to have warned people doomed to die unjustly than to have arrested them. But in fact, your actions reveal you as not being distressed but delighted at what was happening. The jury, therefore, should give their verdict with an eye to your deeds rather than your words. They should use their knowledge of what actually happened as evidence of what was said in the Council on that occasion, since it is impossible to put forward any witnesses. Not only were we prevented from attending any of their meetings : we were not allowed to stay here in Athens at all, so that it is open to these men who committed every infamy against their country to say nothing but good of themselves.

However, I do not contest this point. I grant you, if you like, that you spoke in opposition. But I wonder what on earth you would have done had you supported the motion, when, maintaining you opposed it, you killed Polemarchus.

*(He turns back to the jury.)*

Tell me, gentlemen : even if you had happened to be his brothers, or his sons, would you have acquitted him ? No, for Eratosthenes is bound to prove one of two things : either that he did not arrest Polemarchus, or that he acted justly in doing so. But he has admitted that the arrest was unjust, so that he has made your verdict upon him easy.

Another point : many, both citizens and foreigners, have come to see what view you will take of these men. Those of them who are your fellow-countrymen will go away having discovered either that they will have to pay a penalty for any crime they may commit, or that they can become dictators in the State if they attain their ends, whereas if they fail, they will stand no lower in your opinion. And all the foreigners who are visiting Athens will learn whether they do rightly or wrongly in banning the Thirty from their own cities. If the very people who have been injured let them go after having caught them, certainly foreigners will think that they are wasting their time in exacting punishment on your behalf.

What a shameful contrast! When those admirals who were victorious in the sea-battle pleaded that they had been unable to rescue their men from the sea, you punished them with death, on the ground that you owed it to the valour of the dead to exact a penalty from their leaders. And now you have these men, the defendants, who when they were private citizens, worked with all their might for a naval defeat, and when they came into office, put to death of their own accord, as they admit, many of their fellow-citizens without trial. Is it not fair that they and their progeny should be punished with the extremest of penalties at your hands ?

The reference to the sea-battle in the last paragraph is that of Arginusae, fought between the Athenian and Spartan fleets in the East Aegean Sea. The Athenians were victorious, but owing to the weather, which was stormy, the commanders of the Athenian fleet, eight in number, made off for their harbour instead of attempting to rescue the Athenian sailors on twelve of their war-ships that were sinking. For this, those who returned to Athens were tried and executed. Lysias contrasts this severity with any leniency the jury may show towards the Thirty, who had worked for a Spartan victory in order to get power themselves; the Thirty owed their power principally to Spartan support after the downfall of Athens in 405 B.C.

Lysias then goes on to launch a general attack on Eratosthenes' career and associates in the late government. He ends his speech with a peroration:

THE EPILOGUE

But I will not go on. I do not want to describe future events when I am not able to enumerate the past crimes of these men : that would require not one prosecutor, but two. Still, so far as depends on my efforts, I have spared no pains : in defence of the temples, whose property they have either sold or burgled and defiled ; in defence of the State, which they weakened, and of the dockyards, which they destroyed ; in defence of the dead, whom, since you could not protect them in their lives, I implore you to succour now that they are gone. I believe that they are listening to us, and that they will know what verdict you give. They will think that those of you who vote for the acquittal of these men will be condemning the dead to death again ; and those of you who demand punishment will have executed vengeance on their behalf.

My indictment shall end here. You have heard, you have seen, you have suffered, you wield the power.

Deliver your verdict.

.    .    .    .    .

It might have been expected that this moving speech would be successful, especially since feeling was still running high against the late dictatorial government when it was delivered, and the jury must have included men who had suffered at their hands. Nevertheless, a verdict against Eratosthenes seems unlikely. Lysias was demanding the death-penalty, yet no execution of Eratosthenes is recorded, nor does he seem to have paid a money-compensation, since Lysias had to go on writing speeches for others in order to earn a living.

Perhaps the fact that Lysias was not an Athenian, but a resident alien of Syracusan origin, may have told against him, in spite of the help he gave to the democratic party during his and their exile. It is said that he made over the rest of his fortune to their leaders, including two hundred shields and two thousand drachmas (£400). For this he was granted citizen rights when democracy was restored, but this was later annulled on technical grounds, so that he must have had enemies even under the democratic *régime*.

The speech, whether successful or not, remains for all time a stirring record of political persecution, victimisation and escape.

# VI

## *ON THE MURDER OF HERODES*

Speech written for the defendant, by ANTIPHON. Date about 419 B.C.
Herodes was an Athenian citizen. He disappeared while on a voyage
with the defendant Helos, a young man from Mytilene, the chief town
of the island of Lesbos, which was at that time an Athenian dependency.
The prosecutors were the relatives of the missing man. They alleged
that Herodes had been murdered by Helos and his body thrown into
the sea.

The accused man was obliged to come to Athens for his trial. He
thus laboured under a disadvantage, not only because he was a foreigner,
but also because his fellow-countrymen were unpopular at Athens.
Some years before, in 427 B.C., Mytilene had stabbed Athens in the
back, at the beginning of her long war with Sparta (431–405 B.C.),
by revolting from the Athenian Empire. The prejudice still lingered
in Athens.

The case was tried, not before the Court of the Areopagus, but before
an ordinary jury-court under the presidency of the prison officials, the
Eleven. This was unusual, and the defendant complains of it at length.
It appears that the prosecution had decided not to bring a straight-
forward indictment for murder against him, but to lay information
against him before the Eleven, which gave them the right to deliver
him over to the prison authorities as soon as he landed in Athens,
and to have him kept in prison until the date of the trial. They therefore
indicted him not as a murderer but as a " malefactor ", a vague term
covering theft, house-breaking, kidnapping, and here stretched to include
murder. This procedure held various disadvantages for the defendant,
which are pointed out in his speech: the most serious of these was that
even if he were acquitted, he could still be indicted for murder and
brought before the Court of the Areopagus in the usual way.

·    ·    ·    ·    ·

THE PROEM

I COULD wish, members of the jury, that I were endowed with
oratorical powers and practical experience in a degree proportionate
to the disaster and the mishaps that have befallen me. But as

63

things are, my adversity has been far beyond my deserts, and my inadequacy passes the bounds of safety. Before, when I was faced with physical injury accompanying an unjust charge, I had no experience to come to my aid ; and now, when I am called upon to win liberty by giving a true statement of events, my inability as a speaker damages my cause. Plenty of men before now, among those who have no oratorical skill, have failed to sound convincing, and so have been destroyed by the very facts that they were unable to make clear. Plenty of others, among those who have been orators, have won credence by telling lies, and have been saved by this very ability. And so, of necessity, a man who has no experience of litigation is more dependent upon the arguments of his accusers than upon the facts themselves and the true story of the events.

My request to you, gentlemen, shall therefore not be that of the majority of men who come before the courts—that you will give them an attentive hearing. This implies a mistrust in their own cause, and a judgment, passed against you in advance, of some injustice. It goes without saying that a jury of good men and true will grant the defendant, even without his asking, the same hearing which the prosecution, likewise without asking, was able to obtain. My plea is rather that you will pardon me two things : if my diction is at fault, let the error be attributed to inexperience and not to guilt ; and if I score a verbal point, let that be attributed to truthfulness and not to ingenuity. Granted, it is not right that a man who has transgressed in deed shall be saved by words ; but neither should a man whose acts have been blameless be damned by words : the verbal error is of the tongue only, but the criminal act springs from the purpose of the mind.

Moreover, it is inevitable that a man who is on trial for his life should make some blunders : he has to think, not only of what he is saying, but of what he is going to say. Whatever is still hidden in the future depends more upon chance than upon foresight. Considerations such as these are bound to cause confusion in the mind of the man in jeopardy. My observation tells me that even experienced litigants fall short of their customary skill in speaking when they are in any danger ; they hit the mark far more readily when the matter in hand involves no personal risk. My request, therefore, members of the jury, is in accordance with legal and moral right, and squares with your idea of justice no less than with mine.

As for the accusations, I shall defend myself against them point by point.

First of all, I want to explain to you the violent, illegal method by which I have been brought to trial. I am not trying to evade the judgment of this democratic court. Even if you were not under oath and there were no law on the matter, I would still entrust my life to your vote, because I have confidence not only in my complete innocence, but in your ability to come to a right verdict. But it will show you how violent and illegal their treatment of me has been, in everything that concerned me.

My first point is this : I am on trial for murder, yet they have indicted me as a " malefactor ", a thing that has never happened to anyone before in this country. But I am not a " malefactor ", and not liable to the law against malefactors. The prosecution have borne witness to this themselves : the law is enacted against robbers and bandits, and none of these charges applies to me, as they have shown. And so by causing my arrest in the way they did, they have made my acquittal a matter of strict legality and justice.

They plead that murder is a great crime, and I admit that it is —one of the very greatest. So are temple-robbery and treason ; but there is a separate law laid down for each of these. See what they have done : first, they have caused this trial to take place in the very surroundings from which men accused of murder are excluded by public proclamation—*in the market-place*. Second, they have suggested a money-compensation, whereas the law decrees that a murderer shall give life for life. They did this with a view to their own profit, not out of consideration for me—and so they are assigning to the dead man something *less* than the legal penalty. Third, as you all know, all the law-courts judge murder-cases *in the open air*, with the sole object of safeguarding the jury from entering into the same building as the man whose hands are unclean, and of preventing the prosecutor from being under the same roof as the murderer.

(*He turns to the chief prosecutor.*)

But you have ignored this. You have twisted the law round and made it the exact opposite of what is the common usage. And more than that : you ought by right to have sworn by the greatest of oaths—destruction upon yourself, your house and your family—that you would confine your accusation to the actual charge : murder. In that way, even if I had been guilty of many crimes, I could not be convicted of any except this one thing, and even if I had many good deeds to my credit, I could not be saved by these. But you have ignored this, and have invented a new law, by yourself and for yourself. You, the prosecutor, are not bound by oath, and the witnesses you bring are also unsworn, though they ought to have taken the same oath as you, and given evidence with one hand on the sacred offering. You are asking the jury to condemn a man for murder on the evidence of unsworn witnesses, though you yourself have destroyed their credit by ignoring the enactments of the law. You are asking the jury to set your own illegal invention above the laws themselves.

You say that I would not have stayed if I had been left at liberty —that I would have run away. You talk as if you had dragged me here to this country against my will. But if I had not cared about being banned from this city, it would have been all one to me not to have come when I was summoned. I could have let the case go by default ; or when I had made the first speech in my defence before the Court of the Areopagus, I could have left the country—that is open to everyone. But you are trying to rob me of a right that every Greek shares, by making a private law of your own.

(*He turns back to the jury.*)

Yet everybody admits that your laws on homicide are the best and most sacrosanct. They are the oldest in the land, and have remained unaltered at all points, which is a sure sign that laws are well enacted. It is time and experience that teach mankind when laws are badly made. You do not need to find out from the prosecutor whether your laws are good or bad ; what you must do is to judge by the laws whether what he says is right or not. The Athenian laws on homicide are the best, and no one has ever dared to change them.

(*He turns again to the prosecutor.*)

You alone have dared to set yourself up as a legislator, in order to carry out your wicked schemes. The illegality of your procedure is my best witness—for you knew that no one would give evidence against me if he had first had to swear so solemn an oath.

And therefore you have arranged, not for a single straight-forward trial, as if you trusted your case. No, you have left room for further argument, the idea being not to trust the first jury, so that if I were acquitted here, I should gain nothing. You could say I was acquitted as a " malefactor " only, and not on the charge of murder. But if I am condemned, you can demand my death, on the ground that I have lost a suit for murder. Could there be a more villainous piece of trickery ? If you can convince this jury once, you can have your own way ; but if I get off this time, I am still faced with the same ordeal!

*(He again addresses the jury.)*

More than that, gentlemen : I was imprisoned, with less legal justification than anyone on earth. I was ready to produce three persons as sureties according to law ; but the prosecutor prevented it by working things this way. No other foreigner who has offered to produce three sureties has ever been imprisoned. Even the prison superintendents observe this law. So that I alone was deprived of its benefits, though it applies to all.

This was to the advantage of the prosecution in several ways : first, I would thus present myself here in a state of complete un-preparedness, since I could not handle my own affairs. Second, I would suffer physically, and my physical ill-health would alienate my friends and make them readier to give false evidence against me than to speak the truth on my side. And last, they have inflicted on me and on my family a disgrace which will last my whole life through.

Thus I stand on trial, deprived of all these rights, which are allowed me by your laws and by justice. Yet in spite of everything, I shall try to prove my innocence. It is hard to refute, all at once, false charges which have been concocted over a long period ; and to guard against an unexpected attack is impossible.

THE NARRATIVE

I set out on a sea-voyage from Mytilene, members of the jury, my companion on the trip being this man Herodes, of whose murder I am accused. We were sailing to the north Aegean port of Aenos on the coast of Thrace, I on a visit to my father, who happened to be there at the time, Herodes on business connected with the ransoming of some slaves by their Thracian relatives. With us were the slaves he was to release, and the Thracians who were to pay their ransom. For these facts, I shall bring before you my witnesses.

> (*Witnesses come forward, and their depositions are read, to the effect that the reasons the two men had for travelling together were as Helos states.*)

Such were the respective purposes of our voyage.

However, we were unfortunate enough to experience a storm, which forced us to put back into Methymna (*another port on the coast of Lesbos*). Here was moored a vessel to which we transferred ourselves, the vessel on board which my accusers allege that Herodes went before he met his death.

ARGUMENT ON FIRST PART OF NARRATIVE

Please observe that none of these events was of my choosing: they all happened by chance. There is no proof that I persuaded Herodes to come on the voyage with me. He went of his own accord, on his own private business. Moreover, I too had a fully adequate reason for going to Aenos; and it was not by any machinations of mine that we put back to Methymna—it was through force of inevitable circumstance. Again, when we had dropped anchor, it was not by any trickery or deception that we changed from one ship to another. This too was the outcome of necessity: the ship in which we were sailing had no cover, whereas the one into which we moved was covered in; and we did it because of the rain.

For these facts, I shall bring before you my witnesses.

> (*Further witnesses come forward, and depositions are read, in support of the defendant's statement as to the reasons why they put in to Methymna and why they changed vessels. These witnesses were doubtless members of the crew.*)

THE NARRATIVE CONTINUED

When we had changed ships, we began drinking.

Now it is plain that the deceased left the vessel, and never came back again; but I never left the vessel at all during the whole of that night.

On the following day, as Herodes had disappeared, a search was instituted, by me no less than by the rest of the party. If they thought that it was a sinister happening, so too did I. It was I who caused a messenger to be sent to Mytilene, and by my suggestion that he was sent. When nobody was willing to go—none of the others on board, nor any of Herodes's own party—I offered to send my own servant. It cannot be supposed that I would knowingly send a man to inform against myself.

Well, when Herodes was searched for in the city and could not be found—when he could not be found anywhere—as soon as the weather cleared, all the vessels put out to sea again; and I too continued on my voyage.

For these facts I shall produce before you my witnesses.

*(Witnesses and depositions in support of the above statements.)*

FURTHER ARGUMENTS

The foregoing are the facts. Now consider the probabilities:

In the first place, before I set off to Aenos, after the disappearance of the deceased, nobody brought a charge against me, although they had had the news; otherwise I would not have gone on. But as soon as I had gone, and they had made up this story and concocted this plot against me, then only did they bring forward their accusation.

One of their allegations is that the deceased was murdered on shore—that I hit him on the head with a stone: I, who never once left the ship! They are well aware of this; but they cannot find any likely explanation of the man's disappearance. Obviously this would have happened in all probability near the harbour, seeing that the man was drunk, and that it was night when he left the ship. Doubtless he was not in control of his own limbs, and anyone decoying him could hardly have found a plausible reason for getting him to go very far. But though the search was carried on for two days both near to and far from the harbour, no single witness was found, no blood, nor any other clue whatsoever.

That is the result even if I grant the truth of their lying story—though I am producing evidence that I never left the ship. But even if I *had* left the ship, it is in the highest degree improbable that I could have done away with the body without being seen, unless he had first been taken a long way from the shore.

Well, they say, perhaps he was thrown into the sea. From what ship ? It must have been from one of the ships in the harbour. If so, why has this ship never been discovered ? Surely one might expect to find some clue on the ship, if a man had been murdered and thrown out in the middle of the night.

Now they say that they have found clues on board the vessel on which he was drinking, and which he left, though they admit that it was not here he was murdered. But as for the ship from which he is supposed to have been thrown, they cannot find either the ship itself or any clue thereof.

For these facts I shall place before you my witnesses.

(*Depositions are here read corroborating the defendant's statement that he himself did not leave the second vessel that night ; the prosecution has already admitted that the deceased did leave this vessel and was not murdered there. Witnesses appear also in support of their evidence that no trace of Herodes was found on shore after a two days' search, nor on any other vessel in the harbour which could have been used by anyone wishing to take the body out to sea and throw it overboard.*)

THE NARRATIVE CONTINUED

When I had gone off on my voyage to Aenos, the ship on which Herodes and I had begun our voyage returned to Mytilene. The first action of my accusers was to go on board and make a search. They found some blood-stains ; and they declared that here the murder had been committed. But this turned out to be untenable : it was proved that the stains were sheeps' blood!

So they dropped this theory, and arresting the men, examined them under torture.

Now the man whom they examined then and there had not a word to say against me ; but the man whom they tortured many days later after they had kept him by them for the intervening period—he it was who was prevailed upon by them to tell a false tale of my guilt.

I shall produce my witnesses to these facts.

*(Witnesses are called in support of their depositions that the second man, a slave, was examined a considerable number of days after the first.)*

### ARGUMENTS ON THE EVIDENCE GIVEN UNDER TORTURE

You have heard the evidence, gentlemen: you have heard how much later it was that this second man was examined. Now I want you to pay attention to the circumstances of the examination itself.

The second man was a slave. Probably the prosecution had promised him his freedom if he would speak. Moreover, it rested with them to give the order that would end his sufferings. No doubt it was these two considerations that induced him to denounce me falsely: he hoped to gain his freedom, and he wanted to escape from his immediate agony. You know, I imagine, that the persons who have the greater part of the torture in their hands can compel the victims to say whatever they think will please their tormentors: release is with the latter, especially if the person denounced happens not to be present. If I had been there to order him to be racked as a liar, perhaps he would have been dissuaded from denouncing me; but as it was, my accusers were not only the torturers, but also the assessors of their own advantage.

And so, while he had good hope of gaining something by denouncing me, he persisted in his lying story; but when he grasped that he was to be put to death, then at last he had recourse to the truth—he declared that he had been persuaded by them to denounce me.

But although he had tried his best to maintain the lying story, and then afterwards he spoke the truth, neither course availed him anything: they dragged him off and put him to death, this informer on whose words they rely in bringing their charge against me! In so doing, they reversed the usual procedure with an informer, which is, if he is a free man, to give him money; if he is a slave, to give him freedom. But my accusers here rewarded their informer with death, in spite of the protestations of my friends, who ordered them not to kill this man before I could get back. Obviously therefore it was not his person they had any use for, but only his words. If he had lived, he would have had to undergo the same torture from me, and then he would have turned into a denouncer of their plot. But his death destroyed all chance of proving the truth which has died with him; and I am to be destroyed by his false testimony as if it were the truth!

For these facts, please call my witnesses.

*(Depositions are read and confirmed by witnesses, that the slave who denounced Helos under torture later recanted; and that this slave was put to death by the prosecutors before the defendant's return from his voyage, in spite of the protests of defendant's friends.)*

Their proper course, as I see it, was to produce the informer himself here as evidence against me—to use the man in person as matter for debate, bringing him forward openly and offering him to me for examination; but not to have put him to death. Tell me—which of his tales are they now going to use? The tale he told first? Or the one he told later? Which of the tales is true—his statement that I did the deed, or that I did not? We are forced to judge this question by the standard of probability; and by this it becomes clear that the later story is the true one. He lied at first, for his own advantage; and then, when he found that his very lying was his undoing, he thought that by declaring the truth he might save himself. His true story had no champion: I was not there—I, to whom the truth of his second story was an ally. But his earlier false story brought down on him those who would obliterate it, so that it could never be converted to truth.

Other men when denounced kidnap the man who informs against them, and do away with him. But in this case it is the men who are holding the informer, the men investigating the affair, who themselves have put him out of the way. If I had done away with him, or had refused to hand him over to them, or had evaded any other such test, they would have made use of this as very strong proof,—indeed, as their strongest evidence against me. As it is, I am entitled to use against them the fact that they, at the urgent demand of my friends, evaded further investigation. This proves that the charge they were bringing against me was false.

They further state that the man under torture admitted to having helped me to murder the deceased. I declare that this was not what he said: that he said he conducted me and the deceased off the vessel, and that when the deceased had already been killed by me, he put the body on the other ship and then threw it into the sea. In the first place, please note that the slave did not make this statement until he was placed on the wheel; up to the last compulsion, he kept to the truth and exonerated me. Then he falsely accused me in order to escape the torture. Then, when his torture was over, he ceased to declare that I had done any of these things; and at the very last, he uttered a lament for both himself and me, saying that we were both being destroyed unjustly. This was not because he wished to do me a favour—how could that be, seeing that he was the man who had falsely denounced me?—but because he was driven by the truth itself to confirm the truth of his first statement.

Secondly, the other servant, who sailed on the same ship and was present throughout and constantly with me, though he was subjected to the same torture, confirmed the first and last statements of the slave, exonerating me throughout, and contradicted the statement dragged out of the other man on the rack. The slave said that I left the vessel and murdered Herodes, and that when Herodes was dead, he, the slave, helped me to do away with the body. The other man denied entirely that I ever left the ship.

FURTHER ARGUMENTS OF PROBABILITY

Probability is also on my side.

Do you think that I am so crazy as to have planned this man's death on my own, and then, when the deed was done, to have created witnesses and fellow-conspirators?

Again, their story is that the deceased was murdered near the sea-shore and the ships. Is it possible that a man whose life was being attempted by one single other man did not shout or give any sign to those on shore or on board? But, they say, such a thing can pass unnoticed far more easily by night than by day, on the sea-shore than in a town. Yes, but according to them, he left the vessel while people were still awake.

Again, though he is said to have been murdered on shore, and the corpse placed on a ship, no trace, no blood was discovered on shore or on board. He was murdered, they say, by night, and by night the body was placed on board. But do you think that a man in such a situation as the murderer's could have scraped up the signs on shore, and mopped away the signs on board? Even by day, in one's own home, and uninfluenced by fear, one could not have completely obliterated such traces.

### FURTHER ARGUMENT ON THE EVIDENCE GIVEN UNDER TORTURE

But the point that should have your chief attention—and don't be annoyed with me if I repeat myself : my danger is great, and in so far as you get the correct impression, I am saved, but in so far as you are deceived, I am lost—let no one delete from your minds the fact that *they killed the informer*. They did all they could to prevent his coming here to you, and to prevent my taking him, when I arrived, and submitting him to torture. All this was to their advantage. Instead, they *bought* the slave, and put him to death privately among themselves when he turned informer : this without any State decree, and although he was not the murderer of the deceased. Their proper course was to keep him in chains, or give him out under recognizances to my friends, or hand him over to the magistrates of this city until a vote could be taken about him.

(*He turns to the chief prosecutor.*)

As it is, you yourselves, on your own condemnation, have put the slave to death : a thing which is not allowed even to the State—that any man shall be punished with death without the authorization of the Athenian people. You demand that the jury shall be judges of the slave's words ; but you have appointed yourselves as judges of his deeds. Yet even slaves who kill their masters, even if they are caught red-handed, are not put to death even by the relatives of the deceased. The relatives hand them over to the authorities (*he turns to the jury*), in accordance with your ancestral laws. The law allows a slave to give evidence against a free man in a murder charge, and allows a master, if he so desire, to prosecute anyone who kills his slave. The law has equal force against the man who kills a slave and against him who kills a free man. It would be fair, then, that a trial should be held over the death of this slave, since it was unfair that he was put to death without judgment : (*he turns to the prosecutor*) put to death by you and your friends. And so *you*, all of you, ought more rightly to be on trial than I.

(*He turns back to the jury.*)

Compare the evidence of the two men who were tortured : in which tale do justice and probability reside ? The one man, a slave, gave a double version, at one time affirming, at another time denying, my guilt. The other, a free man, has never to this day said a word against me, though he was subjected to the same torture. The latter could not be influenced, as the slave could, by an offer of freedom ; and further, he preferred to take a risk in company with truth, and bear what had to be. He too knew his own advantage, which was that he would cease being racked just as soon as he said what they wanted. So which is more deserving of credence, the man who gave the same version consistently to the end, or the man who changed it from time to time ? It is always better, even when there is no torture, to believe the man who sticks to the same tale, than the man who changed it. But suppose equal weight be given to both the assertions of the slave : on the prosecutor's side his affirmation of my guilt, on my side his denial. Let equal weight be given also to the evidence of the two men under torture : one affirmed, the other consistently denied my guilt. Even so, when there is equality, the benefit goes to the defendant, since by law, if the number of votes be equal, the defendant is acquitted.

Such then, gentlemen, is the result of the torture, on which the prosecution rely in saying that they are sure that the deceased was murdered by me. Yet if I had been conscious of guilt, I could have got rid of both men, while it was still in my power to have taken them with me to Aenos, or to have shipped them across to the Continent (*i.e. Asia Minor*), instead of leaving behind me people who had knowledge of the crime, so that they could turn informers against me.

ARGUMENT ON AN ALLEGED LETTER TO AN ACCOMPLICE

The prosecution say that they found on board a note which I was sending to Lycinus, to say that I had killed the deceased. But what need had I to send a note, when the bearer of the note was himself an accessory according to them, so that he, who had taken part in the deed, could have given a clearer account himself? Why send a note, when there was no need to conceal anything from him ? One sends letters to explain something which cannot be revealed to the bearer, or else when the story is so long that the messenger cannot carry it in his memory. But in the present instance, the message was short : merely that Herodes was dead. Also, observe that the letter is inconsistent with the evidence of the slave : the slave said that he had had a share in the murder, but the letter revealed me as the sole agent. Which ought to be believed?

At first, when they came on board, they found no such letter : that came later. Why? Because they had not yet thought of this piece of trickery. But when the first man to be tortured said nothing against me, then and not till then they threw the note on board the ship, so that they could have it to use in evidence against me. The note was read ; and then the second man tortured gave evidence against me. This evidence was at variance with the letter, but it was by that time too late to do away with the contents which had been read. If they had thought that they could induce the slave at the outset to denounce me falsely, they would never have devised the contents of the letter.

Please call my witnesses for these facts.

(*The Clerk calls the appropriate witnesses, and reads their depositions, to the effect that the letter to Lycinus was not discovered at·once on board the ship which had returned, but later.*)

ARGUMENT ON MOTIVE

To come to the question of motive : what motive had I for killing this man Herodes? There was no enmity between us. They have the impudence to say that I killed him " to oblige." Whoever did such a thing to oblige another man? No one, I imagine. There has to be great enmity before one conceives such a deed, and the intention has to be clear, from many indications, as a deliberate plot. But there was no quarrel between him and me.

Did I hope to gain money by his death? No, for he had none. Perhaps I feared for myself, in case *he* killed *me*? One might be driven to commit murder from some such motive. But I had no feeling of this kind about him.

(*He turns to the prosecutor.*)

I might rather, and with truth, impute this motive to *you*— that you are seeking my destruction for the sake of gain. My relatives could with much greater justice charge you with murder for my death, than you and Herodes's relatives can charge me. *I* can show obvious intent on *your* part to kill *me* ; but all you have as a basis for your attempt to destroy me is—unfounded gossip.

(*He turns back to the jury.*)

This disproves the existence of any motive on my part.


ARGUMENT ON ALLEGED COMPLICITY OF LYCINUS

But I must also, it seems, speak in defence of Lycinus, and prove the unjustness of their charge.

The same holds good of him as of me, in regard to Herodes. Herodes had no money which Lycinus could gain by murdering him ; nor was there any danger to Lycinus which he averted by Herodes's death. But the chief proof is this : Lycinus, if he had borne Herodes a grudge, was in a position to bring him to trial and place him in great danger and even destroy him, with your laws on his side. He could thus have satisfied his private desire for revenge and at the same time have won your gratitude, by indicting Herodes as an offender against the Athenian State. Yet he refrained, though such an attempt would have been consistent with honour. He let Herodes off on *that* count, when he could have acted without danger to himself or me. Can you believe, then, that he framed his plot in such a way that if he were caught, he deprived me of my native land, and himself of religion and all those other privileges most precious to mankind ?

Again, supposing Lycinus desired Herodes's death with all his heart—for I am now going to bring my arguments to bear on the prosecutor's own version—could I have been induced to do such a deed on his behalf, a deed to which Lycinus himself was unwilling to put his hand ? Was it because I was physically best fitted to do the deed, and he had the money to buy my services ? Certainly not : he had no money, and I had. The exact opposite was true : he could in all probability have sooner been persuaded by me than I by him, because he was in arrears with a payment of seven minas (£140), and could not buy himself out of gaol, and his friends had to pay it for him. Moreover, as showing the degree of intimacy between Lycinus and myself : you have there a very important proof that he was not a very great friend of mine, namely, that I did not pay his debt for him when he was in prison and

77

suffering hardship. And yet I am supposed to have incurred the tremendous risk of murdering a man on his behalf!

I have now proved to the best of my ability that neither I nor Lycinus is guilty of the deed.

### ARGUMENT ON THE DIFFICULTY OF PROVING A NEGATIVE

However, the chief argument of the prosecution is that Herodes has disappeared. Perhaps you too would like to hear more on this point.

If I am to make a guess, my position is the same as yours, members of the jury. I did not do the deed, any more than you did. If the prosecution want the truth, well, they must ask the man who committed the crime : he is the only one who knows. I, who did not do it, can say nothing more in answer to their demand than that *I did not do it*. The man who did can disclose the whereabouts of Herodes quite easily, or if he does not disclose it, he can offer a good guess. Criminals combine with crime an ability to find an excuse for wrong-doing ; but the innocent man is hard put to it if asked to guess about the unknown. You, gentlemen, would be in the same predicament if pressed to answer a question when you had said quite truly that you did not know. So do not place me in a quandary which you yourselves would find awkward to escape from. Do not demand that my acquittal shall depend on my making a happy guess, but let it suffice for me to prove my innocence. This is proved, not by my ability to discover how the man comes to have disappeared or to have lost his life, but by the fact that the charge does not in any way fit me.

I have heard of such occurrences : murdered men, or their murderers, remaining undiscovered. It would be a bad business for their associates if they had to bear the blame in such cases. Actually, many men have perished before now, bearing the blame for the crime of others, before the truth came to light.

For instance, the murder of your fellow-countryman Ephialtes (*democratic statesman, friend of Pericles, assassinated 456 B.C.*) : his murderers have never been discovered to this day. Suppose someone had demanded of his associates that they should either guess who were the murderers or be liable to a charge of murder themselves! They would have been in an awkward position. And what is more, the murderers of Ephialtes did not attempt to do away with the body—did not take the risk of giving themselves away by such an attempt, in the way the prosecution maintain that I did, when I refrained from having an accomplice in the murder-plot, but took one when I did away with the corpse.

Another example : a short time ago, a slave not twelve years old attempted to murder his master. The master cried out, and the slave in his fright ran away leaving the knife in the wound. If he had not done so, the whole household would have paid the penalty, for no one would have thought that the boy would ever have dared such a deed.

Again : once your Imperial Treasurers were charged, as falsely as I am, with embezzlement. They were put to death, through public indignation rather than sane judgment, all of them except one. This one man (Sôsias, I understand, was his name) was already condemned to death, but still awaited execution. At this point, the truth concerning the loss of the money was revealed, and Sôsias, who was already in the hands of the Eleven for execution, was set free by the Assembly of the People ; but the others had already been put to death, though innocent.

These instances are probably remembered by the older men among you ; the young men, like myself, know them by hearsay. They show what a good thing it is to submit matters to the test of time. Perhaps in this case, too, time will reveal how Herodes came by his death. Do not learn this too late, when you have destroyed me who am innocent! Take good counsel in time, without anger or prejudice. You could not have worse counsellors than the prosecution. An angry man is incapable of judgment, because anger vitiates the very organ of deliberation, the mind. Day succeeding day, gentlemen, is a mighty force to convert the mind from wrath, and bring the truth of events to the light. I assure you, I am more deserving of pity than of punishment from you: punishment is for criminals, but pity is for those who are unjustly exposed to danger. Your power to do justice and save me must grow ever stronger than my opponents' wish to do injustice and destroy me. In delay lies the power to prevent these dread deeds to which they invite you ; but in haste there is no possibility of even beginning to deliberate correctly.

CHARACTER OF DEFENDANT'S FATHER

I must also speak in defence of my father.

79

It would be more fitting that *he* should defend *me*, since he is my father, and his age gives him knowledge of my affairs, whereas I am too young to know about *his* past activities. He would have thought himself very badly treated by me if he had been on trial and I had given evidence against him on matters about which I had no real knowledge but had gathered from hearsay. Yet now he compels me to speak in his defence concerning matters about which I am too young to know except by hearsay. Yet he does not see himself as inflicting a great wrong on *me*. However, so far as my knowledge goes, I will not betray my father. His bad reputation with you is unfounded. His conduct was correct, though I may fail by my incorrect explanation of it. Still, this risk must be run.

Before the revolt of Mytilene, he had shown his loyalty to you. But when the whole State so ill-advisedly seceded and lost your good will, he was unable to go against them openly. He could not very well leave the city, as his children and his money were there, and he could not assert his views if he stayed. When you had punished the guilty—my father was not one of them—and had granted leave to the rest to continue inhabiting their territory, he committed no offence thereafter, but fulfilled every one of his duties, omitting no service required by either Athens or Mytilene, even producing dramas at the festivals, and paying his taxes. He may choose to live at Aenos now, but this has not meant any evasion of public duty. Nor has he changed his nationality, as some others I observe have done, who have crossed to the mainland and who live among your enemies and bring mercantile law-suits against you. Nor has he gone there to avoid your democratic government. He has gone there to avoid the class of informers, whom he hates, as you do.

He should not therefore be judged for what he did under compulsion, and not by choice. He should not be judged as an individual for what he shared with the whole State of Mytilene. The people of that city will never forget their past crime. They have exchanged great prosperity for great adversity, and they have seen their country overthrown. As for any of the charges brought against my father personally, do not believe them. This whole process is brought for the sake of money, against him and me.

Many circumstances combine to help those who covet another's goods. My father is too old to help me. I am far too young to be able to avenge myself adequately. It is for you, gentlemen, to come to my aid. You must not let false accusers think that they have more power than you. If, when they come before you, they get their own way, it will be proved that one's best course is to win *them* over, and avoid the judgment of your democratic courts. But if they are shown up as scoundrels, and get no advantage, yours will be the honour and the power, as is just. *You* must lend your aid to me and to the cause of Justice.

ARGUMENT FROM RELIGIOUS OMENS

You have heard all that can be shown by human proof and evidence. You should also consider the signs from heaven when giving your vote. You rely on these for your successful conduct of public affairs, whether involving danger or not ; and these should be considered our most important and trustworthy indications in private affairs.

You know that, before now, many men whose hands are unclean, or who have any other sort of pollution, have gone on board ship, and by doing so have brought destruction on the innocent souls who sailed with them, or have brought them into grave danger. When present at a sacrifice, such people have been revealed as unclean and as preventing the proper performance of the ceremony. My case has been just the opposite : all those with whom I have sailed have had the fairest voyages ; all sacrifices which I have attended have turned out excellently. I claim this as an important proof of my innocence and the falseness of the charge. Please call witnesses to this.

(*The Clerk of the Court reads evidence that the defendant's presence on board ship has not led to shipwreck, and that his presence at religious ceremonies has not resulted in unfavourable omens.*)

One thing, too, I am very sure of : if the facts had been otherwise, my accusers would have used the testimony of heaven as their strongest argument. As it is, since the signs are in opposition to their allegations, and the witnesses support my case as true and denounce their case as false, they bid you disbelieve the witnesses and put your trust in their statements. Other men refute words with facts. They on the contrary are trying to cast doubt on facts by means of words.

I have now answered all the points in the accusation that I remember.

I beg you to acquit me. This same act which saves me is also legal and in accordance with your oath. You have sworn to judge according to law. I was arrested and imprisoned in the name of a law that does not apply in my case ; and a trial on the present charge still faces me. Two trials have been created instead of one : that is the fault of the prosecution. These men, my bitterest foes, have arranged for two trials ; surely you, the impartial arbiters of justice, will not prejudge me and condemn me in this first trial as a murderer ? Do not, I beseech you! Grant something to Time, by whose help those who seek the truth are best enabled to find it!

All I ask, gentlemen, is to be tried according to law. I have no objection to being tried as often as you like in accordance with justice : a multiplication of trials is truth's best ally and falsehood's greatest foe. But an incorrect verdict in a murder trial overrides justice and truth. If you condemn me, I shall be compelled, although I am not the murderer, to submit to your decision and the Law, whatever they decree : no one, however deeply conscious of innocence, would dare to rebel against such a verdict. Thus, justice and truth are overborne, especially if there is no one who will avenge the unjustly punished.

That is the reason why all procedure in cases of homicide is different from any other—the laws themselves, the oaths sworn over a sacrifice, public proclamations and so on—because it is so important to arrive at a true verdict. A correct judgment avenges the injured party ; but condemnation of an innocent man is a crime against Heaven and the laws. An unjust accusation is less serious than an unjust verdict ; the former is not effective, but depends on your verdict at the trial. Your judgment, however, if incorrect, cannot be referred to any court of appeal which can reverse the error.

What, therefore, would be your correct course as a jury ? To allow these men to bring their charge again, after swearing the proper oath, and let me defend myself on the actual charge. How can you allow this ? By acquitting me now. If this is done, I shall not be escaping your judgment : it will be you who will sit in that other Court to exercise your vote on my case. If you acquit me now, you can do with me as you wish on the future occasion ; but if you condemn me, you will lose your power of even deliberating any further on my case.

Observe, too, that if a mistake has to be made, it is more pardonable in the eyes of Heaven to acquit a person wrongfully than to destroy him unfairly : the former is merely a mistake, but the latter is a sin. And so one must exercise great forethought, when one is about to do something irrevocable. When there is a remedy, a mistake arising from indignation or listening to false charges is not so serious : one can change one's mind and recognize one's error. But when there is no remedy, to change one's mind and admit to a mistake merely doubles the injury. Some of you before today have regretted the infliction of the death penalty ; but you have never regretted sparing someone by mistake, however right it may be that deceivers should perish.

Moreover, involuntary crimes can be condoned, but not voluntary ones. An involuntary crime, gentlemen, is a matter of chance, but a voluntary one is a matter of choice. Yet how can anything be more intentional than to carry into immediate action a matter on which one has deliberated ? It is the same thing to kill a man unjustly with one's vote as with one's hand.

You can be certain that if I had been conscious of guilt, I would never have come to Athens. But I relied on Justice, whose protection no man deserves more than I, who am guilty of no act of impiety nor any crime against Heaven. In such straits, when the body grows weary, the spirit comes to its rescue, desiring to share its suffering because of her clearness of conscience ; but if one has a guilty conscience, this psychological effect is one's greatest enemy, because while the body is still in full strength, the spirit deserts it, believing that punishment for sin is at hand. I have come before you with a conscience utterly clear.

The fact that the prosecution maligns me is not at all surprising. This is their business, just as it is your business to refuse to accept what is unfair. If you accept my version, you can change your minds : you have a remedy—future punishment. But if you accept their story and they get their way, there is no cure. It is not as though the time-interval were very great, after which you can do legally what the prosecution ask you to do illegally. This is not a matter for haste but for careful consideration. At present, regard yourself as a jury giving a legal ruling ; later, you can be judges of the evidence. At the moment, express your opinion ; later you can come to a final decision about the truth. It is easy to bring false evidence against a man on trial for his life. If the prosecution merely win their immediate cause and get him executed, vengeance dies with him. His friends will not seek vengeance once he has perished ; and even if they do, what good is that to a dead man ?

Today, therefore, acquit me! In the real murder-trial, they can accuse me again, after swearing the proper oath, and you can decide my case in accordance with the laws. Then, if I fail, I can no longer complain that my destruction was contrary to the laws.

Do this, I beg and implore you! Then you will not be transgressing what is your duty, nor robbing me of justice. My very salvation depends upon your oath. Believe whichever of my arguments you like—but vote for my acquittal!

.    .    .    .    .

This long and brilliant piece of advocacy, to memorise and deliver which must have been a considerable feat for the defendant, shows the powers of the great lawyer fully extended. He concentrates all his force on argument, troubling less about the appropriateness of the speech to the character of his client. Though the Proem offers the conventional plea of inexperience, many of the sentiments that follow suggest the ripe experience of Antiphon rather than the untried youth of the defendant.

Antiphon evidently felt that his client was in a dangerous position. Helos was a member of an unpopular State, and his father's loyalty was suspect, whereas the deceased was an Athenian. Again, the circumstantial evidence was incriminating: the disappearance of Herodes while on a voyage with Helos, the damaging evidence of the tortured slave, the clues alleged to have been found, the suggested conspiracy with Lycinus. Antiphon tackles these points in a carefully-selected order, and with masterly skill.

The recurring appeal for delay and deliberation, as opposed to haste and indignation, is meant to remind the jurors of the famous incident in 427 B.C., when Mytilene, the defendant's native city, revolted against the Athenian Empire and was quelled. The Athenian Assembly of the People, discussing proposals for the punishment of the treacherous ally, was persuaded in the heat of the moment to pass a decree condemning all male citizens of Mytilene to death, and all women and children to slavery. The ship carrying this order set out; but next day the Assembly, their anger cooling, realised what they had done and reversed their decision. A second ship set out from Athens, carrying the reprieve; but it was not certain whether the second ship could overtake the first. However, the second crew rowed in shifts, eating, as they rowed, a prepared mixture of bread with wine and oil, and taking it in turns to sleep. They rowed fast, whereas the first crew, disliking their mission, rowed slowly. Thus the second ship ran into the harbour just as the commanding officer of the first ship had read the decree and was about to execute it; and the people of Mytilene were saved from complete destruction, though they were made to pay severely in other ways, and lost their independence. This was an occasion when the Athenian people repented of a hasty decision, and did not regret their change of mind.

This speech gives much incidental information on Athenian legal procedure—for instance, that witnesses in trials that came before the ordinary courts did not give evidence under oath, whereas in trials that came before the Court of the Areopagus, a solemn oath was required of witnesses. The speech also deals with the examination of slaves under torture. Here its value is questioned, because the evidence of the tortured slave was against the defendant; but elsewhere, when circumstances required, the same advocate will be found arguing that the evidence of slaves is not trustworthy unless given under torture, and that the overthrow of this system would be subversive of public safety.

It will also be noticed that in spite of much scepticism current in Athens at this time, it was still useful to be able to tell a jury that one's presence had not affected religious sacrifices or brought disaster on one's shipmates. The primitive idea of blood-pollution as a physical, contagious thing was still active; a person accused of murder was banned from society until acquitted, and it was taking a dangerous risk to be under the same roof with him. The first act of anyone tried and acquitted by the Court of the Areopagus was to visit the cave of the Furies, the traditional avengers of blood, at the foot of the hill, and propitiate them with a purificatory offering.

Though the verdict in this case is not recorded, there is a strong probability that it was for the defendant. Antiphon's reputation as an advocate for the defence was very great, and it is likely that this speech was preserved as a supreme example of his art: that of extricating a client from a dangerous position, and securing an acquittal in most unpromising circumstances. Whether the defendant was really innocent is perhaps more doubtful. The weakness of the case of the prosecution was that since no body had been found, they could not know exactly when, where or how Herodes had met his death. Of this weakness the advocate for the defence makes the fullest use, showing up the evidence of the prosecution as guess-work, exposing the contradictions in it, and suggesting malice. But suspicion of the defendant's guilt must remain strong.

# VII

# AGAINST A STEP-MOTHER, ON A CHARGE OF POISONING

Speech for the prosecution, written by ANTIPHON. Date unknown: some time between about 450 and 411 B.C.

The deceased had married twice. The prosecutor is his son by his first wife. The accused woman is his second wife, the prosecutor's step-mother. No woman could plead in person, so that her eldest son by the deceased undertakes her defence. The prosecutor and the speaker for the defence are therefore half-brothers.

The charge is of murder, so that the case came before the Areopagus. The accusation is that the defendant brought about the death of her husband by causing poison to be administered to him by a third party, his friend's concubine. The defence is that the accused woman believed the fatal draught to have been a love-philtre. The alleged crime was committed while the prosecutor was still a boy. He has waited to come of age before bringing the charge.

This is the only surviving speech written by Antiphon for the prosecution in an actual trial. We know that he usually wrote for the defence.

.    .    .    .    .

THE PROEM

MEMBERS of the jury:

Young as I am, and still without experience of litigation, I am placed by this event in a position of terrible difficulty. Either I have to disobey the injunction laid on me by my father, that I should seek vengeance on his murderers ; or if I do seek vengeance, I am driven into a feud with those with whom it is least desirable— my half-brothers and their mother. Events, and my half-brothers themselves, have driven me into bringing this suit against them. They are the very men who ought naturally to have come forward as avengers of the deceased, and allies of the avenger. But in fact, the precise opposite has come about : they have taken their stand here as my adversaries, on the side of murder as I and my indictment declare.

My plea to you, gentlemen, is this : if I prove that their mother
did by intention and forethought cause the death of our
father, and that she had been caught before, not once but several
times, in the very act of plotting his murder, inflict punishment!—
avenge, in the first instance your laws, which you have received
as an inheritance from Heaven and your ancestors, and by which
you must be guided when considering condemnation as judges in
this Court ; avenge, in the second instance him who is dead and
gone, and with him me also, who, alone and deserted, am left
to take his part! You, gentlemen, stand to me now in the place
of my family, because those who should have been his avengers
and my allies have come forward as the dead man's murderers and
my opponents. To whom, then, can anyone turn for help, or where
can he go to seek sanctuary, except to you and to Justice ?

## COMPLAINT AT PROCEDURE OF DEFENCE

I am amazed at my half-brother. What possible object can he
have in taking up the *rôle* of advocate against me ? Does he believe
that filial piety lies in not betraying his mother ? My own view is
that it is far more sinful to neglect the vengeance that one owes
to the dead, especially as his death was brought about by conspiracy,
through no fault of his own, whereas her putting him to death
was a deliberate act, planned beforehand.

Moreover, he cannot plead to a sure knowledge that his mother
did not kill our father, because when it was open to him to obtain
sure knowledge on certain points—that is, by means of torture—
he refused ; but on all points where information could not be
obtained, he keenly demanded investigation. His keenness should
have been directed towards the object of my challenge—a strenuous
effort to bring the truth to light. If the slaves had told contradictory
stories, he could have based his defence and his opposition to me
on sure knowledge, and his mother would have been cleared of
this charge. But in a case where he has refused to seek proof of
what has happened, and on matters about which he has refused
to obtain information, how is it possible for him to have knowledge ?
How, gentlemen, is it likely that he has knowledge about
matters of which he has not ascertained the truth?

What possible defence can he put forward against me? He
was well aware that if evidence were obtained from the slaves under

torture, she was bound to be condemned. He believed that salvation lay in refusing the test by torture ; the defence thought by this means to obliterate what had occurred. How then can he have been avoiding perjury when in his counter-statement he declares under oath that he " knows for certain " ? He it was who refused to seek definite information about this crime, when I was ready to employ the method most in conformity with justice—examination by torture.

I desired, firstly, to examine their slaves, because they knew of a previous attempt that this woman, their mother, had made against our father's life by means of drugs : they knew how my father had caught her in the act, and that she did not deny it, except to maintain that she had intended it not as a poison but as a love-philtre. This was the reason why I wished to get evidence by torture on these matters, after having put in a written deposition containing my accusations against this woman. I urged that they themselves should perform the examination in my presence, so that the slaves should not be forced to give answers to any questions I chose to ask. I was willing to content myself with the questions put down in my deposition. This in itself shall stand as my legal proof that I do lawfully and rightly prosecute the murderess of my father. If slaves were to utter denials, or their evidence disagreed, examination by torture would compel them to reveal the incriminating facts. By this method, even those who are prepared to utter falsehoods can be forced to speak the truth that condemns.

And yet I am certain that if they had come to me as soon as they were informed of my intention to prosecute my father's murderess, and had offered to hand over what slaves they possessed, and I had refused to accept their offer, they would have put this forward as their greatest proof of innocence. But in fact, it is I who have shown readiness either to undertake the examination myself, or to let them carry it out instead of me ; so that it is only proper that these negotiations should count as a proof of guilt. If they had offered to submit their slaves to torture, and I had declined the offer, this would have been evidence on their side. Therefore let the same be granted as evidence on my side, that I offered to put the matter to the test, but they refused to let it be so submitted. To my mind, it is a scandal that they seek to persuade you not to vote for condemnation, when they themselves

have declined to be judges of their own case, as they could have
been by handing over their slaves to the examination by torture.

Hence on these matters it is quite clear that they themselves
have avoided the attainment of sure knowledge. They knew, of
course, that the evil which would come to light was in their own
home, and so they preferred to let it pass in silence and without
investigation. But you, members of the jury, will not do so, I
am sure. You will bring it into the open.

## THE NARRATIVE

There was in our house an upper room, which Philoneos used
to occupy whenever he had business in town. This Philoneos
was an honest, respectable man, a friend of my father's. He had
a concubine, whom he was intending to dispose of to a brothel.
My step-mother, having heard of this, made a friend of the woman ;
and when she got to know of the injury Philoneos was proposing
to do her, she sent for her. When the woman came, my step-
mother told her that she herself also was being wrongly treated,
by my father ; and that if the woman would do as she said, she
was clever enough to restore the love of Philoneos for his concubine, and my father's love for herself. As she expressed it, hers
was the creative part, the other woman's part was that of obeying
orders. She asked her therefore if she was willing to act as her
assistant ; and the woman promised to do so—very readily, I
imagine.

Later, it happened that Philoneos had to go down to the Peiraeus
(*the port of Athens*) in connection with a religious ceremony to
Zeus, Guardian of Property ; and at the same time my father was
preparing for a voyage to Naxos. It seemed to Philoneos an excellent idea, therefore, that he should make the same trip serve a
double purpose : that he should accompany my father, his friend,
down to the harbour, and at the same time perform his religious
duty and entertain him to a feast. Philoneos's concubine went
with them, to help with the sacrifice and the banquet.

When they arrived at the port, they of course performed the
sacrifice. When the religious ceremony was over, the woman
began to deliberate with herself as to how and when she should
administer the drug, whether before dinner or after dinner. The
result of her deliberation was that she decided to do so after dinner,

thus carrying out the instructions of this Clytaemnestra, my step-mother.

The whole story of the dinner would be too long for me to tell or you to hear ; but I shall try to narrate the rest to you in the fewest possible words, that is, how the actual administration of the poison was accomplished.

When they had finished dinner, they naturally—as one of them was sacrificing to Zeus and entertaining a guest, and the other was about to set off on a voyage and was dining with his friend—they naturally were proceeding to pour libations, and accompany them with an offering of incense. Philoneos's concubine, as she was serving them with the wine for the libation—a libation that was to accompany prayers destined, alas! gentlemen, not to be fulfilled —poured in the poison. And in the belief that she was doing something clever, she gave the bigger dose to Philoneos, thinking that perhaps the more she gave him, the more he would love her. She still did not know that she had been deceived by my step-mother, and did not find out until she was already involved in disaster. She poured in a smaller dose for my father.

The two men poured out their libation ; and then, taking in hand that which was their own destroyer, they drained their last draught.

Philoneos dropped dead instantly. My father was seized with an illness from which he died in three weeks. For this, the woman who had acted under orders has paid the penalty for her offence, in which she was an innocent accomplice : she was handed over to the public executioner after being broken on the wheel. But the woman who was the real cause, who thought out and engineered the deed—she will pay the penalty now, if you and Heaven so decree.

THE ARGUMENTS

Consider how much more just is my request to you than that of my brother. I am urging you to be avengers of a man who is dead, whose injury is for ever irreparable. His demand will be in no way connected with the dead, who so well deserves your pity and your support in avenging him, who was robbed of his life so wickedly and shamefully before his time, by the last person in the world who should have done him harm. My brother is about

to plead with you on behalf of the woman who took that life—
a plea contrary to religion, deserving of no fulfilment, not even of
a hearing from Heaven or from you ; and he will base his appeal
on a statement which even she herself has not managed to believe
—that she " meant no harm ". But you must be allies, not of
murderers, but of those who are murdered, especially by those
who least of all should have brought about their death. The
time has come when it rests with you to give a correct verdict on
this case ; and this I beg you to do.

My brother's plea to you, however, will be on behalf of his
mother, who is alive, the woman who so recklessly and wickedly
brought about the death of the deceased. He will plead that she
may escape the penalty, if he can persuade you, of her crime. I
am imploring you on behalf of my father, the man who is dead,
that she may pay the full penalty. It is for you to see that the
criminals do pay the penalty : that is the object for which you
have been appointed judges and given this name. I have come
forward as prosecutor to see that she pays the penalty of her
crime. I shall exact vengeance for my father and for your laws.
For this reason it is right that you should one and all support me,
if I am speaking the truth. My brother stands on the opposite
side, as the ally of the woman who has ignored the laws, to prevent
her from paying the penalty.

Which is more just—that the murderer should pay the penalty,
or not ? Which is more just—to pity rather the dead man, or
the woman who killed him ? The dead man, I would say. That
would be the far more just and more righteous course for you,
in the eyes of God and man. And so at this point I demand that
as she destroyed him without pity and without mercy, so she too
shall be destroyed by you and by Justice. She acted of her own
free will and compassed his death with guile ; he died by force,
an unwilling victim. Can it be denied, gentlemen, that he died
by force—a man who was intending to set out on a voyage from
this country, and who was dining with his friend ? She it was
who sent the poison, who gave the order that it should be given
him to drink, and so killed my father. What claim has she to be
pitied or to win consideration from you or anyone else ? *She*
did not see fit to have pity on her husband—no, but she wickedly
and shamefully destroyed him.

Pity, as you know, is more properly bestowed in cases of

involuntary suffering than of crime and offences committed voluntarily and with malice aforethought. Even as she, fearing neither gods nor saints nor her fellow-men, destroyed the dead man, so let her in turn be destroyed by you and by Justice! Let her win neither consideration nor pity nor any sort of compunction from you, and thus meet with the punishment she has so justly earned!

I am amazed at my brother's hardihood, and puzzled as to his object, in declaring on oath, on his mother's behalf, that he " knows for certain " that she has not committed this crime. How can anyone " know for certain " about events at which he was not present ? Naturally, people who are plotting the murder of their neighbours do not prepare their plans and make their preparations in the presence of witnesses. They do so with the greatest possible secrecy, so that no other human soul may know. But the victims of their machinations know nothing until they are caught in the grip of the menace ; not till then do they recognize the destruction that is upon them. And then, if they are able—if they are not forestalled by death—they summon their friends and relatives, and give evidence and tell them the names of their murderers, and enjoin upon them to avenge the crime.—Such was the injunction which my father laid on me when I was still a boy, when he was suffering from his last unhappy illness.—If they fail to achieve this, they make a statement in writing, and call upon their own servants as witnesses, and reveal the names of those who are guilty of their death. Thus did my father, when I was still young, reveal these facts to me, and leave his last injunction with me, not with his slaves.

THE EPILOGUE

I have now completed my account, and my effort on behalf of the dead man and the law. It rests with you to consider among yourselves what is to be done, and to pass a just verdict. It is my belief that the gods of the nether world have at heart the cause of those who are the victims of crime.

.    .    .    .    .

In this case, the facts are not disputed. It is admitted that the accused woman was responsible for the administration of the poison; but intention to kill is denied. No evidence is offered on either side: an assertion of intention is opposed to a denial on oath. The nature of the case, and the passage of time between the event and the trial, accounts for the absence of witnesses; and the defence had refused to allow an examination of their household slaves. The prosecutor does not fulfil his promise to show that the accused woman had made previous attempts on the life of the deceased; and it does not seem that he had any proof of the complicity between the accused and the other woman. On the other hand, the defending side do not seem able to prove their story that the fatal draught was intended as a love-philtre. A busy traffic in such drugs was carried on in Athens; but the seller doubtless could not be traced.

Great use is made of the defendants' refusal to let their slaves be examined by torture. The prosecutor is made to say that this method is " most in conformity with justice", and to suggest that it is an infallible way of extracting the truth. In the previous case the same advocate's exposition of the argument that such evidence is untrustworthy can be found.

Possession of a concubine did not destroy a man's title to respectability. Concubines, as in Sumerian and Semitic law, had a definite status below that of a married woman, if they were freeborn. This woman, however, was a slave: Philoneos had absolute rights over her, even to selling her to a house for prostitutes. For her part in causing the death of Philoneos, his relatives could hand her over for summary execution, though they could not kill her themselves. The cruel manner of her death is also to be noticed: she was first racked, then handed over to the public executioner (himself a slave), probably to suffer the death known as " apotympanism ", the exact nature of which is not known, but which may have been a sort of garroting. Drinking the hemlock was reserved for free men, and was in fact a kind of compulsory suicide. Some think that it was not introduced as a legal penalty until the end of the fifth century, B.C. " Apotympanism " was inflicted on free men also for certain offences: banditry, treason, and probably murder.

An Athenian dinner-party, if ceremonial, was accompanied by libations—that is, the pouring of wine on to the ground as an offering to a deity—and prayers and hymns. The order of dining was: the main course, or first table, consisting of vegetables, meat or fish, eaten with bread: the dessert, or second table, consisting of fruit, sweetmeats, nuts and the like; then the libations and the wine-drinking. The first libation was usually of pure wine in honour of the Spirit of Good Luck. Then wine was mixed with water, according to a ratio arranged beforehand, in a mixing-bowl (*crater*), and further libations were poured out to Zeus and other deities. Then the rest of the mixed wine was served out in cups to the diners, who sang songs, conversed, and if it was a large party, listened to flute-playing and watched variety entertainments. Perfume was often served, and garlands of sweet-scented flowers and foliage were worn.  On the present occasion, only the two men were present; but the occasion was formal, because Philoneos wished to perform a religious duty and the prosecutor's father wished to ask for a blessing on his voyage.  Philoneos's concubine waited until after the dessert had been served and removed; then she poured out the unmixed wine for the first libation, and added the poison to each cup, giving the larger dose to Philoneos. The two men then prayed for good fortune, poured some of the wine on the ground, and drank the rest as was usual.

This speech is far inferior to the preceding one by the same hand. Antiphon was greater in defence than in attack, and here he had to make the best of a weak case.  The prosecutor is clearly (like Hamlet) fulfilling a duty enjoined on him by his father, and there are hints that he finds this duty distasteful, since it means a feud between him and his half-brothers.  Since there is no conclusive evidence of intention to kill, the advocate is driven to appeal to prejudice: the repetition suggests weakness, though it may have been effective before a jury. The horror felt for a woman who attempted to poison her husband would be extreme.  Nevertheless, the defendant's son could also make an emotional appeal for pity, on the ground that his mother was a wronged and innocent woman whose only mistake was in the means she took to regain her husband's love.  The prosecutor calls her Clytaemnestra; the defendant's son might have called her Deianeira. It is impossible even to surmise which way the verdict went in this case.

*THREE*

*TRIALS*

*FOR*

*VIOLENCE*

# VIII

## *WOUNDING WITH INTENT TO KILL : QUARREL OVER A BOY*

Speech written for the defence, by LYSIAS. Date some time later than 394 B.C.

The name of the prosecutor is Simon. The defendant's name is not given. The boy who was the cause of the quarrel was not an Athenian, but a native of Plataea, a town in the neighbouring territory of Boeotia. His name is Theodotus.

The prosecution has alleged wounding with intent to kill, for which the punishment is banishment with confiscation of property. The defendant denies the charge, alleging that Simon was the aggressor, and that any hurt Simon received was greatly exaggerated. The injury had occurred four years before the date of the trial.

The case came before the Court of the Areopagus.

.     .     .     .     .

### THE PROEM

THOUGH I know a great deal to Simon's discredit, gentlemen, I would never have believed him capable of going to such lengths as at present. This is a case in which he himself ought to be punished, and yet he has dared to bring a charge as if he were the injured party, and to come before you after having sworn so great and solemn an oath !

If it had fallen to any other Court to try this case, I should have greatly dreaded the risk, since I notice that factors both designed and accidental can sometimes crop up which result in a number of surprises to those facing the danger of a trial. But coming before *you*, I hope to obtain justice. What irks me most, gentlemen, is that I shall be compelled to speak to you of the facts, whereas it was my feeling of shame about them, in case my conduct should become widely known, which led me to put up with my grievances. But since Simon has driven me to this pass, I shall tell you without concealment everything that has occurred.

I call upon you, gentlemen, if I am in the wrong, to grant me no pardon. If, however, in this affair I shall prove that I am not guilty of the charges sworn to by Simon, but nevertheless am exposed to you as having entertained towards this boy a feeling too silly for my age, do not, I ask you, think any the worse of me! Remember that desire is an integral part of all human nature, and that the best and wisest man may be he who can bear its disasters with the greatest self-control. All my efforts to achieve this have been prevented by this man Simon, as I shall prove to you.

## THE NARRATIVE

He and I, gentlemen of the court, fell in love with Theodotus, a lad from Plataea.

I hoped that by doing the boy services I could make him my friend; but the prosecutor thought that by bullying and rough treatment he could force him to do whatever he wished. To recount the injuries the boy suffered at his hands would be too long a story; but I think it proper that you should hear the crimes he committed against *me*.

Having discovered that the boy was with me, he came to the house at night, drunk; and bursting the door open, he broke into the women's quarters. In here were my sister and her daughters, whose lives are such models of propriety that they shrink from being seen even by the other members of the household. However, he went to such lengths of violence as to refuse to go away until those who came up, as well as those who had accompanied him, disgusted by his behaviour in breaking in upon young and fatherless girls, expelled him by force.

But he was so far from being sorry for his violent deeds that he found out where we were dining, and did a most extraordinary thing, incredible unless one realizes his insane folly: he called me outside, and as soon as I came out, he aimed a blow at me. When I stood up to him and parried his blows, he began pelting me with stones. He missed me, but struck the man who had come with him to see me—his name was Aristocritus—and the stone bruised his forehead.

However, gentlemen: although I thought I had been shockingly treated, I was ashamed, as I said before, over the whole affair. So I put up with it, and chose rather to forgo the redress offered by the law for these offences, than to appear foolish in the eyes of my fellow-citizens. I realized that though such goings-on accorded well enough with the depravity of *his* character, this experience would bring down on *me* a great deal of ridicule from those whose habit it is to feel spite against anyone who tries to be a useful citizen.

I was so completely at a loss, gentlemen, what to do about his mad behaviour, that I decided it would be best to go out of town. So, taking the boy with me—since I must tell the whole truth— I went away, out of Athens.

When I thought that a sufficient time had elapsed for Simon to forget the boy and to regret his previous errors, I came home again; and I myself went to stay down at the Peiraeus.

Simon, however, observed at once that Theodotus was back, and was staying with Lysimachus, who lived near the house which Simon had rented; and so he invited a number of his friends there. These, while they were having lunch and drinking, had placed watchers on the roof, so that when the boy came out of his house, they could seize him and carry him off into theirs.

At this point I arrived from the Peiraeus, and as I was passing, I turned into Lysimachus's house. After a short while, we came out; and this gang, by now quite drunk, leapt out on us. Some of those who had joined him would not share in his crime; but Simon here, and three of his friends, began dragging the boy away. But the boy threw off his cloak and ran away at full speed.

I therefore thought that he would escape, and that these men, as soon as ever they ran into anybody, would give up the pursuit through shame. So with this idea I went off, taking another road, because I felt it very necessary to guard against them, and I regarded all these events which had occurred through them as being a great source of damage to myself. And on that occasion, where Simon says " the battle " took place, nobody either on his side or on ours had his skull broken or suffered any other injury.

This I shall prove by bringing those who were present before you as witnesses.

(*Witnesses are called in support of their depositions that the street fight described by the defendant was started by Simon.*)

That Simon was the aggressor in injury, gentlemen, and that it was he who plotted against us, and not I against him—this you have learnt from the testimony of eye-witnesses.

After that, the boy took refuge in a laundry; and these men, falling on him all together, began to drag him off by force, while he shouted and yelled his protests. A large crowd quickly gathered. There was a hostile demonstration, and voices were heard declaring that it was a shame. But these men took no notice of these comments, and when the laundryman and others tried to rescue the boy, they knocked him about severely.

At last, as they came opposite Lampon's house, I came along, walking alone, and encountered them. I thought it would be a shame and a disgrace to look on and see the boy so lawlessly and savagely ill-treated; so I took hold of him, and asked them why they were handling him so roughly. They made no answer; but instead, they let go of the boy and began hitting *me*.

A general fight began, gentlemen. The boy was hitting at them and defending his liberty. They were hitting at us, and also striking the boy in their drunken state. I was defending myself. The crowd that came up was helping us as being the injured parties. So that in all this confusion, there was not one of us who escaped without a sore head.

The rest of the gang, who had joined with Simon in his drunken bout, as soon as ever they saw me afterwards, begged my pardon: they obviously did not think themselves the injured, but the offending party. And though four years have passed since that time, nobody has ever summoned me. Simon here, the cause of all the mischief, has kept quiet until now, because he feared for himself; but he has discovered that I lost a private suit concerning an exchange of property; and it is because he thinks I am an easy prey that he has so recklessly brought me to court on the present charge.

I shall now put before you witnesses to the truth of this part of my story also, namely, those who were present.

> (*Witnesses of the second street fight are called to support their depositions that Simon was attempting to abduct Theodotus when the defendant encountered him; and that a general brawl occurred in which Simon was not the only person injured.*)

THE ARGUMENTS

You have now heard both from myself and the witnesses an account of what actually happened.

I wish, gentlemen, that Simon's attitude were the same as mine : then you could have heard the truth from both of us before arriving at your verdict. But as he has no regard for the oath he has sworn, I shall try to give you a correct account also of the matter on which he has misled you.

For instance, he has had the impudence to say that he gave Theodotus three hundred drachmas (£60), as part of a compact made with him, and that I by my machinations enticed the boy away from him. But if this were true, his proper course was to have summoned all possible witnesses and taken legal action on the matter. But he is exposed as having never done anything of the kind. Instead, he used violence : he struck us both, and came rioting along, breaking down our doors and bursting in at night upon gentlewomen. This conduct of his, gentlemen, must be regarded as the surest proof that he is lying against us. Consider the absurdity of his statement : his whole property has been assessed at two hundred and fifty drachmas (£50). It would be a miracle if the would-be lover paid more for the privilege than he actually possessed!

But his audacity is such that it is not enough for him to lie about this point only, that is, the gift of the money. He also alleges that he got it back again. Now is it likely that we would previously have committed all these offences with which he charges us for the sake of getting hold of his three hundred drachmas, and then, when we had had our fight, have chosen that moment to repay him the money, without ensuring that he would drop any litigation and without being under any compulsion ? No, gentlemen : the fact is that all these charges are trumped up by him. His reason for alleging a gift is to save himself from the imputation of criminal behaviour in having dared to ill-treat this boy so violently although there was no business arrangement between them. His reason for pretending to have recovered the money is the obvious fact that he never made any legal claim to the money nor any mention of it whatsoever.

He further declares that he was reduced to a dreadful state by a beating which I gave him at his own door. But he is proved to have chased the boy more than half-a-mile from his house with no sign of injury, and his denial of this is in contradiction to the evidence of more than two hundred eye-witnesses.

He also states that we came to his house with broken tiles in our

hands, and that I threatened to kill him—that herein lies the proof
of intent. I think, however, gentlemen, that it is easy to recognize
this lie, not only for you who are accustomed to investigate such
cases, but for everybody. Who could be induced to believe that
I, with premeditated purpose, went to Simon's house in the day-
time, taking the boy with me, when so many men were assembled
there with Simon, unless I had come to such a pitch of insanity
that I wanted to fight the whole crowd single-handed, especially
as I knew that Simon would be delighted to see me at his doors?
Had he not come as far as *my* house, and burst his way in, sparing
neither my sister nor my nieces in his reckless desire to find me;
and when he discovered where I happened to be dining, did he
not call me out and thrash me? On that occasion, to avoid scandal,
I kept quiet, thinking that his wicked nature was just my hard
luck. Was it likely that when an interval has elapsed I would change
my mind, as he declares, and seek scandal?

If the boy had been staying at his house, this falsehood might
have been supported by some argument, such as that I was driven
by desire into committing an act of improbable folly; but the
fact is, the boy was not on speaking terms with Simon, and indeed
hated him more than anyone on earth, so that actually he was
living with me. How then can any of you accept the story that
I previously went off with the boy away from Athens on a voyage,
just to avoid a fight with Simon, and then, on my return, took the
boy to Simon's very house, where I was most certain to find
trouble? Can you believe that I was plotting against his life, and
yet went there completely unprepared, without calling to my aid
either friends or servants or any other person except just this one
lad, who would have been quite unable to assist me, and yet was
capable of denouncing me under torture if I committed any offence?
Had I really reached such a pitch of stupidity that though I was
plotting against Simon I did not look out for him where he could
be caught alone either by night or by day, but went instead to
the place where I myself was bound to be seen by the greatest
number of people and beaten to death—just as if my premeditations
were directed against myself, in order that I should receive the
greatest possible ill-treatment at the hands of my enemies?

Yet another point, gentlemen: even from the actual fight that
occurred, it is easy to discern that he is lying. When the boy
grasped what was happening, he threw off his cloak and dashed

off, with these men after him ; but I went off by another road. Now whom ought one to regard as responsible for such events— those who run away, or those who try to capture ? I imagine it is obvious to all that those who run away are the ones who fear for their own safety, and those who pursue are the ones who wish to inflict some harm. Nor can it be said that though this is the pro- bability, the events were otherwise. They actually caught the boy in the street and dragged him off by force, and I, happening to meet them, left them untouched, only seizing hold of the boy, whereupon they carried him off by force and beat me. All this has been testified to you by eye-witnesses. It is therefore a shame if I am to be thought guilty of premeditation in occurrences in which these men are actually guilty of such disgraceful, lawless behaviour.

What on earth would have been my lot if things had turned out exactly opposite to what has actually happened ? Suppose that I, accompanied by a crowd of my supporters, had en- countered Simon, and had fought with him, thrashed him, chased him and caught him and tried to carry him off by force. Actually, he has done all these things ; but it is I who am on trial, in danger of exile from my native land and the loss of all my property.

To mention the biggest and most glaring discrepancy of all : the fact that this man who was injured and plotted against by me, as he alleges, yet did not pluck up courage until four years later to lay his complaint before you. Other men, when they are in love and are robbed of the object of their passion and beaten besides, feel such anger that they attempt to obtain immediate vengeance ; but this man has waited all this length of time.

That I am not responsible, gentlemen, for any of these happenings has, I think, been sufficiently demonstrated. But further, my attitude towards the dissension arising out of this affair is such that in spite of the many injuries inflicted upon me by Simon— and in particular, a serious head wound—I have never brought myself to lay a complaint in law against him. I have always thought it intolerable to try to hound a man out of his native land just because of our mutual rivalries for the affections of boys.

Further, I did not think that any wound could be said to be inflicted " with intent " if the agent did not mean it to be fatal. Who is such a fool as to plan for a long time beforehand how to inflict a *wound* on one of his enemies ? It is obvious that even those who framed our laws had no wish to impose banishment on men who happened to have been fighting and to have cut each other's heads open—otherwise the number of exiles would be great indeed ! No, the legislators intended this severe penalty for those who while plotting to kill a man merely wounded him, being unable to kill. The idea was that punishment is rightly exacted when there has been planning and premeditation, and that a failure to achieve one's object was none the less a virtual commission of the crime. This view has often before now been expressed by you in your verdicts on premeditation. And indeed it would be intolerable if men fighting under the influence of drink, or rivalry, or for sport, or because of angry words, or over a mistress, should get wounded as a result of an action such as every man regrets when he has come to his senses ; and if for this same action you should exact a punishment so dreadful and so severe as to banish one of your fellow-citizens from his native land.

## CHARACTER OF THE PROSECUTOR

It is this man's character that amazes me most of all. To love, and to bring false charges, do not seem to me to go together. The former belongs to the more simple type of man, the latter to a complete scoundrel. I should have liked to be able to demonstrate his wickedness to you from other examples, so that you might realize how much fairer it would be if he himself were facing a capital charge than bringing other men into the danger of losing their country. The rest I will pass over ; but there is one point I will mention, which I think it right for you to hear and which will be a proof of his reckless audacity : at Corinth, after arriving too late for the battle and the campaign, he had a fight with his company commander, and gave him a beating ; so that when our men marched out in full force, he was adjudged guilty of extreme insubordination and of the worst possible character, and was the sole Athenian to be debarred from the campaign by proclamation of the commanders-in-chief.

## THE EPILOGUE

I could give you a great deal more information about this man ; but as it is illegal in this Court to go beyond the actual charge in one's speech, I will merely suggest one thought to your minds : these are the kind of men who break into our homes, who hunt us down, who seize us forcibly in the street and carry us away. Bear this in mind, and so vote for the just cause! Do not allow me to be unjustly banished from the country for which I have undergone many dangers and performed many acts of special service, the country on which neither I nor any of my forebears have inflicted any hurt, but on the contrary have bestowed numerous benefits. Such a record should earn me pity from you and all others, not only lest I suffer the fate desired by Simon, but also because I have been driven as the result of such events to face so serious a trial.

.    .    .    .    .

As the Court was that of the Areopagus, the speaker is made to adopt a more restrained tone than was necessary before the ordinary law-courts. His Proem is deferential and apologetic. He endeavours by means of frankness to win the pardon of his hearers for conduct which he knows will seem absurd in a man of his age and position. From time to time he throws in a little flattery, suggesting that the Court with their experience will have no difficulty in detecting the falsity and improbability of his opponent's story. Speakers before the Areopagus had to take an oath that they would keep to the charge and not introduce irrelevant matter.

The racy narrative gives a vivid picture of a street brawl. Since there were no regular police in Athens, such street fights were not uncommon, and it lay with the spectators to decide who was in the right and restore order. There is also a glimpse of the cloistered life of the Athenian lady, whose freedom of behaviour was in inverse ratio to her respectability. The woman in the defendant's household was his widowed sister, who with her two daughters had evidently returned to his care after her husband's death; they were so correct that they shrank from being seen by the male members even of their own household.

The principal effort of the advocate, however, is to rebut the charge of " intent to kill " in the wounding of Simon; this he argues in every possible way, from fact supported by the testimony of eye-witnesses, and from probability.

It is reasonable to assume that the defendant was a man of some position, as he mentions the special acts of service to the State (called Liturgies) to which only citizens of a certain standard of wealth were liable. (For an account of these special services, see the next speech.) This would account more particularly for his feelings of shame at confessing to his folly before the Court, and for his wish to avoid any open scandal. The boy Theodotus was a Plataean, and citizens of Plataea had special rights at Athens because of their services in the Persian Wars; but these rights did not include protection against torture. It is unlikely that the boy was a slave: if he had been, the dispute between the two men would have been one of ownership merely; nor could he have been offered a money-gift. Slaves could not own property of any kind.

Pieces of broken pottery, or tiles, which could be picked up in the streets, were favourite weapons or missiles. They also played their part in politics. In the famous institution at Athens called Ostracism, an extraordinary meeting of the Assembly of the People was held, to decide whether certain statesmen should be exiled. The names were written on pieces of pottery (*ostraka*), and if the number of pieces showing the same name passed six thousand, the politician thus designated went into exile for ten years, though without suffering any loss of property or other disability, and with the possibility of being recalled before the time had elapsed if his services were considered necessary. Modern excavations by the American School of Archaeology in the Athenian market-place (*Agora*) have resulted in the discovery of a well, used in the fifth century B.C. as a rubbish dump; and in this well were found numbers of pieces of pottery with the names of famous statesmen such as Themistocles and Aristeides scratched upon them. Broken pottery was also used by the children for some of their games. Plato gives us an excellent description of a street game played by boys, called " Night or Day ", in which a crock was thrown down, and one of the two sides of players had to run according to the side of the crock that fell uppermost. For the use of the broken tile as a weapon, see also the next speech.

The leniency of the commanding officers towards gross insubordination is notable: for striking an officer, Simon was merely forbidden to take any further part in the campaign, if the defendant is to be believed— and it is unlikely that he would minimize Simon's disgrace. During the fourth century B.C., Athenians tended to accept military discipline, and even military service, less and less readily; and in the end, this cost them their independence, in the war against Macedon.

# IX

## *WOUNDING WITH INTENT TO KILL : QUARREL OVER A SLAVE-GIRL*

Speech written for the defence, by LYSIAS.   Exact date unknown: sometime between 400 and 380 B.C.

This speech is incomplete.   The whole of the first part, including the Narrative, is lost, and we pick up the case in the middle of the defendant's argument.   The prosecutor alleges that one night the defendant and his party came to his house with the intention of killing him, and seriously injured him with a broken tile.   The defendant denies intent, says that he came by invitation, and that though a *fracas* arose, the " wound " was a mere black eye.

The cause of enmity was rivalry for the possession of a slave-girl.   This case, like the previous one, came before the Court of the Areopagus, and rendered the defendant liable to banishment and confiscation of property.

Although the Narrative is lost, the story of events is clear from what remains:

Two men had quarrelled over the possession of a slave-girl, to whose purchase both had contributed.   One night, the defendant, accompanied by others, went to the prosecutor's house.   A fight ensued, in the presence of the woman, and the prosecutor was injured by a blow from a tile.

At the trial, the prosecutor contends that the defendant came in order to kill him—that they were enemies of long standing.   This he supports by reference to the past history of their dealings with one another:

The prosecutor had been called upon to fulfil one of those special services to the State known as Liturgies.   The Liturgy in Athens was one of those devices by which the State made up for its lack of regular revenue, there being no income tax or other fixed levy.   Any Athenian citizen who was believed to possess property exceeding a certain amount was liable to be called upon to undertake the financing of some public need, such as the equipment of a war-ship, or the provision of a Chorus to perform at one of the public festivals.   If, however, the person who had been called upon considered that there was someone else wealthier than himself whose turn it was to undertake the Liturgy, he could indicate this other man; and the latter then had to choose whether he would himself fulfil the Special Service in question, or else submit to an exchange of property with the person who had named him. If he accepted the exchange of property, this was held to prove that he was not richer than his challenger; but if he refused, then obviously he must have good reason, and so was liable to the Special Service. Many interesting law-suits arose out of this ingenious system, which was said to have been instituted by Solon himself.

In the present case, the prosecutor had been called upon to fulfil a Special Service, and he had used his privilege of challenging another citizen to the exchange of property. He chose the defendant as the object of this challenge; and this, the defendant maintains, was an act of enmity.

Moreover, the defendant accepted the challenge, and the exchange of property was actually made. The prosecutor took from the defendant a yoke of oxen and a number of slaves. In fact, says the defendant, this was his object when he made the challenge; he wished to get possession of the defendant's female slave, and did so by this means.

However, an agreement was later arrived at, through the mediation of friends. The prosecutor restored to the defendant all the before-mentioned property, except the woman herself. It was arranged, the defendant alleges, that they two should share her; and this constituted a reconciliation between them.

Then there followed a still more shady transaction. According to the defendant, the prosecutor was nominated by him as one of the judges at the spring festival of the Great Dionysia, at which the most important choral and dramatic competitions were held each year. The condition imposed by the defendant as a return for this nomination was that the prosecutor should vote for the victory of the defendant's clan in the competition. The final selection of the judges from the list of nominees was always made by lot; and it happened that the prosecutor's name was not one of those picked. The compact between the two men had actually been recorded by the prosecutor in writing; there were even witnesses to it, though owing to a legal difficulty they cannot appear.

Such was the previous history of their relationship, according to the defence. There had been enmity due to rivalry over the slave-girl, and a reconciliation sealed by two very questionable compacts. He then comes to the story of the crucial evening, and argues the question of premeditation:

·　　　·　　　·　　　·　　　·

## THE ARGUMENTS

According to the prosecutor, I came to his house for the purpose of killing him, and burst my way in. Then why did I not kill him, when I had him at my mercy, and was so much the victor that I was able even to take the woman ? Let him explain that to you ! But he cannot do so.

Again, you all know quite well that he could have been killed more easily by a stab from a dagger than by a blow of the fist. Yet you see that even he himself does not charge us with being in possession of any such weapon : he states that he was struck with a piece of broken earthenware. It is obvious by now, from his own statements, that there was no premeditated intent. We would never have come as we did, not knowing whether we would use this method of killing him ; we would have taken some weapon with us when we started out from home.

In actual fact, we admit that we went there drunk, and were after the boys and the flute-girls. So how can there have been any " intent " in all this ? I see none anywhere.

The truth is, this man's passion takes him in a perverse way, different from other people's. He wants to have it both ways, to keep the woman and yet not pay his share of the purchase-money. Moreover, when he is worked up by the woman, he is very quick with his fists as well as getting drunk, and one has to defend oneself. But she pretends to prefer me at one time, him at another, because she wants to be loved by both of us. For my part, I have kept my temper from the outset, and still do ; but his ill-nature has risen to such a pitch that he is not ashamed to call his black eye a " wound ", and to be carried round on a stretcher, and to pretend to be reduced to dreadful misery for the sake of a common strumpet, when he can have undisputed possession of her by paying me my share of her purchase-price.

Further, though he maintains that a dire plot was formed against his life, and he disputes every word I say, yet when he could have tested these statements by putting the woman to the torture, he refused. She could have told us, to begin with, whether she belonged to us both in common or solely to him, and whether I contributed half the price or he gave the whole, and whether we were reconciled or were still foes. She could also have told whether we came by invitation or unasked, and whether he began the fighting without justification, or whether I first struck him. All these details and all the other facts could easily have been explained by her to others and to this Court.

It has therefore been demonstrated to you, gentlemen, that there was no " intent ", nor have I done him any wrong. On this you have heard a vast number of proofs and witnesses. But I must claim one thing further : if *I* had refused to submit my slaves to torture, it would have counted against the credibility of my statements. I ask that it shall count equally as testimony to my truthfulness that the prosecutor refused to get proof out of the woman. I also ask that no weight be given to his own statement that the woman is now free. I myself have an equal interest in her freedom, since I paid the same sum as he did. But what he says is completely untrue.

It is most unfair! Suppose I had needed money to buy my ransom from an enemy in war : I could then have done what I liked with her. But as things are, I am in danger of exile from my country, and yet I am not going to be allowed even to get the truth out of her regarding the charges on which I am standing my trial. It would have been far more just that she should be tortured than that she should be sold to defray the expenses of ransoming me from an enemy, for the following reason : one can, if the enemy is willing to release one, get from elsewhere the means for one's return home ; but when one falls into the hands of private foes, this is not possible. It is not money they yearn for ; they are trying to expel one from one's country.

Hence it is right that you should reject his statement that he refused to allow the woman to be tortured because she is now free. You should rather condemn him as a false accuser, one who hoped by evading this sure test to practise an easy deception on you.

You will not, of course, think it necessary to regard *his* offer as made in better faith than ours, namely, that we could examine his other slaves under torture. The facts known to them—that we went to his house—are admitted by us as well. But the question of whether we went by invitation or not, and whether I suffered or inflicted the first blow, can better be answered by *her*.

Furthermore, if we had taken his slaves, who are his private property, and had put them to the torture, they would, in an unreasoning attempt to oblige their master, have given me the lie in contradiction to the truth. But *she* was the only one who belonged to us both in common—on the grounds of our both having paid an equal sum of money—and she best knew. She has been the cause of all our actions. Everything can be made clear by reference to her.

I should not have been in a perfectly fair position even if she had been tortured. I should still have been running a risk therein, because she obviously set far more store by him than by me. She did me wrong by joining him, but she never inflicted any injury on him by joining *me*. And yet I was the one who had recourse to her testimony, whereas he refused to put his trust in her.

## THE EPILOGUE

I feel indignation, gentlemen, if on account of a mere prostitute slave-woman I find myself faced with the danger of losing all that is most dear. I ask myself, what wrong have I done either to my country or even to the prosecutor ; or against whom among my fellow-citizens have I committed any crime ? It is not I who have done any such thing ; but I risk bringing on myself a much greater danger, through the action of my accusers—and it is utterly undeserved.

Therefore, in the name of your children, your wives, and the gods who guard this place, I beg and implore you, have pity on me! Do not allow me to be delivered into my accuser's power! Do not involve me in irreparable misfortune! *I* am not deserving of banishment from my country. *He* does not deserve to obtain such a reparation from me in return for the wrongs he says he has suffered, when actually he has suffered no wrong.

·     ·     ·     ·     ·

Both the prosecutor and the defendant in this case seem to have been disreputable characters. The legal difficulty which prevented the defendant from bringing forward witnesses to the shady compact between himself and the prosecutor was a rule peculiar to the Court of the Areopagus: before this body, all witnesses had to give their evidence definitely on one side or the other, and they had first to swear an oath affirming their belief in the guilt or innocence of the accused person. Witnesses to a small side-issue like the promise of a vote in return for nomination to office would not be prepared to express on oath an opinion about the merits of the case as a whole.

The Liturgies or Special Services to the State were divided into two groups, the regular or encyclic, which recurred annually, and the extraordinary, which occurred on particular occasions only. The regular Services were all connected with the mounting of entertainments, for instance, the paying of the expenses of a dramatic or other

Chorus; or of an athletic display, such as the training of runners for the various torch-races held throughout the year; or of competitors in the various competitive Games. All these festivals were basically religious: all were performed in honour of one of the deities. The extraordinary Service of the greatest importance was the Trierarchy, the maintaining and perhaps equipping of a ship of war.

We are not told which Service had been required of the prosecutor in this case; it was evidently one of the many regular charges. No citizen was liable to these for two years in succession, unless he chose; but a property of over three talents (£3,600) made him liable every other year. Nevertheless, wealthy citizens sometimes volunteered out of turn; and the ambitious man sometimes made a point of courting popular favour by spending more than was required; to spend only the necessary amount was regarded as mean. In the present instance, both men seem to have been anxious to avoid the burden; and the defendant regards the prosecutor's challenge as a proof of hostility.

The after-dinner visiting party, or Comus as it was called, was a well-known feature of Athenian social life. A party of diners, after their wine, would sally forth to visit—whether by invitation or not—another house where a dinner-party was being held. As the diners were usually drunk by the time the visitors entered, these encounters were lively. The most famous of such occasions is that described in Plato's *Symposium*, when Agathon's celebration-dinner in honour of his success in the dramatic festival at Athens was invaded by Alcibiades and his party, and Alcibiades made his glorious drunken speech in praise of Socrates. The present law-suit serves as a reminder that these visits were not always so successful.

This speech clearly shows the difference separating the slave from the free man or woman at Athens, and the prevalent opinion regarding their respective importance. The defendant's remark, " I could have done what I liked with her," means that he could have had her sold. If he had been taken prisoner in war and a ransom had been demanded for his release, he could have sold the slave to buy his own freedom. Thus, he argues, it is hard on him that she was not tortured to save him from exile.

The refusal of the prosecutor to allow the slave-girl to be tortured may be thought in this case to be due to his affection for her: it appears that he gave her her freedom, expressly in order to place her out of reach of the defendant's demand. This, however, was not the customary reason for a refusal, if it were given: the slave, like the horse or ox, was a piece of property with a value, and if he or she were handed over to the torturer, the result might be mutilation or even fatal injury, which would mean monetary loss to the owner.

The woman in this case is less passive than is usual. The defendant admits that she preferred the prosecutor, though he accuses her of playing a double game. Not being a free woman, she was not bound by convention; and she had a great deal to gain or lose, according to whether she belonged to one or the other. Her preference was clearly justified, since the prosecutor gave her her freedom. The defendant seems unable to prove his statement that he contributed half the original price; and he has recourse to the allegation of a compact by which they were to share her. This too he seems unable to prove, since he asserts that only the woman—now out of his reach—knows the real situation.

Since the prosecutor had refused to hand over the woman to examination by torture, the defendant is bound partly to defend the system: the orator makes him call it " this sure test." But the prosecutor had offered the rest of his slaves for examination: the defendant is therefore made to say in the next breath that they would have lied to oblige their master, and their evidence would have been worthless. This is a good example of the contradictory reasoning which earned the rhetoricians a bad name, and debased the meaning of " sophist " and " sophistry."

The defendant's peroration pleads with the Court not to deliver him into the accuser's power. This means that if he were condemned, he would be exiled, and would have to obtain the prosecutor's consent, with money and otherwise, before he could return. The State would neither help nor hinder. Thus his future would be in the hands of the prosecutor. There is no means of deciding which of the two litigants obtained the verdict; but one cannot help thinking that the defendant, if banished, would have been no great loss to his native land.

# X

## ASSAULT AND BATTERY: QUARREL IN CAMP

Speech for the prosecution, written by DEMOSTHENES. Date about 340 B.C.

The prosecutor was a very young man called Ariston. The defendant was an older man named Conon. The prosecutor charges Conon and his sons with a series of annoyances, ending in assault and battery.

The case was a private suit, in which the prosecutor claimed damages. No agreement having been reached beforehand by arbitration, the case came before an ordinary jury-court.

．　　．　　．　　．　　．

### THE PROEM

MEMBERS of the jury:

I have experienced an outrage of such violence at the hands of the defendant Conon that for a long time my family and all the doctors despaired of my life. However, contrary to expectation I was saved; and so, having recovered, I brought this action against him for assault.

All my friends and relatives, with whom I took counsel, declared that he was liable to summary arrest as a footpad, and to a public prosecution for violence because of these deeds. Still, they urged and advised me not to show myself as bringing a charge which was beyond my years, when seeking redress for my injuries. So I did as they said, and at their instigation I brought this private suit—though I would have liked, gentlemen, to put him on trial for his life.

I know you will excuse this sentiment, all of you, when you hear the story of my sufferings. Terrible though his violence was on the actual occasion, his disgraceful behaviour since then has been just as bad. I now call upon you and beg you all alike, first to hear me sympathetically while I describe my injuries, and then, if you agree that I have been wronged and criminally treated, to aid me with the just redress.

I shall now tell you the story of the events in detail from the beginning, as briefly as I can.

THE NARRATIVE

Two years ago, I was ordered away on garrison duty to Panactum (*a town on the frontier of Attica*), and I went.

The sons of the defendant Conon pitched their tents near us— to my sorrow, because this was the origin of all our feuds and fights. I will tell you how.

They used to begin drinking immediately after lunch, and continue all day long. This they did every day during all the time we were on garrison duty. Our way of life was the same out there as at home. Thus, when the time came for the others to have dinner, these men would be playing drunken tricks, for the most part on our servants, but in the end upon us too. They used to pretend that the servants annoyed them with the smoke of their cooking, or that they were impertinent—any kind of excuse; and for this they used to thrash them and empty the chamber-pots over them and urinate at them. There was no sort of disgusting outrage they left undone.

When we saw this, we were annoyed; but at first we merely rebuked them. However, they replied with insults, and refused to stop; so we all—my mess-mates as well, not I apart from the others—went in a body to the Commanding Officer and told him. They were very rude to him. He censured them severely, not only for their insolent treatment of us but for their whole behaviour in the camp. Yet far from leaving off or being ashamed, on that very same evening as soon as it was dark they burst in upon us, beginning with abuse and ending by aiming blows at me. They made such a din and uproar around our tent that the Colonel, the lieutenants and some of the men came along; and they prevented any more serious consequences to us at the hands of the defendants in their drunken state.

However, as things had gone so far, you can imagine that when we returned home here, there was mutual bad feeling and hostility: not, I assure you, that I had the slightest intention of bringing a suit against them, or even mentioning what had happened. My sole idea was to take care in future, and to beware of having any dealings with men of this kind.

Now first of all I should like to produce witnesses to the facts I have already told you. Then I will pass on to prove my injuries at the hands of the defendant himself, so that you can see how the man whose duty it was to have censured the original offences has himself added to them by actions far more violent.

*(Depositions are read and witnesses called in support of the prosecutor's account of the violent behaviour of Conon's sons in camp at Panactum.)*

Not long afterwards, I was taking my usual evening walk in the market-place (of Athens) with one of my friends, named Phanostratus, when who should come past us opposite the Monument but the defendant's son Ctesias, in a state of intoxication! Seeing us, he gave a yell, and then muttered something to himself indistinctly, as a drunken man does. Then he went on up towards Honeywood (*a suburb of Athens*). It seems that a drinking-party was being held up there (as I was told afterwards) at the house of Pamphilus the dyer and cleaner. At this party were the defendant Conon, his friend Theogenes, and many others. Ctesias fetched them away from the party, and came back with them to the market-place.

We happened to have turned back, and were again walking in about the same place, near the Monument, when we encountered them. As we came close, one of them, I don't know which, fell upon my friend Phanostratus and held him, while Conon and his son and Theogenes attacked me. First they tore off my clothes, then they tripped me up, threw me into the mud, jumped on me and kicked me with such violence that my lip was cut through and my eyes were closed up. In this state they left me, unable to get up or utter a word.

As I lay on the ground, I heard them use dreadful language, some of it so shocking that I could not bring myself to repeat it before you. One thing, however, I will tell you—a thing that is a sign of the defendant's brutality and a proof that he was the ring-leader : he crowed, in imitation of a fighting-cock that has won a battle, and the others made him clap with his elbows against his sides like wings!

After this, the bystanders carried me off, naked as I was—for these men had gone off with my cloak. When they got me to the door, there was a great outcry and wailing from my mother and the maids. With great difficulty they carried me to a public baths ; there they washed me clean all over, and showed me to the doctors.

I shall now place before you my witnesses to the truth of these statements.

(*Depositions and witnesses regarding the fight in the market-place, and the state of the prosecutor when he was brought home. These depositions would include the evidence of Phanostratus, of bystanders, of the prosecutor's household, and perhaps the attendant at the public baths.*)

It happened, members of the jury, that a relative of mine named Euxitheus, who is here present, and his friend Meidias, had been out to dinner somewhere and were coming away when they met us, while we were still quite near my home. They came with me as I was being carried to the baths; and they were present when the doctor was fetched. And I was so weak that, in order to spare me the long journey back home, it was decided that I should be taken to Meidias's house for that night; and this was done.

(*To the Clerk of the Court.*) Please take now the depositions on this head, so that the jury may know how numerous are the witnesses to the violence I suffered at these men's hands.

(*Depositions are read and confirmed by Euxitheus, to the effect that the prosecutor was too weak to be carried home and that he spent the night at the house of Meidias.*)

(*To the Clerk of the Court.*) Please take now the doctor's deposition.

(*Medical evidence is read, describing the condition of the prosecutor when examined at the baths, shortly after the fight. The damage consisted of cuts, bruises, and facial swelling; the lip had to be stitched.*)

Such, then, was the immediate condition to which I was reduced by the blows and injuries I had received. Later, the doctor said that the swellings on my face and the cuts and bruises gave no great cause for alarm. But a high temperature followed, and continued without intermission, together with sharp and violent pains throughout my whole system, and especially in my sides and abdomen. I was unable to take any food; and as the doctor said, if a sudden discharge of blood had not relieved me at the most painful and critical moment, I should have died of suppuration. As it was, the loss of blood saved my life.

In support of the truth of this further statement, that an illness of such severity ensued that I was in the extreme of danger, because of the beating I received from these men, I now ask the Clerk of the Court to read the deposition of the doctor and of those who nursed me.

(*Further medical evidence is read describing the illness consequent on violence : pain, high temperature, loss of appetite, followed by a haemorrhage, the nature of which was probably specified ; and stating the opinion that the prosecutor's life was for a time in danger.*)

## THE ARGUMENTS

It has now, I think, been sufficiently demonstrated to you that the blows I received were of the utmost force and severity, and that since my life was endangered by these men's unrestrained violence, the action I have brought against them falls far short of the appropriate redress.

Some of you, however, may wonder what possible plea Conon will dare to put forward in his defence. So I wish to tell you in advance the arguments which I am informed he has ready.

I gather that he will try to divert attention from the assault and what actually happened by turning the matter to ridicule and making fun of it, saying that there are plenty of lads in Athens, the sons of respectable citizens, who in sport, as young men will, apply opprobrious epithets to one another, and some of them even have disreputable love-affairs ; that his son is of their number, and has many a time taken and given beatings because of a girl ; that this is the way of young men. He will also describe all of us, me and my brothers, as too fond of drink, and equally rowdy, but spiteful and stupid as well.

For my part gentlemen, deep as is the grudge I bear for what I have suffered, I should resent it no less deeply and should consider myself no less ill-treated—if I may say so—were Conon's version of our characters to be accepted by you as true, and if your knowledge is so limited that your opinion of anyone is derived from his own or his neighbour's assertions, no credit being given to the law-abiding man for his daily life and habits. The fact is that no one has ever seen us the worse for drink or behaving rowdily. We cannot agree that our conduct is in any way spiteful because we demand legal reparation for injuries received. As for the opprobrious epithets, we agree with Conon that they fit his sons very well. May Heaven bring these things and everything like them home to him and his sons ! They are the men who perform obscene rites and do other things which are shameful even to speak of, much less to do, if one is respectable.

However, what is that to me ? I shall be surprised if there is any excuse or plea acceptable to your Court by which a man, if convicted of violence and of inflicting blows, can escape punishment. The law takes a quite opposite view : it has anticipated the inevitable excuses, and tried to prevent them from growing more serious. For instance—and this research has been imposed on me by the defendant's conduct—take the process for verbal abuse : this, it is asserted, exists to prevent men from being led on from angry words to blows. Then there is the process for assault, to prevent a man when he is getting the worst of it from defending himself with a stone or any other such weapon, and induce him to seek legal redress. Then there is the indictment for inflicting wounds, to prevent murder following on wounding. The least important of these, I take it—the process for verbal abuse—looks ahead to the last and most terrible, by endeavouring to prevent murder and the gradual passage from angry words to blows, from blows to wounding, and from wounding to loss of life, and by making legal provision for these various kinds of law-suits, so that differences shall not be settled by the fury or caprice of any individual.

Such is the attitude of the law. But suppose Conon says : " We are a wild lot when we get together, and in pursuit of a love-affair we hit and even throttle anyone we like ! " Will you laugh and let him off ? I imagine not. None of you would have felt inclined to laugh if you had been there when I was dragged about and my clothes were torn off and I was so roughly handled. I had left home fit and well : I was brought back on a stretcher. My mother rushed out. The screaming and crying of the women filled our house as if someone were dead, so that some of the neighbours sent to inquire what was the matter.

To generalize, members of the jury : justice demands that no excuse and no pardon shall be available for anyone brought before you, by means of which violence is encouraged. If, however, any allowance is made, it should be to those who act thus because of their youth: only for them must these loop-holes be reserved, and even in their case not in order to punish them less than they deserve. But if a man of over fifty years is in the company of young men, and these young men his own sons, and if instead of dissuading or preventing them, he himself becomes their leader and chieftain and the most scurrilous of them all, what reparation can be made that is adequate to his deeds? Myself, I consider death itself insufficient. Even if he himself had taken no actual part in the affray, but had looked on while his son Ctesias did the deeds now proved to have been done by Conon, the latter would justly have been regarded with loathing. But if he has brought up his sons in such a way that they can do wrong under his eyes—commit crimes such that for some of them death is the penalty—without feeling any fear or any shame, what punishment exists, do you think, too great for him? My own view is that we have here a proof that he never respected his own father. If he had honoured and feared him, he would have insisted on the same treatment from his sons.

(*To the Clerk of the Court.*) Please take up the laws on assault and on foot-pads.

(*To the jury.*) You will see that the defendant is liable under both these laws.

(*To the Clerk.*) Please read.

(*The Clerk reads aloud the laws on assault and on highway robbery.*)

Conon by his actions has rendered himself liable under both these laws: he both assaulted me and committed highway robbery. If we had not chosen to seek redress under these laws, we should still have the reputation of inoffensiveness and respectability, quite rightly, whereas he would have his own reputation for depravity. I ask you, what if anything had happened to me? He would have been facing a charge for murder, with all its terrible consequences. One may cite the case of the father of a local priestess, who was admitted not to have laid a finger on the dead man, yet since he had encouraged the man who struck the blows, he was banished by the Court of the Areopagus—and rightly so. If bystanders, instead of preventing men who are trying to commit injuries through drunkenness or bad temper or any other cause, themselves egg on the offenders, there is no hope of salvation for the man who encounters ruffians, but they can carry on with their violence until they grow tired. This is what happened to me.

## COMPLAINT OF DEFENDANTS' CONDUCT AT ARBITRATION

I shall now describe their conduct during the arbitration. In this too you will observe their recklessness. They fixed the time at after midnight. They refused to read depositions or put in written copies. They took our witnesses one by one up to the altar and made them swear oaths. They entered depositions which were quite irrelevant, such as that Conon's son was illegitimate and he had suffered this and that. Their behaviour earned the censure and disgust of everyone present, including, in the end, their own party. When at last they grew tired and had had enough of this sort of thing, they began issuing challenges, with a view to delay and in order to prevent the deed-boxes from being sealed up. They offered to hand over some slaves to be examined on the question of the blows given, and mentioned these by name. And now, I gather, this point will play the largest part in their defence.

In my submission, however, you must all consider this one point : if the defendants had issued this challenge with the genuine object of holding an examination under torture, and if they had had confidence in this plea, they would not have waited until the actual arbitration to make the challenge, at night, when no other pretext was left, but would have made it at the outset, before I brought my suit, while I was still in bed and, not knowing if I would recover, was naming Conon to all who visited me as the man who had struck the first blow and perpetrated most of my injuries. *Then* immediately Conon would have come to my home with a large number of witnesses : *then* he would have offered the slaves and called in some members of the Court of the Areopagus, since if I had died, the case would have come before that body. Even supposing he was ignorant of this, and, as he will now tell you, did not make preparations against such a serious contingency because he intended to make the challenge—still, when I was out of bed and had issued my summons, he would have shown himself ready to offer up the slaves at the first meeting before the arbitrator. But he did nothing of the kind.

To support the truth of my assertion that his challenge was issued for the sake of delay (*to the Clerk*), please read this deposition, which will make it clear.

(*A deposition regarding the proceedings of the defendant before the arbitrator is read.*)

As regards the examination by torture, therefore, bear these points in mind : the late hour at which he issued the challenge ; the reasons for his attempted delay ; and the previous interval during which at no point did he show any wish to exercise this right, not even issuing the challenge nor yet claiming the privilege of doing so.

ALLEGATION OF FALSE DEPOSITION

When, however, all the facts had been proved, as now, before the arbitrator, and the defendant was clearly proved to be liable to the whole of the charges, he put in a false deposition, and enrolled as witnesses men whose names will not, I think, be unfamiliar to you when you hear them :

" Diotimus son of Diotimus, of the deme Icaria ; Archebiades son of Demoteles, of the deme Halae ; Chaeretimus son of Chaerimenes, of the deme Pitthos : The above-named bear witness that they left a dinner-party with Conon, and in the market-place encountered Ariston and Conon's son having a fight ; that Conon did not strike Ariston."

He imagines that you will at once be convinced, and will not be able to work out the truth, namely that in the first place my own witnesses—Lysistratus, Paseas, Niceratus and Diodorus—have expressly testified to seeing me beaten by Conon, stripped of my cloak, and otherwise roughly handled as I was ; and these men, who were strangers to me and merely happened to come along, would never have been willing to give false evidence and testify that they had seen me thus treated if they had not. Secondly, I myself, if I had not suffered these injuries at his hands, would never have let off these who are admitted by their own party to have struck me, and chosen to go first for the man who had not laid a finger on me. Why should I ? Naturally I bring my suit against the man by whom I was first struck and from whom I suffered the most injuries. *He* is the object of my enmity and my retaliation.

On my side, as you see, all the facts are correct and shown to be so. But if Conon had not put forward these men as witnesses, he would certainly have no defence; he would have been liable to immediate condemnation because he had nothing to say. But they are his cronies, the partners in all his nefarious deeds; so naturally they bear false witness. Yet if things come to this pass—if certain persons once lose all sense of shame and openly dare to give false evidence, if there is to be no advantage on the side of truth, what a disastrous state of affairs!

But, he will say, they aren't that sort of men. However, many of you, I imagine, have personal knowledge of (*he points out Conon's witnesses who are in Court*) Diotimus, Archebiades, and Chaeretimus here with his grey hairs, men who during the day-time put on a severe expression and pretend to have Spartan habits like wearing a threadbare cloak and thin-soled shoes. But when they get together and are in each other's company, there is no base or shameful deed they leave undone. Hear their brilliant and high-spirited defence!—"Why shouldn't we give evidence for one another? Isn't that the duty of comrades and friends? And what is there to be afraid of in the charges he will bring against you? Some people say they saw him being beaten? Oh, but we will testify that he was never even touched! He was stripped of his cloak? Oh, but we will swear that they began it! He had to have his lip stitched? Oh, but we will say we had our heads cut open or some other part of us!"

Yes, but I am offering medical evidence in corroboration, which, members of the jury, is impossible for the defence. Apart from their own allegations, they will have difficulty in finding anyone to testify against us.

But indeed, I could not even describe their unlimited readiness to do anything whatsoever. To let you know, therefore, the deeds they go about doing (*to the Clerk of the Court*), please read to the Court these depositions. (*To the timing-official.*) Please stop the water-clock.

(*Depositions are read alleging that Conon and the before-mentioned witnesses have been guilty on other occasions of assault and house-breaking.*)

Housebreakers, men who strike anyone they meet: do you think that such men would hesitate to give false evidence in one another's interests, on a scrap of paper, when they are confederates in such utter riotousness, villainy and brazen-faced violence ? All these qualities seem to me inherent in their behaviour. Actually, they have even more serious crimes to their credit, but I should not be able to track down all the persons they have injured.

## FURTHER ALLEGATIONS AGAINST CHARACTER OF DEFENDANT

The most scandalous device, however, which I hear he is going to try, I think it best to warn you of in advance. I am told that he is going to bring his children into court, and swear an oath on their heads, invoking certain dire and awful curses, so terrible that someone who heard them was amazed and passed the information on to us. Such acts of audacity, gentlemen, are hard to combat, because, as I see it, the best people, those who would least think of telling a lie themselves, are most easily deceived by them. But one must not accord belief without due regard to life and character. Conon is completely without respect for oaths, as I shall show you : I have found it out through hard necessity. I learn, gentlemen, that a certain Bacchius, who was executed by order of your Court, and Aristocrates, the man with the bad eyes, and other men of the same sort, including Conon here, were comrades in their boyhood and called themselves the Huns. They used to collect the food offered to the dead whenever they were dining together ; and they found oaths and perjury the easiest thing on earth. So that Conon, such being his character, cannot be trusted when he swears an oath. Quite the contrary, in fact : the man who would not even swear a true oath, who would never even think of swearing on the heads of his children—an oath you do not recognize—but who would suffer anything sooner ; the man who would, if it were necessary, take the recognized oath of destruction on himself, his family and house : *he* is more deserving of credence than the man who swears by his children, and who offers to go through fire!

## CHALLENGE TO DEFENDANT

(*To Conon.*) I am more worthy to be believed throughout than you, Conon ; and I volunteered to swear the following oath, not, like you, to avoid punishment for any offence, whatever I may do, but for the sake of truth and to avoid being further mishandled, and in the spirit of one who refuses to gain his case by perjury.

(*To the Clerk*.) Read my challenge!

(*The Clerk reads the oath voluntarily sworn by the prosecutor at the arbitration, that he actually suffered the injuries he alleges and for which he claims damages*.)

Such was the oath I then volunteered to swear; and I swear now, gentlemen, for the benefit of yourselves and all present, in the name of all the gods and goddesses, that I verily did suffer at Conon's hands the injuries about which I am now at law; that I was struck, that my lip was cut through so badly that it had to be stitched, and that it is for this assault I am seeking redress. If I swear truthfully, may many blessings befall me, and may I never again have such an experience as this; but if I swear falsely, may I perish utterly, both myself and all that is or ever shall be mine!

## THE EPILOGUE

But I do not swear falsely, no, not though Conon bursts himself to prove it! I therefore call upon you, gentlemen, since I have put before you everything I am justified in pleading, and have supported my case with a solemn oath, to do as you would if you experienced what I have. Just as each one of you would hate his attacker, so now on my behalf show your anger towards Conon, when it is done to someone else. Whenever such a thing happens to anyone, come to his aid, mete out due punishment, and regard with hatred those who before the offence are reckless and headstrong, and when they are brought to justice, show themselves hardened in sin—who care neither for their good name nor for social usage nor anything else whatever, except only to avoid the penalty!

Conon will importune you and shed tears. But consider which of us is the more deserving of pity: the man who suffers injuries like mine at his hands, if I am to be sent away with added insult and without redress; or Conon if he pays the penalty? Which is to the advantage of each one of you: that there shall be license to beat and assault people, or not? The latter, in my submission; If, then, you acquit him, the number of criminals will be multiplied; if you punish him, they will be reduced.

I could tell at great length, members of the jury, of our good record, both mine and my brother's, and our father's when he was alive : how we contributed to the equipment of a war-ship, and did our military service, and performed every duty laid upon us. I could also show that the defendant and his sons have done none of these things. But the time will not suffice, and also these matters are not in question now. Even if we were, as it happened, admittedly more worthless and wicked than they, this still does not give them the right to beat and assault us.

I do not see that I need say any more. All of you, I believe, are fully aware of what I have told you.

. . . . .

Demosthenes, the advocate in this case, thought little of forensic work, his ambition being towards political oratory as a part of statesmanship. He was already famous for his speeches on foreign affairs when this case was tried; but he still undertook forensic cases, and could write with all the verve, humour and penetration of Lysias, and with the same keen appreciation of his client's character. In the present case, he knew that it would be easy for the defendant to throw ridicule on his client's story; he therefore anticipates this line and robs it of its effectiveness. He seems willing to let the jury laugh at his young client (who certainly seems something of a " mother's boy ") so long as they granted him the damages to which he was entitled for his injuries.

Garrison-duty was obligatory on all Athenian men between the ages of eighteen and twenty. Nevertheless, it seems as if military service were sometimes avoided, since the defendant claims it as a virtue that he, his father and his brother have fulfilled theirs. By this time, the Athenians had certainly become lax about service overseas. Eleven years earlier, Demosthenes was already begging them, in the face of the threat to their independence from the dictator Philip of Macedon, to serve abroad themselves and not delegate these duties to hired soldiers: " In matters connected with war and preparation for war," he said, " all is irregular, unorganised, undefined. . . . Be sure that there will be disaster, unless you give these matters your attention and agree to do your duty." (Demosthenes, *First Philippic*, § § 36, 50: date 351 B.C.)

In this speech as in the last, the lack of discipline is notable. Fighting and disorderly behaviour were apparently common, and though the officers intervened, no punishment is mentioned either for the behaviour itself or for rudeness to the Commanding Officer. It is well to remember that there were only about two years still to run before the Athenians suffered their defeat at Chaeronea at the hands of Philip, and lost their independence: " The disaster at Chaeronea was the beginning of calamity for the Greek States, both for those who had ignored the danger, and those who had taken sides with Philip: all were enslaved," wrote a Greek tourist visiting these parts five centuries later. (Pausanias, *Tour of Greece*, Book I, Chapter XXV: date, second century A.D.) The garrison-town of Panactum was on the frontier between Attica and Boeotia; it had been a bone of contention in the past, and was a key-point for the invasion of Attica.

The Athenians liked to walk in the market-place in the cool of the evening, as they now walk in the public gardens. The large market-place here referred to was on the north side of the Acropolis; it was the centre of the business and social life of the city. In the morning it was full of people shopping, meeting their friends, discussing various news and arranging transactions, or attending the law-courts. At noon, it emptied for lunch. Later, it filled up again. The Monument referred to in the speech was called the Leokorion, and had stood there for two centuries: it commemorated the three daughters of Leos, who were said to have sacrificed their lives for their country in obedience to an oracle. It was here that the most famous assassination in Athenian history had taken place in 514 B.C., when two young men, Harmodious and Aristo-geiton, killed Hipparchus, the brother of the dictator Hippias, in order to free Athens of tyranny.

Cock-fighting was a favourite sport in Athens, and the possession of a good bird ranked with that of horses and hounds; hence Conon's triumphant crowing over Ariston's prostrate body would be thought a good joke by the victors.

It will be noticed that at Athens doctors were within call then as now, and that the stitching of cuts was practised. It was convenient to take the patient to the baths, where water was plentiful, rather than wash him at home. These baths were of course places where one went to get a bath, not to swim. The customer sat in a sort of basin on legs, and a slave poured water over him. He was then rubbed with olive oil.

The prosecutor's allegation that Conon in his youth had belonged to a band of rowdies who used among other things to go round collect-ing the offerings to the dead for their dinner-parties, is a deep insult. These offerings of food were placed monthly at cross-roads; they were called " offerings to Hecatê ", the goddess of the underworld, and were eaten by beggars, but no respectable person would touch them. The word in the speech which is translated " Huns " is " Triballi ", the name of a Thracian tribe with a reputation for savagery; it was apparently adopted by a gang of young men at Athens, in the same way as the London street-brawlers of Queen Anne's day called themselves Mohocks, after a North American tribe.

It is interesting to observe that the Athenian law on homicide recognised the guilt of an accessory. We learn that the father of a local priestess (the priestess of Artemis at Brauron in Attica) was exiled for encouraging another man to strike a blow which proved fatal. It is clearly recognised as a duty of bystanders to help any victim of violence; this was very necessary in a city so ill-policed as Athens, for the safety of the community depended upon active support of the law by all well-constituted citizens. The highly-civilised conception of law and social order bequeathed to us by Heleas runs all through this speech: it is nowhere more clearly expressed than in the passage showing how the law, by attempting to check violence in its early stages, endeavours to prevent greater crimes, and to see that no quarrel is settled " by the fury or caprice of any individual " by giving to every citizen an opportunity for legal redress.

---

*FOUR*

*TRIALS*

*CONCERNING*

*PROPERTY*

---

# XI

## EMBEZZLEMENT OF TRUST FUNDS: AGAINST A GUARDIAN

Speech for the prosecution, written by Lysias.  Date 400 B.C.

This is a prosecution of a guardian, named Diogeiton, for malad-ministration of the property held in trust by him for his three wards, two boys and a girl.  The person addressing the Court on behalf of the wards is the girl's husband.

The advocate has expounded with perfect clarity the rather compli-cated family relationships; but in order to enjoy the situation, it is well to have the following table before one:

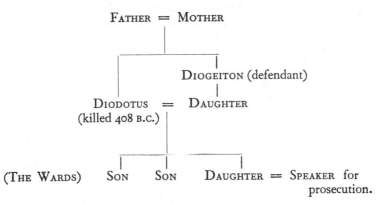

That is to say, the daughter of the defendant Diogeiton had married her uncle, Diogeiton's brother, as was allowed in Athenian law; and their children were the wards whom Diogeiton is alleged to have defrauded. The children were therefore at the same time both the nephews and niece, and the grandchildren, of the defendant.

It is quite easy to follow the money-accounts if it is remembered that the basis of the Athenian coinage-system was the silver drachma, the famous coin stamped on one side with the head of Athena, and on the other with the owl and olive-branch.  There were 100 drachmas to a mina, and 6,000 drachmas to a talent; the drachma was worth 6 obols.

Nevertheless, in order to give a rough scale of relative values, the drachma has been treated as equivalent to four shillings or a dollar.

The action was brought eight years after the death of the children's father Diodotus, by the eldest son on the attainment of his majority. He is, however, too young and inexperienced to state his own case with force, and so his sister's husband does so on behalf of all the wards. The case came before a jury-court presided over by the Chief Magistrate, the Archon Eponymus.

The speaker begins with a quiet and modest statement of his reason for bringing a family dispute into the open: he tried, he says, to get the matter settled by arbitration in order to avoid publicity, but was prevented by Diogeiton, who refused to do justice to his wards. He then recounts the facts:

•　　•　　•　　•　　•

### THE NARRATIVE

THERE were two brothers, members of the jury, Diodotus and Diogeiton, who had the same parents, both father and mother. The money they inherited was divided between them; the real property they used in common.

As Diodotus had made a large fortune in commerce, Diogeiton persuaded him to take as his wife his (Diogeiton's) only daughter. From this marriage sprang two sons and one daughter.

After some years, Diodotus was called up for service in the infantry, under General Thrasyllus. He therefore summoned a meeting of his wife (*who was also his niece*); and her father Diogeiton (*who was both his father-in-law and his full brother, as well as both the grandfather and uncle of his [Diodotus's] children*); and believing that by reason of these near ties, no one was better equipped to be a just guardian of his children, he handed Diogeiton his will, and a deposit of 5 silver talents (£6,000). He also declared that his investments in sea-going commerce were 7 talents 40 minas (£9,200), as well as 2,000 drachmas (£400) owing to him in the Chersonese. (*Total property, 78,000 drachmas, about £15,600.*) He directed that in the event of his death, 1 talent (£1,200) and the furniture of the house were to go to his wife; and 1 talent (£1,200) to his daughter. He left to his wife a further 20 minas (£400) and 30 Cyzicene staters (*about 800 drachmas or £160*).

After doing this and depositing a copy of these provisions at his own home, he went off for the campaign under General Thrasyllus, and was killed at Ephesus.

Diogeiton concealed from his daughter the fact of her husband's death; and he took the document (*the will*), which Diodotus had left under seal, his pretext being that he had to refer to these papers in order to recover the money invested at sea.

Then, after a while, he revealed Diodotus's death to the wife and children; and they, when they had performed the customary dues to the dead man, stayed on at the Peiraeus for the first year, as all the necessaries of life that had been left them were there. When these gave out, Diogeiton sent the children up to the city, and married off their mother (*his* daughter) with a dowry of 5,000 drachmas (£1,000)—1,000 (£200) less than her first husband had left her.

Eight years later, when the elder of the two boys reached his majority, Diogeiton summoned them, and informed them that their father had left them 20 minas of silver and 30 staters (*a total of* 2,800 *drachmas :* £560 *instead of* £15,560).

"Hence," he said, "I have spent a good deal of my own money on your upbringing. While I had it, I didn't mind; but now, I'm badly off myself. So therefore, as you have come of age and reached manhood, you must begin now and see about earning your own living."

When they heard this, they were dumbfounded. They went in tears to their mother, and bringing her along with them, they came to me. They were reduced to a pitiable state by the blow, miserably expelled as they were from participation in their property; and with tears and prayers they besought me not to look on indifferently while they were robbed of their patrimony, and reduced to beggary by the outrageous action of the man from whom, of all others, such treatment was least justifiable. They begged me to help them, for their sister's sake and their own.

It would require a long speech to describe the lamentations witnessed in my house on that occasion. In the end, their mother begged and implored me to call a meeting of her father and the family connections. She said that although previously she had not been accustomed to speak before men, the magnitude of the calamity would drive her into explaining to us the whole story of their wrongs.

I therefore went and expressed indignation to Hegemon, who is married to one of Diogeiton's daughters; and I had conversations with the other members of the family. I then demanded of Diogeiton that he should submit to an examination of these affairs.

At first he refused; but finally he was persuaded to it by his friends.

When we were assembled, the mother asked him what sort of a heart he had that he could bring himself to carry out such a policy towards her children—" You who are their father's brother," she said, " and also my father, and so both uncle and grandfather to them! If you felt no shame before any human being, you ought to have dreaded the anger of Heaven—you, who to start with, when their father set sail, received 5 talents (£6,000) from him as a deposit! On this point I am willing, in defence of my children —both these and the children who have since been born to me— to take an oath, wherever you care to specify. And I am not so worthless, nor do I set such a value on money, that I would go to my grave burdened with the crime of perjury against my own children, and the wicked theft of their patrimony."

She further convicted him of having received 7 talents (£8,400) shipping investment, and 4,000 drachmas (£800). In support of this she produced the written documents; for in the moving, when she had moved from her old home in Collytus to the house of Phaedrus, her second husband, her children had happened to find the book thrown out, and had brought it to her.

She also proved that Diogeiton had recovered 100 minas (£2,000) lent out at interest in the form of a land mortgage, and a further 2,000 drachmas (£400), and very valuable furniture; and also that corn had come annually from the Chersonese as part of their income.

" And then," she said, " you dared to say, when you held all this money, that their father left them only 2,000 drachmas and 30 staters (£560), which was the sum he had left to me, and which on his death I gave to you! And you did not hesitate to turn out these children, your own grandsons, from their own home, dressed in rags, barefoot, without an attendant, without a coverlet, without a cloak, deprived of the household goods which their father had bequeathed them, and of the money which he had deposited with you. And now you have children by my step-mother, and these you are rearing in the enjoyment of all the blessings of wealth.

That is all as it should be ; but at the same time you wrong my sons, turning them ignominiously out of their home with the determination to reduce them from wealth to beggary. In these actions, you show no fear of Heaven, no shame before me, your daughter, who share with you the knowledge of the facts, and no respect to your brother's memory. No : we are all, in your eyes, subordinated to money! "

Then, gentlemen, when she had finished this long and terrible list of accusations, all of us who were present were deeply affected by this man's deeds and by her words. We looked at the children and thought of their sufferings. We remembered their dead father, and thought how unworthy was the man whom he had left to be the trustee of his property. We reflected how hard it is to find anybody whom one can trust over one's own affairs. All this affected us so deeply that not one of us there present was able to utter a sound ; but shedding tears no less than the victims, we all went silently away . . .

This ends the narrative proper.

Witnesses are called in support of the facts therein stated. The arguments then follow.

The adversary's case is dealt with in two halves: the speaker discusses, firstly, the money which Diogeiton admits to having received, but which he declares he has spent on the children's maintenance; and secondly, the money which he denies having received. He remarks:

### THE ARGUMENTS

Diogeiton has gone to such lengths of brazenness that, being unable to explain what he did with the money, he reckoned the food of two boys and their sister at 5 obols a day each (*about ten shillings*). As for shoes, laundry and hair-cutting, he possessed no account either for the month or for the year, but lumped it all together at more than a talent of silver (£1,200) for the whole period of eight years.

Moreover, though he spent on their father's tombstone not 25 minas (£500) out of 5,000 drachmas (£1,000), he puts down only half to himself, and has debited them with the other half. And for the Dionysiac festival, gentlemen (I think it is not out of place to mention this as well), he wrote 16 drachmas (£3 4s.)

as the price of a lamb, and of this he put down 8 drachmas (£1 12s.) to the children's account—a fact which aroused in us as great an indignation as anything. Thus, gentlemen, when great losses are involved, sometimes trifles sting the mind of the injured person just as much, because they show up all too clearly the baseness of those who are wronging them.

Further, for the other festivals and sacrifices he set down to their account an expenditure of more than 4,000 drachmas (£800), as well as a vast number of other items which he put down as a round sum. It is as if the purpose for which he had been left as guardian to the children was that he might display bills to them instead of money, and prove them to be, instead of wealthy, complete paupers; and in order that the children might forget any hereditary enemy they had, and contend instead with this man, their grandfather, by whom they found themselves deprived of their inheritance.

Yet if he had wanted to be just to the children, he could have conformed to the laws in force regarding fatherless children, laws which apply to all guardians, whether capable or incapable of maintaining them—and rid himself of a great deal of trouble, by letting the house; or he could have bought land and reared the children from the proceeds. Whichever of these he had done, they would have been as rich as anyone in Athens. As it is, it seems to me that he never gave a thought to laying out the money in real estate. He was preoccupied with the question of how to get hold of their money for himself, in the belief that such wickedness as his was destined to succeed to the wealth of the dead.

But the following, gentlemen, is the most monstrous of all:

The defendant shared a State Service, the equipment of a warship, with Alexis son of Aristodocus; and he says he contributed 48 minas (£960) as his share. Half of this he entered against the account of the orphans, whom the State not only relieves of taxation during their minority, but also, even when they reach their majority, exempts from all contributions for one year. And this man, their grandfather, in exact opposition to the law, mulcts his own grandchildren of one-half the price of his own State Service!

Further, when despatching to the Adriatic a cargo vessel of two talents' freight (£2,400), he remarked to the boys' mother, as it was setting out, that the risk was on the children; but when the boat came back safely and doubled her cargo's worth, he claimed the profit of the voyage as his! But if he is going to set down all losses as theirs, and keep for himself whatever profits come in safely, then he will feel no difficulty in entering all expenditure against their account, while he himself gets rich with ease on what does not belong to him.

However, gentlemen, to give you an account of every detail would be a heavy task. But as I had great difficulty in getting the papers out of the defendant, I went, accompanied by witnesses, to Aristodocus the brother of Alexis (Alexis himself being dead) and asked him if he had the record of the State Service of equipping the warship. He said that he had. We went to his house, and found that Diogeiton had paid to Alexis 24 minas (£480) as his share towards the Service. But Diogeiton here has declared that he spent 48 minas (£960), so that he has debited the children's account with the whole of his expenditure! How much, then, do you suppose he has done of which no one knows but himself, on occasions when he has handled any matter alone?—seeing that in transactions which were carried out through others, and about which it was easy to find out, he has dared by false deductions to mulct his own grandchildren of four-and-twenty minas (£480)?

Witness to these statements, please come forward.

*(Aristodocus the brother of Alexis, and others, come forward in support of their depositions as to the expenditure on the State Service of equipping a warship.)*

You have heard the witnesses, gentlemen.

I shall take the sum which he himself has at last admitted to having received, that is, 7 talents 40 minas (£9,200) and base my calculations on that, without reckoning any revenue, but counting expenditure as being from capital. I shall set down a sum such as no one in this city ever does, for maintenance of two boys, their sister, a male attendant, and a female servant, namely, 1,000 drachmas a year (£200)—a little under 3 drachmas (12 shillings) a day. In eight years, this adds up to 8,000 drachmas (£1,600), which gives a balance of 6 talents out of the 7, and 20 minas (£7,600). He cannot prove that he lost them through the action of pirates, nor that he sustained any loss or had to pay them to creditors. . . .

*(The rest of the speech is lost.)*

.    .    .    .    .

This speech was taken as a model of ancient oratory by the literary critic Dionysius of Halicarnassus, who deeply admired Lysias. It differs from most of those by Lysias in that the character of the speaker is not important, since he is speaking on behalf of the injured party; and so he is made to keep himself in the background. The writer's dramatic skill is therefore directed elsewhere : to the pitiable plight of the children when the wicked grandfather-uncle revealed their penniless condition to them; and to the resolute stand taken by their mother, Diogeiton's daughter, who for the first time in her life ventured to speak before a meeting of male *relatives* in defence of the children of her first marriage! This latter example shows how complete was the segregation demanded of an Athenian married woman.

Lysias in his portrait of the untrustworthy guardian has tried to touch the imagination of every man in the jury. When the relatives had heard the mother's tale, they "reflected how hard it is to find anyone that can be trusted to handle one's affairs." It is not the least of the orator's functions to make the jury feel that in punishing the opponent they will be protecting themselves.

*Diodotus's Will.* A lump sum and the furniture to his wife, a lump sum to the daughter: these bequests were intended actually as dowries, for the wife on her remarriage, for the daughter on her marriage. Athenian women could not own property. Hence the wife handed the money to her father, until such time as he should again dispose of her: this was the ordinary procedure. When her husband died, she returned to the jurisdiction of her nearest male relative, until her remarriage. If she had property, it was attached to her: she could not handle it or dispose of it.

The remainder of Diodotus's property was automatically divided between his two sons; there was no need to state this in the will. The will would give an exact account of the deceased's property: this was why Diogeiton took care to get and keep possession of it.

The accounts, which might have been dull, are expounded with great skill and clarity by Lysias. They give some idea of the value of money in Athens round about 400 B.C. A property of 6 talents (say over £7,000) was a considerable fortune; a little over double this placed one in the wealthiest circles. Twenty-five minas was a paltry sum (say about £500) for the tombstone of a rich man; 5 obols a day (about three shillings and fourpence) was an absurdly high sum for a child's food; a sacrificial lamb cost 16 drachmas (on the same reckoning, over £3). We further learn what were the main items of expenditure on children of wealthy parents. They had to have their own slaves—a servant-escort for the boys, a waiting-woman for the girl. Boys were taken to and from school by a slave, usually of foreign birth, called *paedagogus* (boy-escort), who waited for them while they had their lessons or played their games; this was because of the very real danger of theft or even kidnapping in the unpoliced Athenian streets. There is a vivid picture in one of Plato's dialogues, *Lysis*, of boys who have spent the day at the gymnasium being called to come home by their escorts. Two boys, Lysis and Menexenus, have left their games to come and sit with Socrates and the grown-ups and join in a long discussion on friendship. In the end, says Socrates: " I was thinking of rousing up one of the other adults; and then, like evil genii, up came the servants to fetch Lysis and Menexenus, bringing their brothers, and they began calling them and telling them to come away home, for it was late by now. Well, first of all we and the bystanders tried to drive them off; however, they took no notice of us, but went on scolding in their foreign accent and calling no less than before; also we noticed that they had got tipsy at the Hermes-festival and were therefore difficult to deal with; so in the end, defeated by them, we broke up our conference . . ."

Two of the heaviest items of expenditure were laundry and hair-cutting. Athenians of the leisured class spent much of their time at the barber's having their hair attended to; evidently this began in childhood.

*Law on Wardship.* Two provisions are mentioned: that a guardian, whether able or unable to maintain his wards may, if he prefers, invest the patrimony in real estate, and maintain the children from the proceeds; or make other arrangements of a similar kind. Also, that the property of fatherless children is not liable to taxation of any kind for the duration of their wardship and for one year after.

The double relationship of this guardian to his wards is treated by the prosecution as an added reason for his looking after his wards with every care. In Athens it was customary to seek as husbands for the girl-children the nearest possible kinsman, so that such doubling of ties was not unusual. The whole basis of the Athenian marriage-law was to continue the family, and to keep the property in the family—a provision particularly necessary because there was no system of primogeniture in inheritance. The property was divided equally between all the sons, with dowries for the daughters. Thus in this family the two brothers Diogeiton and Diodotus shared their patrimony: they divided the money, and made common use of the real estate.

# XII

## *DAMAGE TO A FARM : DEFENCE AGAINST CALLICLES*

Speech for the defence, written by DEMOSTHENES.   Date 359 B.C.

These two litigants owned adjacent farms on the side of a mountain; and between the farms ran a road.   The prosecutor, Callicles, alleges that the defendant has walled off a part of his land through which water from the mountain used to flow, and so diverted this water on to the road; the result has been damage to the prosecutor's farm.   The defendant maintains that the charge is false, frivolous, and has an ulterior motive, namely that of securing the defendant's land.

It appears that this is only one of a series of law-suits that have arisen between the two farmers, although formerly their families had been on friendly terms.   A previous claim against the defendant had been brought before an arbitrator, and had succeeded because of the defendant's non-appearance.

The present suit is a claim for damages of 1,000 drachmas, (£200), and comes before an ordinary jury-court.


THE PROEM

IT seems, gentlemen of the jury, that there is no greater affliction than a wicked and grasping neighbour—which is my present fate.

Callicles has conceived a desire for my farm ; he has therefore attacked me with malicious litigation.   First, he suborned his cousin to claim the farm from me ; but his case was clearly disproved, and I was victorious over their machinations.   So they tried again ; and going to arbitration, obtained two awards against me by default : one for 1,000 drachmas (£200), claimed by the present prosecutor ; and another claim put forward at his instigation, by his brother here.

Now I do beg all of you to listen to me and give me your attention—not because I think *I* am going to make a good speech, but because I want *you* to discover from the actual facts that the case brought against me is obviously inspired by malice.

## PRELIMINARY PROTEST

There is one retort I have to offer against all their arguments—and it is true : this farm was enclosed with a wall by my father almost before I was born. Their own father, Callippides, was still alive and was our neighbour, so that he surely knew the facts better than they do. Callicles himself was already grown-up and living in Athens. My father survived more than fifteen years longer ; and their own father no less. Yet in all these years no one ever came to complain or object—although clearly even in those days it often rained—nor did anyone offer any hindrance at the outset, when, if at all, my father was committing an offence by building the wall round his farm. No one prohibited it or lodged a protest.

(*He turns to the prosecutor.*)

Yet, Callicles, it was open to you, I suppose, at the time, when you saw the water-course being blocked by the wall, to have come at once and expressed your annoyance, and to have said to my father : " Teisias, what is this you are doing ? Are you blocking the water-course ? If so, the water will flow on to our land." Then, if he had chosen to stop, there would have been no unpleasantness between you ; but if he had ignored your remarks and damage had resulted, you could have produced as witnesses those who had been present on that occasion . . .

Now, gentlemen, I beg of you in the name of all that is sacred, to give me your close attention.

## THE NARRATIVE

The division between my farm and theirs is a road ; and since both the farms are encircled by a mountain, the water which flows down runs partly on to the road, partly on to the farms, as it happens. Further, the water that runs on to the road, where it finds a clear passage, is carried on down along the road ; but where there is any obstruction, then this water is bound to over-flow on to the farm lands. And of course, gentlemen of the jury, it came about that after a heavy downpour the water flooded this farm under discussion, as well as others.

The matter was neglected. This was before the prosecutor's father owned the farm; it was then in the possession of a man who utterly detested the district and preferred a city life. And so the water overflowed a second and third time, and damaged the farm lands and was making a channel for itself, more and more. My father saw this—as I gather from people who know—and also the neighbours began grazing their flocks and trespassing over his land; and this was the reason why he built the boundary wall.

THE ARGUMENTS

In support of what I say, gentlemen, I shall produce as witnesses those who know the facts. But I have much more cogent proof than witnesses. Callicles says that I am injuring him by having blocked the water-course; but I shall prove that this is farm land, and not a water-course. If they did not admit that it was our own private property, perhaps we should be at fault in this, if we were building at all on public land. But they do not contest this; and furthermore, there are trees planted on the land—vines and figs. Yet who would choose to plant such trees in a water-course? No one, surely! Or who would choose such a place for a family burial-ground? No one would do that either, I imagine. And yet, gentlemen of the jury, both these conditions exist: the trees have been there since before my father built the enclosing wall; and the tombs are ancient, having been erected before my family acquired the land. This being so, what more cogent argument could there be, gentlemen? The facts clearly prove my case.

However (*to the Clerk of the Court*), take up all the depositions, and read.

(*Depositions are read in support of defendant's statement that the boundary-wall was built on their own land; and that there are figs and vines on this land, as well as an ancient burial-ground.*)

It is worth your while, gentlemen of the jury, to hear me on the other points raised by Callicles. Firstly, ask yourselves, has any of you ever seen or heard of a water-course running along a road? No, for I imagine none exists, in the whole countryside.

What reason was there why anyone should have made a channel for water which was bound to take its natural course down the public highway? And further: who among you, either in the country or in the town, I ask you, would receive on to his own land or into his house the water that runs through the street? Do we not do the exact opposite?—if it tries to force a way in, do we not all keep it out, with dams and walls? Yet the prosecutor here demands of me that I first receive on to my own farm land the water from the road, and then, when it has flowed past *his* land, conduct it back on to the road again! But if I do that, my neighbour the man who has his farm below mine will lodge a protest: clearly if the prosecutor's claim is legal, then it is open to all. I suppose he thinks that if I shrink from conducting the water on to the road, I can cheerfully let it loose on to my neighbour's land! How shall I fare, I wonder, at the hands of those who suffer damage from water coming direct from my land on to theirs, when I find myself the defendant in a claim for damages because the water that flows down the road has broken through on to the prosecutor's farm? And if I am not going to be allowed to let the water that comes my way flow either on to the road or on to other land, what remains, gentlemen, in Heaven's name? Callicles can hardly make me drink it!

If, gentlemen, there were a channel to receive the water again, perhaps I should be at fault in not receiving it: on certain other of the farms, there are admitted water-courses. Where these exist, the first persons receive the flow—just as in the case of rain-water that runs off houses—and the next receive it after them, and so on; but in this case, no one passes it on, no one receives it after me. How then can it be a water-course? Water flowing in has, I imagine, many a time before now done damage to many who have not taken precautions; and so it is with the plaintiff now. . . .

You shall presently learn more clearly from the depositions of witnesses how he himself has committed offences, first in making the road narrower by carrying his wall further out, with the object of enclosing the trees belonging to the road; second, by throwing out his rubbish on to the road, and so making it higher and narrower. The point I wish to put before you at the moment is this: that he has suffered no loss or damage worth mentioning—nothing warranting a law-suit such as he brings against me.

### FURTHER NARRATIVE

My mother was on friendly terms with their mother before they began this malicious litigation. The two women used to visit each other, as was natural seeing that they both lived in the country and were neighbours, and also that their husbands had been friendly while they lived. My mother went to call upon their mother; and the latter lamented the accident and showed the damage—this was how we found out everything, gentlemen of the jury. Now I am telling you exactly what I heard from my mother, so help me God! If I lie, may bad luck attend me! I swear that she said she saw—and was told of by their mother—some barley which had been drenched and which she saw being dried, not so much as three bushels, and about half a bushel of barley meal. Also she was told of a jar of olive oil that had fallen over, but had not been damaged at all!

Such, gentlemen of the jury, was the extent of their misfortune, for which I am sued for a fixed sum of 1,000 drachmas (£200)—when their total loss does not amount to 50! (£10).

### FURTHER ARGUMENT

Don't be surprised, gentlemen of the jury, at his eagerness, nor that he has had the nerve to bring a false charge now. Even before, when he suborned his cousin to claim my farm, he produced forged agreements; and now he himself has obtained an award by arbitration on a similar claim, which went against me by default. In this, he issued a writ against Callarus, one of my slaves. You see that in addition to their other attempts to harm, they have discovered this device also—they bring the action against Callarus. Yet what servant would enclose his master's land without his master's orders? They could find no one else to charge; and so they bring a suit about land enclosed by my father fifteen years before he died—and bring it against Callarus!

Now if I give up my farm to them, either by sale, or by removing myself to other land, then Callarus is not guilty; but if I refuse to relinquish my property to them, then Callarus is guilty of inflicting every possible hurt upon them, and they hunt for an arbitrator who will adjudge the land to them, or a settlement by which they can obtain it.

So, gentlemen, if it is right that plotters and dishonest litigants should succeed, then there is no point in my talking; but if you detest such people and vote for what is just—since Callicles has suffered neither loss nor injury either through Callarus or my father—then I don't see that I need say any more. But in order that you may know how, even before, he put his cousin up against me as part of his plot to get the land; and how he has now himself obtained an arbitrator's award in another similar action against Callarus—to spite me, because I set a high value on the man; and how he has brought yet another action against Callarus to prove all this; the Clerk will read you the depositions.

(*Depositions are read regarding the other actions brought by the prosecutor against the defendant and Callarus his slave, in an attempt to get his farm.*)


THE EPILOGUE

Do not, therefore, gentlemen of the jury, in Heaven's name, give me into their hands, when I have done no wrong! It is not the fine that I care about so much—although that is a severe blow to men of small property—but they are driving me completely out of the district with their harrying and litigation. In support of our innocence, we were prepared to submit the quarrel to those who knew the facts, and who were fair and impartial; and we were prepared to swear the customary oath. We thought that that would be the strongest testimony to put before you who are yourselves under oath.

(*To the Clerk.*) Please read my challenge, and the remaining deposition.

· · · · ·

This lively and sarcastic speech, written for a defendant much younger than the plaintiff, was clearly meant to entertain as well as convince the jury. It may be compared with the other speech by Demosthenes given in this book (Chapter X) where a possible attempt at ridicule is forestalled.

The "challenge" mentioned in the last paragraph was one of the devices of litigants. This, in law, could take various forms. It was the technical term for an offer to give up one's slaves to be examined under torture (as in Chapter X), or a challenge to the other party to do so (as in Chapters VII and XIII). One could also challenge the opponent to produce a document, or offer to allow him to inspect one. In the present case, as in that against Conon (Chapter X), we have the challenge by oath. The challenger offers to swear a solemn oath that his charge, or his defence against a charge, is true, if the opponent will accept this as evidence. The offer was usually made in the hope that it would be rejected. The challenger would then make great play with the refusal, and pretend that it implied that the opponent had no faith in his case. The opponent would maintain that the challenger's oath was valueless because it would be perjured.

These oaths, if accepted, were very solemn: the person taking the oath swore destruction on himself and his children or his whole race, if he were committing perjury. The challenge was always put into writing, and it formed part of the documents in the case, depositions and other material sealed up in the deed-box after the preliminary investigation, which were read at the trial when the challenger so requested. In this speech, the challenge is read out at the very end, as an effective climax.

The speech gives a vivid glimpse into life in the country as opposed to that of the city: the mountainous conditions in Attica, the severe winter rains which turned roads into water-courses, the exchange of visits between neighbours, and complaints of damage to stores through damp; the figs and vines, the old cemetery. It will be noticed that women living in the country, unlike those in the city, were able to pay visits without hindrance or ceremony: they had to work harder, but they enjoyed more freedom.

The suit brought against the slave was apparently a legal device to get hold of him and detain him or do him injury: a slave could not take any active part in a law-suit or appear as a witness. Callarus was valued by the defendant, and so the prosecution tried to harm him: this certainly supports the defendant's contention that the claim for damages is malicious and has an ulterior motive.

The orator does his best to bring home to the jury the unpleasantness of having a spiteful neighbour, especially in the country, and to gain their sympathy for his client.

# XIII

## CLAIM TO A LEGACY : THE ESTATE OF CIRON

Speech for the defence, written by ISAEUS. Date 375 B.C.
" The speeches of Isaeus are the oldest documents in the world which illustrate with minuteness of detail the workings of a Testamentary Law."
JEBB, Attic Orators, II, p. 315.

In order to enjoy this speech, it is necessary to understand the relationship of the rival claimants to the testator Ciron; and how these claims were regarded in Athenian law.

Ciron married twice. His first wife was his cousin, her mother and Ciron's mother being sisters. His second wife was the sister of a man named Diocles, who plays an important part in the story.

Ciron had children by both his wives. By his first wife he had one daughter. By his second wife he had two sons who both died young.

Ciron's only daughter also married twice. Her first husband was called Nausimenes, and he died before there were children. Her second husband was a man not named, by whom she had two sons. One of these two sons is the Speaker in this case for the defence.

The Speaker (whose name is not given) is therefore the grandson of the testator Ciron, through Ciron's only daughter. He has therefore the strongest claim to the legacy.

Ciron, however, had a brother; and this brother had a son. This son was persuaded by Diocles (mentioned above) to contest the will.

The Claimant, being only a nephew (brother's son) of the testator Ciron, has a weaker claim than the defendant, who is a grandson (daughter's son), though he tries to contend that descent through the female line *via* a daughter is a weaker title than claim *via* a male relative. This is glaringly invalid according to Athenian law.

His second point therefore is that the defendant's mother was not the daughter of Ciron—that Ciron never had a daughter; and this is the point with which the speaker really has to deal.

Diocles, who is behind the claimant, is no relative of any of the parties. He is merely the brother of Ciron's second wife, whose sons, had they lived, would have inherited the property. Presumably he and his sister would retain their hold over the property if Ciron's nephew got it; but they would lose all control of it if it passed down in the direct line. Naturally Ciron's second wife would be loth to see the property passing from her to the older line, Ciron's descendants by the daughter of his first marriage.

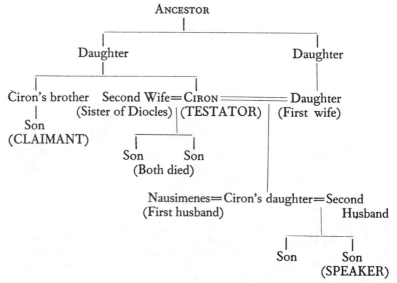

The chief rules governing succession and bequest in Athenian law are as follows:[1]

1. When a citizen died leaving sons, they shared the inheritance equally, the eldest having priority of selection.
2. Failing sons and sons' issue, daughters and daughters' issue succeeded.
3. A daughter was never, in our sense, an heiress. She was, properly speaking, a person who went with the estate. The heir was either her nearest kinsman, who was bound to marry her, or that person to whom her father had devised the property on condition of his marrying her.
4. Failing lineal descendants, the succession passed to collateral kinsfolk on the paternal side, as far down as to children of first cousins, with a preference to males. Failing these, it passed to the maternal side, with the like limit and preference. It then returned to the paternal side.
5. A man could not disinherit his son. Nor could he separate his estate from his daughter, though he could select the person whom she was to marry.

[1] Jebb, *Attic Orators*, II, pp. 318–9.

6. A childless man might, either during his life or by testament, adopt any Athenian citizen as his son and heir.

7. Mothers certainly, fathers probably, could not inherit from their children. But an inheritance could ascend collaterally; e.g. an uncle could inherit, or could marry the daughter with whom the estate went.

.   .   .   .   .

THE PROEM

GENTLEMEN :

In cases like this, one is bound to feel indignation, when people not only have the hardihood to lay claim to the property of others, but even hope to annul by their own arguments the justice that is set forth in the legal code. This is what the claimants are now trying to do.

My grandfather Ciron did not die childless. He left us as his descendants, born from his legitimate daughter. Yet the plaintiffs both claim the inheritance as being the nearest relatives, and also insult us by declaring that we are not the sons of Ciron's daughter —that Ciron never had any daughter at all!

The motive of their action is their own greed, and the large estate which Ciron has left. They have seized this by force, and so hold and have control of it. And they have the brazenness at one and the same time to declare that Ciron left nothing—and also to lay claim to his legacy!

Now you must not imagine that this suit of mine is being fought against the person who has brought the claim for the inheritance ; no, it is against the brother of Ciron's second wife, Diocles of Phlya, surnamed Orestes. He is the man who has suborned the claimant to give us trouble ; he is trying to rob us of the money which Ciron my grandfather bequeathed as he was dying, and to bring this risk upon us, so that he need restore none of the property —that is, if you are won over by his arguments and are deceived.

It is therefore necessary, in view of their machinations, that you should learn all the events, so that you may not be in ignorance of any of the facts, but may give your vote with a clear knowledge of them. And so I beg you, if ever you gave your close attention to any lawsuit, do so now no less, as is also just. This city has seen many law-suits, but never shall litigants be shown up to be making a more scandalous, more obviously unjustifiable claim. It is not easy, gentlemen, to come forward in a case of such magnitude, and defend oneself against concocted arguments and false witnesses, when one is completely without experience of the law-courts. Yet I have great hopes that I shall obtain justice from you, and shall myself speak adequately, without of course overstepping justice—*unless something happens of the kind which, as a matter of fact, I am now dreading.* . . . And so, gentlemen, I beg you to hear me with good will, and if I appear to have been unfairly treated, to come to my aid with justice.

First of all, that my mother was Ciron's legitimate daughter— this I shall prove to you, by report of conversations and witnesses' evidence, when the events are in the remote past; and when they are within memory, by the testimony of those who know; further, by proofs which are stronger than the depositions of witnesses. Then, when I have made that clear, I will show that we are more entitled than they are to inherit Ciron's wealth. I too will begin my account from the point at which they started.

### THE NARRATIVE

My grandfather Ciron, gentlemen, and his wife, my grand-mother, were first cousins, as his mother and hers were sisters. She, however, did not long survive the marriage, but died after four years. My grandfather, as he had only one daughter, married again, taking as his second wife the sister of Diocles; and by her he had two sons. He brought up his daughter in the same house with his second wife and their sons; and while the sons were still alive, when his daughter reached marriageable age, he gave her as wife to Nausimenes of Cholargus, with a dowry of clothes and gold jewellery amounting to 25 minas (£500). The husband, three or four years later, fell ill and died, before any children had been born to him and my mother. So my grandfather received her back, without reclaiming the dowry, which had been large on account of Nausimenes's poverty; and he gave her in second marriage to my father, with a dowry of 1,000 drachmas (£200).

### THE ARGUMENT

Now how can all these facts be clearly demonstrated in the face of my adversaries' present charges? I have made inquiries and found out.

The question whether she was Ciron's daughter or not, and whether she lived in his house or not, and whether he celebrated two marriages of hers or not, and what dowry each of her husbands received with her—all these points must be known to the slaves, male and female, who belonged to Ciron. I wished, therefore, in addition to the witnesses I have, to make an examination of these slaves by torture, in order that you might put more faith in the witnesses, as they would not be merely facing a possible future examination, but would have already provided proof of their evidence ; and I demanded of the claimants that they should give up their slaves, male and female, to be examined on this and all other points about which they happen to know. But the claimant, who is now about to ask you to believe his witnesses, refused the test by torture. Yet if he shall be shown to have been unwilling to do this, what remains for his witnesses except the appearance, now, of giving false testimony? Nothing, I imagine.

To prove the truth of my statement, first take this deposition and read it.

*(A document is read recording that the speaker challenged the plaintiff to give over his slaves for examination, and that the latter refused.)*

Now it is your belief, gentlemen, that in public and in private, examination by torture is the most accurate test. And whenever both slaves and free men are present, and it is required to find out some unknown point, you do not take the depositions of the free men, but you seek by torturing the slaves to find out the truth about what has happened. Rightly so, gentlemen : for you are aware that before now there have been witnesses who have been thought not to give true evidence ; but of those examined by torture, none has ever been proved to have spoken what is untrue during the torture. But this man, the most shameless in the world, will expect you to believe fictitious statements and witnesses who give false evidence, although he has evaded this exact test. We shall not, however! Even before this, we claimed the right of recourse to torture on behalf of those who were to give evidence ; and thus we shall suppose you are bound to give our witnesses credence.

*(A number of depositions are read, testifying that Ciron's daughter was legitimate : the witnesses are Ciron's friends ; relatives of the two husbands of Ciron's daughter, and other friends of the family who testify that she was brought up in Ciron's house after his second marriage.)*

Who is likely to know about long past events? Obviously, the friends of my grandfather. These have told you what they heard said. Who must necessarily know the facts about the marriages of my mother? Those who conducted the betrothals, and those present when the betrothals took place. The relatives of Nausimenes, and those of my father, have given evidence. Who would know that she was brought up in that house and was the legitimate daughter of Ciron? The present claimants, it is obvious, virtually testify that this is true, in refusing the test by torture. So that you have no grounds for disbelieving our witnesses, but far more grounds for disbelieving theirs.

However, we have further proof that we are the sons of Ciron's daughter.

FURTHER NARRATIVE

As was natural, seeing that we were the sons of his own daughter, he never performed a sacrifice without us, but whether the occasion was trivial or important, we were always at his side, taking part with him in the ceremony. And not only were we invited on these occasions, but he always took us to the Dionysian festival in the country, and we used to go in the procession with him, seated by his side; and we celebrated all festivals in his presence. And when he sacrificed to Zeus, Guardian of Property—a festival by which he set the greatest store, refusing to admit either slaves, or freemen who were illegitimate, and doing everything by himself —*we* shared in the ceremony and helped to carry the sacrifices and lay them on the altar and do all the other offices; and he prayed that we should be granted health and a goodly property, as was natural seeing that he was our grandfather. Yet if he had not believed us to be his daughter's children, and seen in us the only descendants left to him, he would never have done any of these things, but would have had at his side the claimant here, who now declares himself to be Ciron's nephew.

That what I say is true is best known to my grandfather's servants, whom the claimant has refused to surrender to the torture; but the most prominent facts are known also to certain of Ciron's acquaintances, and these I shall put forward as witnesses.

(*To the Clerk.*) Please take the depositions and read.

*(Depositions are read of friends of Ciron, testifying to having seen the speaker and his brother taking part in the family ceremonies with Ciron.)*

However, it is not only this evidence that proves our mother to have been the legitimate daughter of Ciron, but also the actions of our father, and the knowledge that the wives of the local inhabitants had of her. For when our father was taking her to wife, he celebrated a marriage feast and invited three friends of his, together with his relatives, and he also celebrated the marriage-sacrifice before the clansmen, in accordance with their laws. Later, the wives of the local inhabitants chose her, along with the wife of Diocles of Pitthos, to preside at the Thesmophoria, and to carry out the customary rites with her colleague. When we were born, our father presented us to the clansmen, taking the oath in accordance with the existing laws, that we were born of a pure-bred and legally married woman. None of the clansmen challenged or disputed the truth of this statement, though there are plenty of them, and they scrutinize such matters with minuteness. But do you imagine that if our mother had been the kind of woman they allege, our father would have celebrated his wedding and offered a marriage-sacrifice? No, he would have concealed all this. And would the wives of the neighbourhood have chosen her as joint-official with Diocles's wife, and put her in charge of the sacred ceremony? No, they would have entrusted this to some other woman. The clansmen would not have accepted us, but would have denounced and exposed us, unless it were admitted on all sides that our mother was the legitimate daughter of Ciron. And today, owing to the patent truth of the matter and the number of persons who share in the knowledge of it, from no quarter has any such challenge been brought. In proof of this (*to the Clerk*), please call witnesses on these points.

*(Witnesses are called who were present at the marriage of Ciron's daughter to the speaker's father; at the ceremony of the Thesmophoria at which she was joint president; and at the presentation of her children to the clansmen.)*

Furthermore, gentlemen, it is easy to recognize from the behaviour of Diocles when our grandfather died that we were acknowledged to be the sons of Ciron's daughter.

I went to fetch the corpse, intending to hold the funeral from my own house; I took with me one of my relatives, a cousin of my father. I did not find Diocles at home; but I went in, and I was in a position to take away the body, as I had brought bearers. However, my grandfather's wife implored me to let him be buried from her house; and when she said she would like to join with us herself in laying out and adorning the corpse, and added her supplication and tears, I consented, gentlemen; and approaching Diocles, I told him in the presence of witnesses that I would hold the funeral from that house, as his sister had implored me to do so.

Diocles, hearing this, made no objection, but said that he had made some purchases towards the funeral necessaries, and had paid a deposit on certain others. He asked for the money from me, and he agreed, if he were paid the price of the things actually purchased, to put me in touch with the people who had received a deposit for the other goods. And he immediately threw in the remark that Ciron had not left anything at all—although I had not yet made any mention of Ciron's property.

But if I were not the son of Ciron's daughter, he would not have made such an agreement. He would have spoken like this: "Who are *you*, pray? What affair of *yours* is the burial? I don't know you. I forbid you to enter the house." These would have been suitable remarks—and indeed he has now induced others to make them. But at the time he said nothing of the kind—he asked me to bring the money next morning.

(*Witnesses are called in support of the defendant's account of the arrangements made for Ciron's funeral and the attitude of the widow and her brother Diocles.*)

However, not only Diocles but also the present claimant refrained from saying any such thing—though the latter now denies this, having been put up to it by Diocles.

Diocles, when I brought the money, refused to accept it; he said that he had received it the previous day from the claimant. However, I was not prevented from sharing in the funeral. I did everything with them. But do not imagine that either the claimant or Diocles spent anything: the funeral expenses were paid out of the money left by the deceased.

Yet if Ciron was not my grandfather, the claimant likewise could justifiably have used force and turned me out, and prevented me from sharing in the funeral, as I should have had no connection with him. *I* was allowing him to share in all the preparations because he was the son of my grandfather's brother ; but *he* was behaving improperly in admitting *me*, if what they now have the impudence to say were really true. But he was quite paralysed by the facts of the matter, so much so that when I made a speech at the grave, and denounced Diocles for trying to rob me of the property by persuading the plaintiff to lay claim to it, even then the claimant had not the courage to utter a single squeak, much less to say what he now dares!

(*Witnesses are called in support of the defendant's account of the scene at Ciron's funeral.*)

Then follows an argument proving that a daughter's son is nearer in the line of succession than a brother's son. The speaker then explains what he alleges to be the real reason why the case was brought:

ALLEGATIONS AGAINST DIOCLES

Ciron had property, gentlemen,—a field at Phlya worth easily a talent (£1,200), and two houses in the city, one near the temple of Dionysus in the Marshes, worth 1,000 drachmas (£200), which was let ; the other, in which he lived himself, worth 13 minas (£260). Further, he had slaves whom he hired out, and two female slaves and a small girl ; also the furniture of his dwelling-house, worth, together with the slaves, practically 13 minas (£260) : making a total value for the visible property, of 96 minas (£1,920). Apart from this, there were a considerable number of loans, from which he drew interest.

It is for this money that Diocles, together with his sister, has been plotting, for a long time, ever since Ciron's sons died. Diocles did not give her again in marriage, though she was still capable of bearing children to some other man, because he did not wish her to be divorced, nor Ciron to take counsel about his own affairs, as was proper. No, Diocles persuaded her to stay—to say that she thought she was with child by Ciron, and then pretend that she had had an abortion, so that he might continuously hope for children, and thus not adopt either of us as his son. And he was unceasingly decrying our father, pretending that he was plotting to get Ciron's money.

And so he persuaded Ciron to let him administer all business concerning debts owing to Ciron, and interest on loans, and real estate. He seduced the old man by flattering attentions, until he got the whole of his affairs into his own hands. But he knew that I would seek to become the owner of all these things as was my due; and so, when my grandfather died, he did not hinder me from entering the house, tending the dead, and passing time there, lest I should be exasperated and lose my temper with him; but he suborned someone to lay claim to the estate, promising him a small share if the claim succeeded, but intending to get the whole property for himself. Even to his accomplice he did not admit that my grandfather had left money; he declared that there was nothing at all.

The moment my grandfather was dead, Diocles, having made the funeral arrangements in advance, requested me to bring the money for them, as you have heard from the witnesses. Then he pretended that he had received it from the present claimant, and he now refused to accept it from me, the idea being gradually to edge me out, so that the claimant should appear to be burying my grandfather, and not I. And when Diocles, while laying claim to Ciron's house and everything else he had left, was also maintaining that he had left nothing, still I felt it impossible, at such a time of mourning, to use force and remove my grandfather's body—with which decision my family concurred—but I chose rather to join with them in the funeral, the expenses being paid out of my grandfather's estate.

Such was the compulsion under which I acted in this way; but to make certain that they should not score any points over me through this, I consulted a priest, and by his instructions I contributed to the expenses, and provided the ninth-day sacrifices, the finest I could procure, so that I could disarm Diocles of this sacrilege; and also to avoid the appearance of leaving the expense to them while I spent nothing, and to show that I too was doing my share.

You have heard, gentlemen, practically the whole story of the events, and the causes which have brought on us all this trouble. If you knew the brazen character of Diocles, and the way he behaves in other matters, you would not refuse credence to anything that has been narrated. The property he holds and from which his grandeur is derived is not his own: he has three half-sisters on the mother's side, who were left as " heiresses " with their father's property; and as the father made no deposition concerning them, Diocles constituted himself adopted son and heir. And when the husbands of two of the sisters put in a claim to the father's estate, Diocles made the husband of the elder sister a prisoner, and succeeded by a plot in causing his disfranchisement. A charge of assault was laid against Diocles, but he has not paid the penalty so far. As for the husband of the second sister, he gave orders to a slave to murder him; and then, getting rid of the slave, he turned the accusation upon his sister. Then, having crushed her with his calumny, he proceeded to rob the dead man's son, whose guardian he had become, of his property: Diocles is in possession of the farm land, and he has given the son a piece of stony ground. They will perhaps—although they are afraid of Diocles—be willing to bear me witness that these statements of mine are the truth; but if not, then I will produce as witnesses persons who know the facts.

(*To the Clerk.*) Please take the latter first.

(*Witnesses appear in support of the speaker's account of Diocles's treatment of his half-sisters, their husbands, and one of the sons. These persons were bound to appear in support of already-existing depositions: the pretence that they may not do so for fear of Diocles is a device to emphasize the speaker's version of Diocles's violent character.*)

Thus, though he is so unrestrainedly violent, and has robbed his sisters of their property, even their possessions do not satisfy him, but since he has suffered no penalty for these crimes, he has come here to rob us also of our grandfather's property; and by giving a bribe of—as we learn—no more than 2 minas (£40) to the plaintiff here, has put us in danger of losing, not only our property, but also our country; for if you are deceived by him into believing that our mother was not of pure blood, then neither are we, since we were born after the magistracy of Eucleides. Can it be said that this suit in which he has involved us deals with matters of small importance? While our grandfather and father were alive, no charge was brought against us; we remained throughout the whole time unchallenged. But now that they are dead, even if we win our case, we shall suffer reproach, because our legitimacy has been questioned—all through this Orestes here, who is destined to come to a bad end. He is a man who has been convicted as an adulterer, and has paid the proper penalty for such a crime; and yet he by no means desists from it, as those who know will testify.

And so his character is revealed to you; and it will be revealed still more accurately later on, when *we* bring *our* suit against *him*. And you—I beg and beseech—do not see me violently swindled over the property my grandfather left, but come to my rescue to the utmost of each man's power. You have sufficient guarantee, from depositions, from the evidence under torture, from the laws themselves, that we are the children of Ciron's legitimate daughter, and that it is for us and not for our opponents to inherit his property, as we are our grandfather's direct descendants. So, remembering both the oaths you swore as members of the jury, and our declarations, and the laws, give your verdict on the side where justice lies!

I see no reason for continuing. You are, I think, in possession of all the facts. (*To the Clerk.*) Please take the remaining deposition, concerning his conviction for adultery, and read.

(*A document is read recording Diocles's conviction for adultery and his payment of a fine.*)

. . . . .

This case really turns on the character of Diocles, who is behind the claimant's action, and who looms as a sinister figure in the background. He was his sister's legal guardian, if anything—death or divorce—happened to dissolve her marriage with Ciron. Her two sons by Ciron died; and it is suggested by the defendant that as she was not likely to have more children by him, it was her brother's duty to take her away from her husband and give her in marriage to another man, but that he did not do so because he had designs on Ciron's estate. It is extremely unlikely that a brother ever had the right to act thus unless the husband consented.

When Ciron died, his wife returned by law into her brother's keeping. Diocles, however, had evidently taken advantage of the situation to install himself in Ciron's house, so that he was in possession of the property. Diocles is depicted by the defendant as a violent, dissolute man, with a conviction for adultery against him, and the suspicion of worse crimes. The actual claimant, Ciron's nephew, is hardly mentioned, and remains quite characterless. The defendant's remark, "unless something happens of the kind which I am now dreading," is a hint that he himself fears foul play, as do his witnesses; it is suggested that all who stand in the way of Diocles's rapacity are eliminated, as, for instance, his other two sisters and their husbands.

It appears that Diocles's mother married a second time, and by her second husband—Diocles's step-father—had three daughters, with whom their father's property would go unless he made a will adopting a male heir, who would then have to marry one of them. It is not known whether, if the daughters were already married, the father had the right to dissolve such a marriage and adopt another heir to marry one of them. If the father made no special stipulation, then the property would go automatically to the nearest male relatives who were able to marry the daughters, or to the daughters' sons if such existed.

Diocles, being their half-brother on the mother's side, was out of the running; for by Athenian law, marriages between half-brothers and half-sisters on the father's side were allowed, but not between half-brothers and half-sisters on the mother's side. However, Diocles appears to have constituted himself the heir, his half-sisters being already married; and to have ousted the true claimants.

The plot by which he got rid of the husband of the eldest half-sister is not clear. Probably he managed to keep the husband a prisoner in such a way that he failed to fulfil some obligation to the State, such as paying a debt or presenting himself for military service when called up, and so lost his Athenian citizenship.

The husband of the second half-sister was still more dangerous, as this couple had a son, who was therefore the rightful heir to the grand-father's estate. So Diocles caused this husband to be murdered, got rid of the only witness—the slave who had done the deed—and apparently fastening the guilt of the murder on the wife, obtained legal guardianship of the son, whom he was then able to cheat of the best part of the estate. So at any rate it is alleged by the defendant.

The third half-sister is not mentioned further. Perhaps she was Ciron's wife; or she may have been an unmarried sister, for whom no provision by means of a dowry had been made. If so, Diocles could not marry her without incurring a charge of incest, but he could prevent her from marrying, and so from raising up heirs, by robbing her of her dowry.

He had thus, according to the defendant, acquired wealth, and lived in considerable style. At the outset of the speech, he is mentioned as the real power behind the scenes; and it is a conviction against him for adultery with which the speech closes. It is suggested that he wormed his way into the old man's confidence and obtained control of his property before his death; and after his death, he was cunning enough to prevent the rightful heirs from taking a full part in the funeral rites, without openly showing them what he was doing and so provoking their opposition. Allowing for all exaggeration on the defendant's part, it is notable that Diocles did rely, among other things, on the patently inadmissible argument that the nephew had a better claim than the grandsons through the female line; and therefore he must have had a weak case. It was fairly easy to allege illegitimacy, for although careful records were kept, it could often be suggested that names had been inserted by an official who had been bribed.

The commonest way of challenging legitimacy was by alleging that one of the parents was not of pure Athenian birth, for by the law of Pericles, only the children of Athenian parents on both sides were eligible for Athenian citizenship, or in the case of women, could convey it to their sons. This law apparently fell into disuse during the Peloponnesian War, which lasted from 431 to 405 B.C. After the War, in 403 B.C., the magistracy of Eucleides, a law was passed reaffirming that of Pericles. It was not retrospective, and therefore did not affect men who had married foreign wives during the War; but it was intended to guard the purity of the race once the War was ended; and children born after that date had to be of pure Athenian parentage to claim legitimacy.

This case contains another example of a challenge to be allowed to examine slaves under torture. The request was refused, and this gives occasion for the usual claim that such a refusal implies a mistrust in one's opponent's case. The general claim that evidence of slaves under torture is dependable is here put forward with amazing exaggeration, the orator going so far as to say that no slave examined under torture has ever been proved to have spoken what is untrue, and that the evidence of slaves under torture is preferred to that of free men, as being the most accurate obtainable. This was not the unanimous view, as we see from the variety of pleas put forward on this topic, nor perhaps the view of Isaeus, but merely what it suited him to maintain in this case.

An interesting passage for comparison occurs in a speech of Antiphon, *On the Death of the Choir-Boy*. In this case, the deceased boy was training for a festival choir, and was given a drink by the choir-master to improve his voice; but instead, he died. The choir-master was prosecuted by the brother of the deceased, on a charge of unintentional homicide, and tried before the Court of the Areopagus. The defendant, as part of his defence, offered his slaves for examination, and the offer was rejected. He says:

"I urged my accuser to take with him as many witnesses as he liked, and visit those who had been present when the boy took the poisonous draught. I named the latter individually to him, and told him to question and examine them, the free men as befits free men, who would tell the truth for their own sake and for the sake of justice, the slaves if they seemed to him to be telling the truth in answer to questions. If not, I was prepared to hand over all my own slaves to be tortured, and if he wished to examine anyone else's slaves, I agreed to get the consent of the master and hand them over to him to torture in any way he pleased."

This attitude—that free men are more likely to tell the truth without compulsion, and that therefore a slave, not having a natural sense of right, will yield better results under torture—is probably more representative of the perverse logic on this subject current in ancient Athens than the uncompromising declaration of Isaeus. Still, Isaeus could not have said this to a jury-court if it had been an unpopular point of view. Incidentally, we learn from the passage quoted above that slaves belonging to persons other than those concerned in the case could be tortured if their evidence was of any value to either side, and if the master's consent could be gained, doubtless in return for a money-compensation.

To turn to something pleasanter, there are several pictures of Athenians on holiday, enjoying festivals in the home and out of it. The Dionysian festival to which Ciron used to take the children was a winter celebration held in the country; it took place in December, when the new wine was broached. There were rustic sports such as dancing on wineskins which were blown up and greased; and there were performances of plays. Ciron lived in the city; but he made the expedition into the country each year, to his estate in Phlya.

The Thesmophoria, at which Ciron's daughter was chosen to act as joint president, was a religious festival celebrated by women only, in honour of Demeter (see also Chapter IV). The ceremonies varied in different cities. At Athens they consisted of a preparatory day or two in which the women underwent purification and refrained from any "unclean" behaviour such as sexual intercourse; then a procession from Athens to Demeter's holy temple at Eleusis, fourteen miles away; then a night service, followed by a day of mourning and fasting; a return procession to Athens; and finally a day of jollity and fun. At the beginning, each village appointed two married women to superintend the ceremonies; and their husbands who had received a dowry amounting to three talents (£600) had to pay the expenses for that village. The speaker's mother had received a dowry (on her second marriage) of only one-third that amount; nevertheless, she was chosen, doubtless because there was no one whose husband was wealthier; and he would have to contribute his share.

Most interesting of all is the account of what happened at the funeral. According to Athenian belief, it was highly important that the next of kin should perform the funeral rites: otherwise the dead man's spirit would be offended, and would seek vengeance. These funeral rites continued after the body was buried, at regular intervals—the speaker mentions the ninth-day sacrifices, and there were occasions throughout the year when the ghosts of the dead were a special care to the State and to families. In the present case, each party was anxious to have the body and perform the burial rites in order to substantiate his claim to the heritage. No incongruity was felt, apparently, between the outward show of respect and the scene at the grave when once the body was buried: the speaker addressed the assembled relatives on his claim, and was surprised that his rival did not reply! This cannot have been as shocking to Athenian opinion as it would be to us, otherwise the speaker would not have mentioned it so casually.

The defendant seems to have a strong case, provided that his claim to legitimacy is as sound as he maintains. It is probable that he was successful, and that the speech was preserved as an outstanding example of Isaeus's skill. It seems that he was planning further litigation, against Diocles,—doubtless in connection with the estate of Ciron, alleging that Diocles had appropriated goods that were not his when he was in possession. But no record of this has survived.

# XIV

## *DEFENCE OF A STATE PENSION*

Speech for the defendant, written by LYSIAS. Date: after 403 B.C.

The defendant in this suit is one of the unfit, who were in receipt of a small State pension—one obol (about eightpence) a day. The pension-lists were scrutinized annually, and it was then open to any citizen to lodge an objection against any person on the list. The objector stated his case for the deletion of the name, and the pensioner stated his case for its retention.

The case came before the Council of Five Hundred.

The prosecutor has attacked the defendant's right to a pension on the ground that he is not actually unfit, and that he is a skilled craftsman who can maintain himself without State aid. He has also attacked the defendant's character.

There is no Narrative, as the case is concerned with the defendant's fitness to receive the pension, not with any event or events. In a brief Proem he alleges that the prosecutor's motive is jealousy, and then plunges directly into his arguments.

·  ·  ·  ·  ·

THE PROEM

I FEEL something not far removed from gratitude, gentlemen, towards my accuser, for having got up this case against me. Previously I never had any excuse for giving an account of my life, but now through him I have got one. I shall try to show you in my speech that this man is lying, and that I have always up to this day lived in a manner more deserving of praise than jealousy. I say jealousy because I can see no other reason why he should have brought this anxiety upon me, except that of jealousy. But when a man is jealous of someone whom all others pity, of what villainy, do you suppose, is he not capable?

. He surely does not hope to get money out of me by bringing these false charges? And if he says I am an enemy on whom he is seeking vengeance, he lies: owing to his villainous character, I have avoided all contact with him as enemy or friend. So, gentlemen, it now becomes clear that he is jealous, because in spite of my affliction I am a better citizen than he is. And it is true, gentlemen, that I think one ought to remedy bodily afflictions with habits of mind. If I bring my mental condition down to the level of my physical state and so conduct the rest of my life, in what way shall I be different from my accuser?

However, let that be enough on this subject. I will come to the point at issue, and speak as briefly as I can.

### ARGUMENT

My accuser says that I am not entitled to receive the gratuity from the State, because I am an able-bodied man and not of the class of unfit, and because I have a skilled trade by which I can live without this contribution.

The proof he adduces of my physical soundness is that I ride on horseback; and the proof of the large income I derive from my work, that I am able to mix with men who have money to spend. Now as for my affluence derived from my work, and the rest of my way of life, I imagine that all of you are familiar with it; still, I shall speak of it briefly.

My father left me nothing, and it is now just over two years since I ceased to maintain my mother, on her death. I have, so far, no children who will look after me. As for my work, I have a skilled trade, but it is of little help, seeing that I myself can now practise it only with difficulty, and that so far I am not able to get hold of a man who will take it over for me. I have no other source of income than this pension; and if you deprive me of it, I shall in all probability be reduced to the direst straits.

Do not, therefore, gentlemen, when you can save me with justice, ruin me with injustice! You granted me my pension when I was younger and stronger; do not take it away now that I am older and feebler! You have always before now had a reputation for extreme compassion even towards those who are not in any distress; do not now let this man persuade you to deal harshly with those who are objects of pity even to their enemies! Do not, by hardening your hearts to do me a wrong, inflict despondency on all who are in the same position as I am!

It certainly would be an anomaly, gentlemen: when my affliction was single, it is seen that I was receiving this money;

but now, when old age, sickness and all the ills that come in their train are added to me, my pension is to be taken away!

I imagine that the depth of my poverty could be demonstrated most clearly by no one but my accuser. If I were chosen for the State service of producing a play at the festival of tragic drama, and I challenged him to an exchange of property, he would choose to undertake the production of the play ten times rather than make the exchange once. Surely, then, it is disgraceful that he should today be accusing me of such great affluence that I can associate on equal terms with the richest men, whereas if something like what I have just mentioned were to happen, he would do as I say? What could be more wicked?

As for my riding on horseback, which this man has the effrontery to mention before you—for he had no fear of fortune's reversals, and no respect for you—I can deal with that quite briefly. I imagine, gentlemen of the Council, that all those who have any affliction like mine seek for some alleviation, and study how to deal with their misfortune in such a way as to make it least painful to them. I am one of these. Since it is my lot to be thus afflicted, I have discovered in riding a means of alleviating the discomforts of my longer journeys. The greatest proof, gentlemen, that it is because of my ailment and not through disrespect that I ride on horseback, is easy to convey to you : if I possessed wealth, I should ride on a saddle-mule—I should not be mounting borrowed nags. As it is, since I cannot rise to anything so grand, I am often obliged to make use of borrowed horses. And yet, gentlemen of the Council, is it not absurd that this same man, if he saw me riding on a saddle-mule, would hold his tongue—for what could he say?—and yet should try to convince you that because I ride on horses begged from others, I am not therefore unfit? He does not, because I use two sticks whereas others use only one, denounce this practice also as being that of the hale and hearty; yet he wishes to make use of the fact that I ride on horseback, as evidence of my belonging to that class, whereas I use both for exactly the same reason.

So far does his lack of decency surpass that of all other mortals, that he, one man, is trying to convince you who are so many, that *I* am not one of the unfit. But if he succeeds in convincing any of you, gentlemen, what is there to prevent me from being chosen as one of the magistrates? What is there to prevent you from not only taking away my pension on the ground that I am in good health, but proceeding unanimously to vote it to *him* as being disabled? It is surely not possible that *you* should cancel a man's pension on the ground of his physical fitness, and that the same man should be debarred from standing as a candidate for the magistracies, on the ground of his physical disability!

But you do not take the same view as the prosecutor; and he will alter his views if he is wise. *He* has come here to dispute about my complaint as if it were the hand of an heiress, and he is trying to convince you that I am not such as you all see me. But you, like sensible men, must trust, not to his words, but to your own eyes.

He says further that I am violent, insolent, and of an excessively licentious disposition—as if by calling me hard names he was bound to be speaking the truth, but not if he applied mild terms— as if his object in speaking like this were to avoid falsehood. But I imagine, gentlemen, you are bound to distinguish between persons for whom it is possible to behave with arrogance, and those for whom it is impossible. Arrogant behaviour is certainly not *probable* in those who are poor and in greatly straitened circumstances, but rather in those whose possessions far exceed their needs. Nor is it possible in those who are physically disabled, but in those who have complete confidence in their strength; nor in those who are already advanced in years, but in those who are still young and who have equally youthful minds. The rich can use their wealth to buy off any danger that threatens them; the poor are compelled by their ever-present necessity to exercise moderation. The young expect to be excused by their elders; but the latter when they commit an offence meet with reprobation alike from young and old. The strong have it in their power, even when they themselves are in no way ill-treated, to browbeat whomever they wish; the delicate are unable to defend themselves against the aggressor when they are ill-treated, or, if they wish to inflict injury, to get the better of their victim. Thus it seems to me that my accuser, in speaking of my violent conduct, cannot be serious. He must be joking, and his object must be, not to convince you that I am as he says, but to make me into a comic character—as if that were a clever idea!

He further states that I am visited by large numbers of persons of bad character, who spend their own money, and plot against those who wish to save theirs. I ask all of you to reflect that in making such a statement he is no more accusing me than he is accusing every other man who plies a trade. His words apply no less to those who call upon every other tradesman than to those who call on me. Every one of you is in the habit of visiting, say, the perfumier, or the barber, or the cobbler, and so on. The greatest number go to those who have set up shop nearest the market-place, and the least to those who are farthest away from it. So that if any of you means to condemn the character of those who visit me, obviously he will equally be condemning those who spend time in other establishments. If he does this, then he is condemning the whole of Athens—for all of you are accustomed to call on tradespeople and pass your time somewhere or other.

However, I see no reason why I should trouble you at any greater length by a too-detailed defence against each of his statements. If I have answered the major charges, why should I seriously deal with the remaining points, which are as trivial as my accuser? I implore you, gentlemen, retain towards me the same attitude as of old: do not deprive me of the only share in my country which fate has granted me—do not let this one man persuade you to take back what you long ago, unanimously, as a public body, bestowed! It was because, gentlemen, Providence had denied us a share in the great public offices that the State decreed us this money, thinking that all fortune, good or bad, is to be shared in common by the community as a whole. Surely, then, my lot would be wretched indeed if, while debarred by my affliction from any share in the greatest and most splendid activities, I were further to be stripped, through the agency of my accuser, of that which the State granted expressly with a view to compensating those who are in this position. Let nothing, gentlemen, induce you to give such a verdict!

What have I done that I should receive such treatment at your hands? Has anyone, through me, ever been brought to the law-court and lost his means? Not a man could maintain it. Am I a meddler, reckless, a stirrer-up of quarrels? My resources in life are not such that I can have recourse to these pursuits. Am I bullying and violent? Not even my accuser could say so, unless he wished to add this lie to all the others. Did I, during the rule of the Thirty, climb into a position of power and ill-treat numbers of my fellow-citizens? No, I accompanied the democrats and went into exile with you to Chalcis on the Euripus. I could have lived on unharmed under their *régime*, but I preferred to take the risk along with all of you.

EPILOGUE

Do not, therefore, gentlemen of the Council, when I have done no wrong, mete out to me the same treatment that you do to those who are loaded with crimes ! Pass on me the same verdict as you did at all your other sessions, bearing in mind that I am not here as the administrator of public funds, to render account of my office ; nor as the holder of any magistracy, to submit to an examination of my tenure. No, I am here to defend my pittance merely. Thus, gentlemen, you will all show your recognition of justice. I, in return for your bounty, shall be filled with gratitude ; and my accuser here will have learnt his lesson for the future : not to attack the weak, but to win his victories over those who are a match for him.

     .     .     .     .     .

This speech is a masterpiece of dramatic characterisation. The litigant, in defence of his daily eightpence, is equipped by Lysias with a kind of querulous sarcasm which must have exactly fitted him. The sarcasm rises to its height in his remarks about his horse-riding, but there are many shrewd hits, such as that the accuser is a rival for the complaint which incapacitates him, as if it were the hand of an heiress. But the purpose of the defence is never forgotten. The picture of the defendant as poor, crippled, and getting on in years is steadily built up, and the jury is made to grasp that the loss of the pension, a small thing to the State, is life and death to him.

We are not told what was his trade, but only that he plied it near the market-place. He had, or could have, plenty of customers, though he was hampered by lack of help, that is, he could not afford to buy a slave to assist him. His trade was the customary legacy of father to son, if he could not leave him money: by a law of Solon, it was obligatory on a father to have his son taught a trade, and the son in return had to maintain his parents in their old age. The latter duty was remitted if the father failed to do his duty by the son. In this instance, both sides of the bargain had been fulfilled.

His affliction, too, is not described, except that it obliged him to walk with two sticks, or, on longer journeys, to ride. It cannot have been acquired in military service, or he would have said so. Probably this information was superfluous, as all the jury-members knew him well. When younger, he had been one of those who left Athens on the seizure of the government by the cabal of thirty, and returned when that government was overthrown and democracy restored; but otherwise he had been debarred from public life; and we learn from this speech that physical debility or unfitness debarred one from standing for any of the higher magistracies, which were otherwise open to all citizens, rich and poor.

The barber, the perfumier and the cobbler played a great part in the life of all Athenians: shoes, laundry and hair-cutting are mentioned in the speech against the fraudulent guardian (Chapter XI) as a heavy item in the expenses even of children. The Athenians walked a great deal about the streets of the city, and seem to have worn out many shoes: Socrates in his conversations often uses the cobbler's trade to illustrate a point in the argument. Athenians were also exceedingly fond of perfume, so much so that this tendency was deplored among the more ascetic, who favoured Spartan austerity. There was an oriental streak in the Athenian blood and character—shown also in their treatment of women—which made them tend towards luxury. The lawgiver Solon is said to have enacted a law prohibiting men from engaging in the manufacture of perfume. It was offered to guests at dinner-parties as part of the service; and Socrates is depicted by his biographer Xenophon as refusing perfume at a dinner, with the remark that scent is for women, oil for men (that is, the oil used to rub down the body in training for gymnastic exercises). The barber's shop was visited daily by those who could afford it, for attention to the hair and beard; it was a favourite *rendezvous* and centre for gossip, as we shall see in the next speech, against Pancleon (Chapter XV).

The prosecutor had evidently suggested that the defendant's shop or booth was a resort of shady characters. His spirited retort that this applies to any shop in Athens if it is near the centre of business is in Lysias's best vein. So too is the rather cynical passage arguing that licentious behaviour is a privilege reserved to the wealthy, young and strong.

This speech was evidently a favourite at the time, otherwise it would not have been preserved, as it concerns such a trifling matter. It is difficult to believe that it was not successful.

---

*A*

*TRIAL*

*CONCERNING*

*CIVIL*

*STATUS*

---

# XV

## A CLAIM TO CITIZEN RIGHTS : AGAINST PANCLEON

Speech written for the respondent, by LYSIAS. Date unknown: some time between 403 and 387 B.C.

The speaker, wishing to bring a charge against a man named Pancleon for some unspecified offence, and believing him to be a resident alien, summoned him before the appropriate magistrate (the Archon Polemarchus).

Pancleon put in a special plea alleging that he was a native of Plataea, a town whose inhabitants enjoyed citizen rights at Athens; and that he was therefore entitled to be tried by an ordinary jury-court.

The speaker now undertakes, before a jury, to disprove Pancleon's plea, as a preliminary to proceeding against him with the original charge.

.    .    .    .    .

### THE PROEM

To speak at length, members of the jury, on the present matter is beyond my power, and also seems to me unnecessary. I shall try to prove to you that the indictment which I brought against Pancleon was in the correct form, since he is not a native of Plataea.

### THE NARRATIVE

As he persistently committed offences against me over a long period of time, I went to the laundry where he was employed, and summoned him to appear before the Polemarch, believing him to be a resident alien.

He declared that he was a Plataean. I asked him in what district he was registered : this was on the advice of a bystander, who suggested also that I should summon him before the local group of which he should declare himself a member. He replied that his district was Deceleia. I therefore summoned him to appear also before the arbitrators of the local group in question.

Then I went to the barber's shop in the Hermae Street—this being the one patronized by the men of Deceleia—and made enquiries. I asked any Deceleans I found there whether they knew of a fellow-member called Pancleon. Not one of them said that he knew him.

I also discovered that there had been other law-suits, in some of which he was defendant, others of which he had lost, and that in these he had appeared before the Polemarch. So I too brought my indictment in the same form.

*(Witnesses from Deceleia are called in support of their testimony that they do not know Pancleon.)*

Pancleon then lodged a counter-plea against me that the summons did not apply to him. I thought it important, therefore, not to look as though I were wanting rather to persecute someone than to get redress for my injuries ; so I first approached Euthycritus, whom I knew to be the oldest of the Plataeans and thought most likely to know, and I asked him if he knew a man called Pancleon, a Plataean, son of Hipparmodorus. He answered that he knew Hipparmodorus, but that Hipparmodorus had no son at all, neither Pancleon nor any other so far as *he* was aware.

I therefore went on to ask any others whom I knew to be Plataeans. All said that they did not know the name, but that I should find out for certain if I went to the Green Cheese Market on the last day of the month, because on that day every month the Plataeans forgather there.

So I went to the Green Cheese Market on that date, and made inquiries there, if any of them knew a fellow-member of theirs called Pancleon. All said they did not—except one man who said that he knew the name, but that it was not the name of any of the citizens : he had a runaway slave named Pancleon—and he mentioned the age, which was the same as the appellant's, and the trade, which is the one in which Pancleon actually is engaged.

*(Witnesses are called in support of the above testimony.)*

A few days later, I saw this man Pancleon being dragged off by Nicomedes, who alleged that he was his master ; and I approached, wishing to find out what would be done with him. At last, when they had stopped fighting, some of the men who were with Pancleon said that he had a brother who would vindicate his claim to freedom.

Pledges were therefore given that they would produce him in the public market-place, and they then went off.

Next day, I thought that as there was this counter-plea and also the law-suit itself, I had better be present myself with witnesses, in order to find out who would substantiate his claim, and by what arguments. However, there appeared no brother to answer to the terms of the bail he had been allowed, but a woman, who alleged that he was *her* slave, and disputed his possession with Nicomedes, and refused to allow the latter to carry him off.

Well, to relate all that was said there would be a very long story; but his supporters and he himself became so truculent that although Nicomedes and also the woman were quite ready to relinquish him if anyone should vindicate his claim to freedom or should declare him to be his slave, they did none of these things, but took him forcibly away and went off.

(*Witnesses are called in support of the respondent's statements regarding the above scene.*)

## THE ARGUMENT

It is therefore easy to see that Pancleon himself does not believe even that he is a free man, much less that he is a Plataean. A man who was ready, by letting himself be abducted by force, to expose his own friends to the penalties for violence, instead of legally vindicating his title to freedom and then taking proceedings against those who had seized him—that man, anyone can see, was well aware that he was a slave, and was afraid to put forward guarantors and contend in law for his own person.

That he is far from being a Plataean, therefore, you can judge pretty well, I imagine, from the preceding statements. But that even he himself, who best knows his own business, did not expect you to believe that he was a Plataean, you can easily learn from his actions. In the suit brought against him by Aristodicus here present, he put in a counter-deposition maintaining that the proceedings against him did not come under the jurisdiction of the Polemarchus; and he was then, on the evidence, adjudged not to be a Plataean. He denounced the witness, but did not carry the matter through, and allowed Aristodicus to get a verdict against him. When he failed to pay the damages on the given date, he settled the case on the best terms he could arrange.

175

I will bring witnesses to the truth of this. (*To the Clerk.*) Please stop the water-clock.

(*Witnesses in support of the statements regarding the law-suit with Aristodicus are brought forward.*)

However, before making this agreement with Aristodicus, he was so much afraid of him that he left Athens and lived as an alien in Thebes. But you know, I am sure, that if he had been a Plataean, Thebes was the last place he was likely to have chosen to live in as an alien. But the fact is, he did live there for a long time. I shall bring witnesses to prove it.

(*Witnesses are called in support of the respondent's statement regarding the law-suit with Aristodicus.*)

THE EPILOGUE

What I have said is enough, I think, gentlemen of the jury.

If you will run over it in your minds, I know that you will vote in accordance with justice and truth, which is all I ask of you.

.      .      .      .      .

This little narrative, small as is its scope, is none the less a masterpiece. There is no passage in Athenian literature which gives more concretely the sensation of actually walking about the streets of the city, in and out of shops and markets, and conversing with other citizens.

As the " I " of the story is merely responding to a counter-plea, no appeal to feelings is necessary. It would be Pancleon's part to try to arouse the sympathy of the jury in his favour, and complain of persecution. The respondent here merely has to sound like an honest man relating plain facts, and this he does. He is also made to show indirectly that he took pains to arrive at the correct procedure. Throughout his speech, the impression is made by subtle hints that those who threatened Pancleon's liberty are exceedingly reasonable, ready to let him go at once if he could substantiate his claim, whereas Pancleon and his friends had recourse to violence and are not willing to submit to the ruling of the law.

Plataea, in the neighbouring territory of Boeotia, had been a friend and ally of Athens. A thousand of her men fought with Athens against Persia at the battle of Marathon in 490 B.C., when the rest of Greece held aloof. Thebes, the chief city of Boeotia, was as hostile to Athens as Plataea was friendly, and this hostility included Plataea. In the year

427 B.C., the Thebans, helped by the Spartans, took Plataea and utterly destroyed it, the Athenians failing to send adequate assistance. Hence the remark that Thebes was the last place in which Pancleon would have chosen to live if he had been a Plataean.

Plataea rose again; but it was again destroyed by the Thebans, in 372 B.C., after Lysias's day. It was restored by Philip of Macedon again in 338 B.C. After the first destruction in 427 B.C., the Athenians always had a tender conscience about the Plataeans—hence the popularity of the plea of Plataean blood. The story of the part played by Plataea in the cause of Greek freedom, and of their acts of friendship towards Athens which earned them the grant of citizenship, are told by the second speaker in the case against Neaera (Chapter XVII). It appears that in Lysias's day they were the chief vendors of fresh cheese, and used to call on retailers in the market-place on the last day of the month for the settlement of their accounts. The boy who was the cause of the quarrel described in Chapter VIII also came from Plataea.

It is odd that the speaker in the present suit did not consult some official source such as the district register, when combating Pancleon's claim. He seems to have relied solely upon hearsay, although a bystander suggested an action before Pancleon's alleged local group, or tribe as it was called. Every person registered as a citizen on the local rolls automatically became a member of one of the ten Attic "tribes", membership of which entitled one to all citizen privileges. Confusion sometimes occurred in local registers, and even corruption: a bribe could sometimes secure inclusion. It may be that the registers of Deceleia were particularly unreliable, as this place was occupied by the Spartans during the latter half of the Peloponnesian War (431 to 405 B.C.) Perhaps, therefore, it was a favourite device of those claiming Athenian citizenship to say that they belonged to Deceleia.

In Athens at this time it was a common occurrence for a slave to try to run away. In one of Plato's dialogues (*Protagoras*) a speaker mentions casually that he got home late the previous evening, as he had to go in pursuit of an escaped slave; he does not bother to say whether the chase was successful—it was part of the business of the day.

The barber's shop was the place to go for news and information. Each barber evidently had, then as now, his regular daily *clientèle*.

It will be noticed that the State made no provision for arrest and bail; these were private transactions. This led to abuses, such as the wrongful detention complained of in the previous speech; but each man involved took care always to provide himself with witnesses, and even, as here, with a bodyguard of supporters. There was no police-force; hence the bystanders took a lively interest.

---

*A*

*TRIAL*

*CONCERNING*

*SACRILEGE*

---

# XVI

## DEFENCE OF A FARMER: ON THE SACRED OLIVE-TREE

Speech for the defence, by Lysias.   Date about 395 B.C.

This case came before the Court of the Areopagus, under the presidency of the King-Archon, as it was ostensibly concerned with a religious matter.

The defendant was accused by one Nicomachus of the destruction of a sacred olive-tree on a farm belonging to him.  The sacred olives, supposed to be propagated direct from the tree originally presented by Athena, were State property, and any revenue from them was payable to the Treasury, no matter where they stood—for some of them stood on private lands.  Any injury to such a tree, or the removal even of the stump of a dead tree, was illegal.  Such a stump had to be fenced in and preserved.

There was naturally a tendency on the part of landowners and farmers to get rid of these dead stumps and work the land; but if they did so, they were liable to prosecution for sacrilege, for which the maximum penalty was exile and confiscation of property, and the minimum penalty a fine.  As the sacred olives were visited once a month by Inspectors, and once a year by Commissioners, anyone injuring them ran a serious risk of detection.

The present defendant had originally been accused of destroying a living olive-tree; but for lack of evidence the charge had been altered to one of destroying a fenced-in stump.  After explaining this, he passes on to the narrative, which takes the form of a history of the farm.

.        .        .        .        .

THE NARRATIVE

THE farm in question formerly belonged to Peisander; but after his property had been confiscated, Apollodorus of Megara received it as a gift from the State.  He farmed it for some time.  Then, shortly before the usurpation of the Thirty, Anticles bought it from him and rented it out.  I bought it from Anticles when peace was re-established.

I think, therefore, gentlemen, that it is my task to show that when I acquired the farm there was no olive on it, either ordinary or sacred. I suppose I cannot justly be punished for what happened before then, even if in the past there were vast numbers of sacred olives. If their disappearance was not due to *us*, it is not proper that we should incur risk for offences committed by others.

You are all aware that the War was responsible for many ills, amongst which was the damage inflicted on more distant property by the ravages of the enemy, and on property nearer home by the depredations of friends. Surely, therefore, I cannot justly be made to suffer, at this time of day, for misfortunes which then fell upon the city, especially as the farm, having been confiscated during the War, lay idle for more than three years. It was not strange if the sacred olives were cut down at that time, when we were unable to defend even our own. You are aware, gentlemen—those of you who take a special interest in these things—that there were many farms at that time which were thick with private and sacred olives, the majority of which are now cut down, leaving the land bare. Yet where the owners have remained the same throughout the War and during the peace, you do not demand punishment of them for the destruction inflicted by others. But if you exempt from blame those who have been farming throughout the whole period, it is surely right that those who merely bought property during the peace should go unpenalized by you.

However, gentlemen, much as I could say about the past, I judge that what I have said is sufficient. When I took over the farm, I let it, before five days had elapsed, to Callistratus during the magistracy of Pythodorus. He farmed it for two years, not having taken over either private olive or sacred olive or fenced-in stump. In the third year, Demetrius here present worked it for a year. In the fourth year, I let it to Alcias son of Antisthenes, a freedman, who has been dead these three years. In the same way, Proteas rented it in his turn.

(*To the above-mentioned*) : Come forward, please, as witnesses.
(*Previous tenants of the farm come forward in support of the defendant's statements.*)

Since his time elapsed, I have farmed it myself.

## THE ARGUMENTS

My accuser says that a fenced-in stump was cut down by me under the magistracy of Suniades. But you have heard the evidence of the previous tenants, who rented it from me for many years, that there was no stump on the farm. What clearer proof could there be that the prosecutor is lying? It is impossible, when a thing was not there before, for the next farmer to destroy it.

In the past, gentlemen, if anyone used to say that I was able and accurate, and would do nothing without reflection or carelessly, I used to get annoyed, thinking that more was being said than I deserved. But today I could wish that every one of you should hold that opinion of me, so that you can believe that if I set my hand to such deeds, I also considered what gain accrued to the destroyer—what penalty to the doer; what penalty I paid at your hands if I were caught, as well as what I gained if I escaped detection. Everybody does this sort of thing for the sake of gain, not out of lawlessness. And that is how you ought to look at it—that is how my opponents ought to build up their accusation: they ought to show what profit accrued to those who committed the crime.

Now my prosecutor cannot show either that I was obliged to take to such action through poverty; nor that the olive-stump was in the way of the vines; nor that it was near the house; nor that I was ignorant of the risk I ran of punishment by you if I attempted anything of this kind. I myself could show the great penalties accruing to myself: in the first place, I was cutting out the stump *by daylight*, as if it were not essential that no one should see—as if all Athens had to be aware of it! If the act had been merely dishonourable, possibly one or two of the passers-by would have ignored it; but as it was, I was braving, not merely moral condemnation, but liability to the greatest punishment. Surely I should have been the most wretched of men if for the rest of my life I were doomed to have in my servants no longer slaves but masters, since they shared the knowledge of such a deed—so much so that however great their delinquencies against me, it would no longer be open to me to inflict punishment, since I should have been well aware that I was in their hands: they could wreak vengeance on me, and win their own freedom by laying information against me!

Further, even supposing I took it into my head not to bother at all about the slaves, how could I have dared, when there were so many hired hands and every man was an accessory, to have destroyed the enclosed tree, when the gain was so small and there was no time-limit set for denunciation; when it was equally in the interests of all who had occupied the farm that the enclosure should be preserved, in order that, if anyone accused them, they could refer him to the man to whom they had handed it over? As it is, the previous tenants have all plainly exculpated me; and just as plainly, if they lie, they are taking on a share of the responsibility.

But suppose that I had arranged all this, even: how could I have suborned the passers-by, or the neighbours, who not only know as much of each other's business as is open to all to see, but also find out what we try to hide from the sight of everybody? Some of them are my friends, others are hostile to me and my fortunes; my accuser should have produced these as witnesses, and not merely made his reckless charges. He says that I stood by while the slaves cut out the stump, and the waggoner loaded it up and went off with the timber. (*He turns to the prosecutor.*) But, Nicomachus, it was then that you should have called the passers-by as witnesses, and revealed the deed. By so doing, you would have left me no defence. If you were acting for the good of the State, you could, by thus exposing me, have avoided the reputation of a calumniator. If it was gain you wanted, it was then that you would have reaped the most: once my deed was exposed, I would have thought that I had no other escape except to suborn you. But you did nothing of the kind. You think that you will compass my ruin by your words, and you declare in your accusation that through my influence and my money, no one is willing to give evidence on your side.

You say you saw me destroying the sacred olive. Why did you not bring up the Nine Archons or other members of the Areopagus? Then you would not have needed any further witnesses, because those who were to judge the cause would also have been convinced of your truthfulness. (*He turns back to the jury.*)

It is extremely hard on me!—If he had produced witnesses, he would have expected them to be believed; but since he has none, he thinks that this too should contribute to my disadvantage.

His conduct does not surprise me : a calumniator may lack witnesses, but he is not going to be at a loss for arguments of this kind. But you, I hope, will take a different view. You know that I have many olives on the Plain, and many burnt stumps on my other farms—stumps which, if I had wanted to do such a thing, it would have been much safer for me to cut down and destroy, and then to have worked over the ground : the number of trees made it so much the less likely that the crime would come to light. But actually I value these as highly as my other property, thinking that the danger is the same to me from both. However, I shall put forward you yourselves as witnesses of this, since you send Inspectors every month and Commissioners every year, not one of whom has ever fined me for having worked the land belonging to the sacred olives. . . .

How is it possible—unless of all men I am the most ill-disposed towards myself, that when you keep such a strict supervision, I should have attempted to destroy the olive on that very farm on which there is not a single tree, but only an enclosure for one sacred tree, according to his account ; and when a road goes round it in a circle, and neighbours live on both sides, and all is unfenced and open to view ? Who would have had the daring, in these circumstances, to attempt such a deed ?

The defendant then goes on to say that he has fulfilled all the duties proper to a man of his wealth towards the State, including Special Services such as furnishing of warships and paying for the production of plays at the dramatic festivals, as well as payment of special property-tax during the war. He goes on to state that the prosecutor refused his offer to give up his slaves for examination by torture.

REFUSAL OF DEFENDANT'S OFFER OF SLAVES

I went to him, gentlemen, accompanied by witnesses, and declared that I still have all the slaves which I possessed when I took over the farm ; and I was prepared, if anyone wished it, to hand them over to be tortured. I thought that this proof would be stronger than his arguments or my deeds. But he refused, saying that no trust was to be put in what was said by slaves.

In my opinion, however, it is incredible that slaves, who under torture bring accusations against themselves that they well know will mean death to them, should in the cause of their master, towards whom they have the greatest natural hostility, prefer to endure torture rather than get out of their immediate afflictions by denouncing him. I think, therefore, gentlemen, it is obvious that if at Nicomachus's request I had refused to hand the men over, it would have seemed as if I had a guilty conscience ; but since on my offer he refused to accept them, one must take the same view of *him*, especially as his risk was by no means equal to mine. If they had denounced me, no defence was left to me ; but if they refused to admit what he wished, he was not liable to any penalty. So that his obligation to accept the offer was far greater than mine to make it. My reason for showing such readiness was my belief that it was to my advantage that you should learn the truth about the matter, both from examination by torture, and from witnesses, and from proofs.

It is your duty to consider, gentlemen of the Court, to which story you should give credence : that supported by many witnesses, or that which no one has dared to support. Which is the more likely—that he, who runs no risk, should be lying, or that I, whose danger is so great, should have committed such a crime ? Which do you believe—that he is acting in the interests of the State, or that he has brought this charge with a view to incriminating me ? I am sure you believe that Nicomachus has brought this charge against me under persuasion from my enemies, not because he hoped to expose a wrong-doer, but because he expected to get money out of me. This type of charge is the most invidious and difficult to refute, and men are proportionately anxious to avoid it. But I, gentlemen, did not choose this course. Instead, when he accused me, I put myself in your hands, to deal with as you please. I did not come to terms with any single one of my enemies because of this trial, although they are readier to slander me than to praise themselves ; and obviously not one of them has ever attempted to do me any harm, but they send against me men who are not worthy of your credence.

I should indeed be the most unfortunate of men if I am to be driven into undeserved exile, severed from my children, and alone ; if my house is to be deserted, and my mother left in direst want; if on the most shameful charges I am to be deprived of a native land like mine, though I have fought on her behalf many a sea-fight and many a battle on land, and have been a law-abiding citizen under the democratic and oligarchic governments likewise.

## THE EPILOGUE

Well, gentlemen, I think I need say no more. I have proved to you that there was no enclosed olive-stump on the farm, and have supported this statement with witnesses and argument. This you should bear in mind when deciding on your verdict; and you should ask the prosecutor why, when he could have caught me in the act, he has brought this serious charge against me after such a long interval. He produces no witnesses, but tries to win credence by words, when it is open to him to bring home my guilt by facts; when although I offered him all my slaves, who according to him were present, he refused to take them over . . .

.    .    .    .    .

This speech has no narrative, except the bare history of the farm; the facts are interwoven with argument. But the characterisation is lively, and an interesting light is thrown on the times.

The offence, technically one of sacrilege, was really against the Treasury. At first sight it is hard to see why the stumps as well as the live olive-trees should have been protected; the reason was that farmers were thus prevented from pretending that State trees had been destroyed, and taking over the land for other uses. The necessity for monthly and yearly inspections shows that there were attempts to evade the law; the farmers found the tax burdensome, and wished to till the land, or found the olives in the way of their vines, or too near the house, and so on.

The defendant in this suit is depicted as a large landowner, with no need to cheat in small matters. He claims to have lived peaceably and to have done all his duty to the State. His shrewd remarks on the inquisitiveness of neighbours, the hostility of slaves to their masters, the motive of the accuser in bringing the charge, and the question of motive in general when fixing a crime on the guilty person: all show that Lysias in writing this speech judged his client to be a man of the world.

In this suit, the defendant claims to have offered his slaves to be tortured; it is therefore in his interest to maintain that they would be only too ready to speak and say what they knew, owing to their natural hatred of their owners, and that if they had spoken they would have told the truth. The accuser Nicomachus, who has for some reason declined the offer, has to argue the opposite: that the testimony of slaves is valueless. This shows yet another aspect of the question, and reveals once more that there were two opinions on it prevalent in Athens at this time. It also shows the miserable position of the slave, when on the one hand refusal of a challenge, and on the other hand refusal of an offer, to have the other party's slaves tortured constituted a grave suspicion. It is indeed remarkable that they ever escaped at all.

The accuser Nicomachus is much younger than the defendant: he is referred to in one place contemptuously as " too young to know about these things". It may be that he was acting under the instigation of more important persons who did not choose to come forward themselves. He seems to have a rather weak case, from the legal point of view. He alleges having seen the defendant commit the offence, but is unable to produce witnesses, he says, because they were all intimidated by the defendant. But this charge, like all accusations of sacrilege or impiety, was very difficult to meet, as the defendant says; and the usual way out was by bribery. The penalty was the heaviest possible, short of death, and meant not only exile for the accused, but complete ruin for his family. The farm in question had already been confiscated from a previous owner, possibly on the same grounds.

The defendant states that he has enemies. It is possible that these were political, since he was one of those who did not leave Athens during the brief reign of the Thirty Tyrants, and therefore did not identify himself with the democratic party, but lived on peacefully under both *régimes*.

Nothing is known of the result of this trial, nor of the fate of the anonymous defendant.

# A

# TRIAL

# CONCERNING

# MARRIAGE

# XVII

## *AN ILLEGAL UNION : AGAINST NEAERA*

Speeches for the prosecution, written by an unknown author; included among the speeches of DEMOSTHENES. Date: about 340 B.C.

There are two speakers for the prosecution. The first is a young man named Theomnestus, who introduces the case; the second is his brother-in-law and father-in-law Apollodorus, the double relationship being due to the fact that Apollodorus had married the sister of Theomnestus, and Theomnestus had then married one of the children of this marriage (his own niece). Apollodorus was a prominent Athenian citizen, son of a banker Pasion; he figures in several cases for which the speeches are preserved. At least two of these are actually by Demosthenes, though the present speeches seem to have wrongly attached themselves to his name because of their subject-matter and general outlook.

The ostensible defendant is the woman Neaera, the charge being that she lives with Stephanus, an Athenian citizen, as his wife, whereas she is an alien. The real object of attack is Stephanus himself, who has previously attacked Apollodorus in a lawsuit and earned his enmity. Neaera is present in court, but is not allowed to take part, and her case is handled by Stephanus. She must at this time have been not far short of sixty years of age. The prosecutor Apollodorus is aged about fifty-four.

The case for the prosecution consists in tracing Neaera's career from childhood. It is alleged that she was originally a slave brought to the profession of a prostitute. Her children are therefore illegitimate, derived from former irregular unions; but one of them, a daughter, has twice been given in marriage to an Athenian citizen, by Stephanus, who sponsored her as his own daughter.

The case for the defence appears to have been that Neaera lives with Stephanus not as his wife but as his mistress; and that the children are not hers, but his from a former marriage.

Neaera, if the case went against her, was liable to be sold into slavery, together with her children. Stephanus was liable to loss of citizen rights; and this was the real object of the attack. The speeches of the prosecutors, though not by Demosthenes (they were recognised as probably not his even in ancient times) are nevertheless genuine in the sense that they were written for delivery in the law-court, and not as exercises; and they are an important source of information on Athenian law and social conditions in the days immediately preceding the loss of Athenian independence.

The case, which was really concerned with the importance of the status of citizenship, came before an ordinary jury-court. It was obviously regarded as of high importance, judging from the length of time allotted to the speakers, and the careful composition of the main speech for the prosecution, that of Apollodorus.

.    .    .    .    .

## I. THE SPEECH OF THEOMNESTUS.—THE PROEM

THERE are many reasons, members of the jury, which impel me to bring this indictment against Neaera, and put my case before you. We have been deeply wronged by Stephanus, and have been brought into a most precarious position by him, both I and my father-in-law, my sister and my wife; so that I shall be playing my part in this trial not as the aggressor but by way of a reprisal. It was he who started this quarrel, though he had never been injured by us in word or deed. I wish to give you a preliminary account of the injuries he has done us, so that you will be more inclined to pardon me for defending myself. I wish to show you how we were driven into the most serious danger of exile and loss of our citizen status.

## THE NARRATIVE

When the Athenian people granted the citizenship to Pasion and his descendants on account of services to the State, one of those who agreed with the People's generous act was my father. He gave his daughter, that is, my sister, in marriage to Pasion's son Apollodorus, and she is the mother of Apollodorus's children.

Apollodorus was good to my sister and to all my family. He regarded us as really related to him and therefore entitled to share all that was his. Seeing this, I took as my own wife Apollodorus's daughter, that is, my niece.

Time passed; and the lot fell upon Apollodorus to sit as a member of the Council. He passed his entrance test, and took the customary oath.

It was at a time of crisis during war. A choice of the utmost importance lay before you : either to win a victory which would establish you as masters of Greece, so that you regained and held your own possessions with undisputed right, and finally crushed King Philip ; or to send your reinforcements too late and betray your allies, bringing about the dissolution of your army for lack of funds, which would mean the loss of your own forces and a reputation for perfidy in the eyes of the rest of Greece. Other consequences were that you would jeopardize your remaining possessions—the islands of Lemnos, Imbros, and Scyros, and the Straits.

At this juncture, you had resolved to despatch the whole of your forces to Euboea and Olynthus. Apollodorus, then acting as Councillor, framed a resolution to put before the Council, and having carried it there, brought it before the Assembly. His proposal was that the Assembly should decide whether to apply the budget surplus to military or to ceremonial purposes,—it being the law that in war-time any budget-surplus should be devoted to military expenditure. He accepted the principle that the Assembly has the right to do whatever it chooses with its own ; but he was under oath to give, as Councillor, the best possible advice to the Assembly, and you yourselves bore witness to his uprightness on that occasion, for when the voting took place, not a single man voted against the proposal to devote this money to military needs ; and even today, if ever the matter is discussed, everybody agrees that he suffered unjust treatment in return for having given the best advice.

One is justified, therefore, in feeling indignation, not against those who were misled, but against the man who misled them. What happened was that the defendant Stephanus here brought an indictment against this proposal as illegal. When he brought his case before the Court, he produced false witnesses to say that Apollodorus had owed money to the Treasury for twenty-five years. He also brought forward many other charges outside the scope of his indictment, with the result that he won his case.

Now if he thought fit to do this, I am not complaining. But when it came to a vote on the assessment of the fine, he refused our suggestion of a compromise, and put in a suggestion that the amount should be fifteen talents! (£18,000). He wanted to rob Apollodorus of his citizenship, and reduce his children, my sister and all of us to utter destitution—for Apollodorus's property did not amount to so much as three talents (£3,600), far from enabling him to pay such a huge fine. If the fine had not been paid by the ninth presidency of the Council, it was to have been doubled, and Apollodorus would have been entered as owing the Treasury thirty talents! (£36,000). When his name had thus been entered, Apollodorus's whole property would have been written off as confiscated to the State; and when it had been sold up, he himself, his wife, his children and all of us would have been reduced to beggary. Further, the other daughter would have been left unmarried—for who would ever have accepted as a wife this dowerless girl whose father was a debtor to the State, and a pauper?

Such, then, were the injuries which Stephanus was trying to bring upon all of us, though he had never suffered any wrong through us. However, I am deeply grateful to the jury that tried the case in question, for one thing at least: they did not allow Apollodorus to be despoiled, but they fined him one talent (£1,200), so that he was just able to pay, though with difficulty. But as for Stephanus, we have, with justification, tried to give him back a taste of his own medicine.

This, however, is not the only way in which Stephanus has sought our ruin. He has also tried to bring about Apollodorus's banishment. He brought a false accusation against him, to the effect that once when Apollodorus had gone to Aphidna to look for a runaway slave, he struck a woman, and that she died of the blow. He suborned a number of slaves to pretend that they were natives of Cyrene, and summoned him before the Court of the Palladion on a charge of homicide. Stephanus there conducted the prosecution, and declared on oath that Apollodorus had killed the woman with his own hand; Stephanus invoked destruction on himself, his family and his household, affirming as facts things that had never happened, things that no one had ever seen or heard of. It was proved that he was committing perjury and had brought a false charge; and he was shown up as having been bribed by two men, Cephisophon and Apollophanes, to bring about Apollodorus's banishment or disfranchisement. Hence he obtained only a small proportion of votes out of a jury of five hundred, and left the Court as a perjurer, with a criminal reputation.

## ARGUMENT

Consider for yourselves, gentlemen of the jury—weigh the probabilities among yourselves! What would have happened to me, to my wife, and to my sister, if Apollodorus had actually suffered any of the disasters contrived against him by the defendant Stephanus, either in the former or in the latter of the two trials? Think of the disgrace and the misery in which I would have been involved! I have been approached in private, and urged by all to seek requital for the wrongs we have suffered at his hands. They reproached me as the most cowardly of men, if being so closely connected with the injured persons, I failed to exact punishment on behalf of my sister, my father-in-law and my nieces, including my own wife, and refrained from bringing before you a charge against this woman who is openly flouting the gods, defying the State and despising your laws, when I can prove by a reasoned statement that she is guilty, and can put her in your power to do with as you think fit.

And so, just as Stephanus here tried to rob me of my relatives, contrary to the law and your ordinances, so too I have come before you to prove that he is living with a foreign woman as his wife, contrary to the law, and has introduced children who are aliens to his clansmen and fellow-members of his district, and that he has been giving in marriage the daughters of prostitutes as being his own, thus offending against Heaven, and depriving the people of their rightful privilege of granting citizenship to whomsoever they please. Who would try any longer to obtain this grant from the people, seeking the citizenship at a price of great expenditure and effort, if it became possible to get the same thing exactly from Stephanus, and with less expense?

## THE EPILOGUE

I have now therefore described to you the wrongs which Stephanus first inflicted on me, and which have led me to bring this indictment against him. It now remains for you to hear proof that Neaera here is a foreigner, that she lives with Stephanus, and has done many illegal acts. I therefore ask you, gentlemen of the jury—and I think my request is proper for a young man inexperienced in speaking—to allow me to call, as my supporter in this case, Apollodorus. He is older than I, he has much greater experience of the law, he has given close attention to all these matters; and further, he has been injured by the defendant Stephanus, so that no reproach can attach to him for wanting to obtain requital from the man who started the quarrel. It is also necessary for you to hear the words of truth itself revealing the exact nature of the prosecution and the defence, before you give your vote in support of religion, law, justice and your own selves.

.     .     .     .     .

*(After this introductory speech, the prosecutor Theomnestus steps down, and his supporter Apollodorus takes his place.)*

## 2. THE SPEECH OF APOLLODORUS.—THE PROEM

The wrongs inflicted on me by Stephanus, gentlemen, which have induced me to appear before you as the accuser of Neaera, have been recounted to you by Theomnestus. What I now wish to prove to you beyond all doubt is that Neaera is of foreign birth, and that she lives with Stephanus as his wife, which is illegal. First of all, therefore, the Clerk shall read you the law, in accordance with which Theomnestus framed his indictment and this trial has come up for your judgment.

*(The Clerk of the Court reads the following law)* :

If an alien shall live as husband with an Athenian woman by any plot or machination whatsoever, he shall be indicted before the Thesmothetae by any person who possesses the right. If he be convicted, he shall be sold himself, and also his property, and a third part of the proceeds shall go to the prosecutor. The same shall apply to any female alien who lives as wife with an Athenian citizen, and further the man who has lived as husband with the female alien so convicted shall pay a fine of 1,000 drachmas (£200).

You have now heard the law, gentlemen, which prohibits co-habitation as husband and wife between Athenians and aliens, and also the procreation of children, by any plot or machination whatsoever. If anyone act contrary to this law, it is provided that an indictment shall be brought before the Thesmothetae, against such persons, whether the alien offender be male or female, and if he or she be convicted, he or she is to be sold. I now wish to prove to you that this woman Neaera is an alien, by giving details from the beginning.

## THE NARRATIVE

She was one of seven little girls bought when small children by Nicareté, a freedwoman who had been the slave of Charisius of Elis, and the wife of Charisius's cook Hippias. Nicareté was a clever judge of beauty in little girls, and moreover she understood the art of rearing and training them skilfully, having made this her profession from which she drew her livelihood. She used to address them as daughters, so that she might exact the largest fee from those who wished to have dealings with them, on the ground that they were freeborn girls ; but after she had reaped her profit from the youth of each of them, one by one, she then sold the whole lot of them together, seven in all : Anteia, Stratola, Aristocleia, Metaneira, Phila, Isthmias, and the defendant Neaera.

Now who were their respective purchasers, and how they were set free by those who bought them from Nicareté, I will explain in the course of my speech, if you wish to hear, and if I have enough time. But the fact that the defendant Neaera did belong to Nicareté and worked as a prostitute open to all comers—this is the point to which I wish to return.

Lysias the professor of rhetoric was the lover of Metaneira. He decided that in addition to the other expenses he had incurred for her, he would like to get her initiated. He thought that the rest of his expenditure went to her owner, but whatever he spent on her over the festival and the initiation ceremony would be a present for the girl herself. He therefore asked Nicareté to come to the Mysteries and bring Metaneira so that she could be initiated, and he promised to instruct her himself in the Mysteries.

When they arrived, Lysias did not admit them to his house, out of respect for his own wife, who was the daughter of Brachyllus and his own niece, and for his mother, who was somewhat advanced in years and lived in the same house. Instead, he lodged them—that is, Metaneira and Nicareté—with Philostratus of Colonus, who was still a bachelor and also a friend of his. The women were accompanied by the defendant Neaera, who was already working as a prostitute, though she was not yet of the proper age.

As witness to the truth of my statements, namely that she was the slave of Nicareté and used to accompany her and was hired out to anyone willing to pay, I now call upon Philostratus himself.

(*Philostratus comes forward, and his deposition is read out, as follows*):

Philostratus son of Dionysius, of the district Colonus, gives evidence that he knows Neaera to have been the slave of Nicareté, who was also the owner of Metaneira, and that she lodged at his house when they came to Athens for the Mysteries, they being natives of Corinth; and that it was Lysias the son of Cephalus, an intimate friend of his, who brought them to his house.

On a later occasion, gentlemen, Simos the Thessalian brought Neaera here to the Great Panathenaic Festival. Nicareté also accompanied them, and they put up at the house of Ctesippus son of Glauconidas. The defendant Neaera drank and dined with them in the presence of a large company, as a courtesan would do.

I now call witnesses to the truth of these statements. (*To the Clerk.*): Please call Euphiletus son of Simon, and Aristomachus son of Critodemus.

(*Euphiletus and Aristomachus step forward in support of their deposition, which is now read out, and is as follows*):

Euphiletus son of Simon and Aristomachus son of Critodemus give evidence that they know that Simos the Thessalian came to Athens to see the Great Panathenaic Festival, and was accompanied by Nicareté and Neaera the present defendant; that they lodged at the house of Ctesippus son of Glauconidas, and that Neaera drank with them after the manner of a prostitute, in the presence of many guests and fellow-diners of Ctesippus.

After that, she worked openly at Corinth as a prostitute, and became famous. Among her lovers were Xenocleides the poet and Hipparchus the actor, who had her on hire. For the truth of these statements, I am unable to put before you the deposition of Xenocleides, because he is debarred by law from giving evidence. . . . But I now call Hipparchus himself, and I shall compel him to give evidence or else take the oath disclaiming knowledge of the facts, according to the law ; otherwise I will *subpoena* him.

*(Hipparchus comes forward reluctantly in support of his deposition, which is read aloud and is as follows)* :

Hipparchus of Athmonia gives evidence that he and Xeno-cleides hired Neaera, the defendant in this case, at Corinth, as a prostitute who could be had for a fee ; and that Neaera used to drink at Corinth with him and with Xenocleides the poet.

After that, she acquired two lovers, Timanoridas of Corinth and Eucrates of Leucas. These men found Nicaretê's charges excessive, as she expected them to pay all the daily expenses of her household ; so they paid down to Nicaretê 30 minas (£600) as the purchase-price of Neaera, and bought her outright from her mistress, according to the law of that city, to be their slave. They kept her and made use of her for as long as they wished. Then, being about to get married, they informed her that they did not wish to see the woman who had been their own mistress plying her trade in Corinth nor kept in a brothel : they would be glad to receive less money for her than they had paid, and to see her also reaping some benefit. They therefore offered to allow her, towards the price of her freedom, 1,000 drachmas (£200), that is, 500 each ; as for the 20 minas (£400) remaining, they told her to find this sum herself and repay it to them.

Neaera, on hearing these propositions from Timanoridas and Eucrates, sent messages to a number of her former lovers, asking them to come to Corinth. Among these was Phrynion, an Athenian from Paeania, the son of Demon, and the brother of Demochares, a man who was living a dissolute and extravagant life, as the older of you remember. When Phrynion arrived, she told him of the proposition made to her by Eucrates and Timanoridas, and handed him the money which she had collected from her other lovers as a contribution towards the purchase of her freedom, together with her own savings, asking him to make up the amount to the 20 minas (£400), and pay it to Eucrates and Timanoridas, so that she should be free.

Phrynion was delighted to hear this proposition of hers. He took the money which had been contributed by her other lovers, made up the deficit himself, and paid the 20 minas (£400) to Eucrates and Timanoridas as the price of her freedom and on condition that she would not practise her profession in Corinth. As a proof of these statements, I will call the man who then witnessed the transaction.

(*To the Clerk*): Please call Philagros of the suburb Melitê.

(*Philagros comes forward in support of his deposition, which is as follows*):

Philagros of Melitê bears witness that he was present at Corinth when Phrynion the brother of Demochares paid 20 minas (£400) for Neaera, the defendant in the present case, to Timanoridas of Corinth and Eucrates of Leucas; and having paid the money, he took Neaera away with him to Athens.

When they arrived here at Athens, he kept her and lived with her in a most dissolute and reckless way. He took her out to dinner with him wherever he went, where there was drinking; and whenever he made an after-dinner excursion, she always went too. He made love to her openly, anywhere and everywhere he chose, to excite the jealousy of the onlookers at his privilege. Among the many houses to which he took her on an after-dinner call was that of Chabrias of the suburb Aexone, when the latter had won a victory at Delphi with a four-horse chariot team which he had bought from the sons of Mitys the Argive, and on his return from Delphi was celebrating victory down at Colias. On that occasion, many men made love to Neaera when she was drunk and Phrynion was asleep, including even some of Chabrias's servants. In proof of this I shall produce before you the actual eye-witnesses. (*To the Clerk*): Please call Chionides and Euthetion.

(*The two witnesses named come forward in support of the deposition, which is read aloud*):

Chionides of Xypete and Euthetion of Cydathenaea bear witness that they were invited to dinner by Chabrias, when Chabrias was celebrating his victory in the chariot-race, and that he entertained them at Colias, and that they know Phrynion to have been present at this dinner with Neaera the defendant in the present case; and that they fell asleep, as did Phrynion and Neaera; and that they (the witnesses) saw various persons getting up during the night to go to Neaera, including some of the servants, domestics of Chabrias.

However, finding herself treated with the most outrageous brutality by Phrynion, instead of being loved as she had expected, or having attention paid to her wishes, she packed up the goods in his house, including all the clothes and jewellery which he had provided for her personal adornment, and taking with her two servants, Thratta and Coccalina, ran away to Megara.

This happened when Asteius was Chief Magistrate at Athens (373–2 B.C., *thirty years or more before the present trial*), during your second war against Sparta. Neaera spent two years in Megara; but her profession did not produce sufficient income to run her house, as she was extravagant, and the Megarians are mean and stingy, and there was no great foreign colony there because it was war-time, and the Megarians favoured the Spartan side, but you were in command of the seas. She could not go back to Corinth because the terms of her release by Eucrates and Timanoridas were that she should not practise her profession there.

However, peace came under the Magistracy of Phrasicleides (371–70 B.C.), after the battle of Leuctra between Sparta and Thebes (July, 371 B.C.). It was then that our opponent Stephanus visited Megara. He put up at her house, as that of a prostitute, and became her lover. She told him her whole life-story and of her ill-treatment at the hands of Phrynion, and gave him the things she had taken with her when she left Phrynion. She longed to live in Athens, but was afraid of Phrynion, because she had done him wrong and he was furious with her. She knew the violence and arrogance of his character. She therefore made the defendant Stephanus her protector, and while they were still in Megara, he talked encouragingly and filled her with hope, saying that Phrynion would be sorry for it if he laid hands on her, as he himself would take her as his wife, and would introduce the sons she already had to his clansmen as being his own, and would make citizens of them. No one on earth, he said, should do her any harm.

And so he arrived here at Athens from Megara with her and her three children, Proxenus, Ariston and a daughter, who now bears the name of Phano. He took her and the children to the little house which he owned, alongside the Whispering Hermes, between the house of Dorotheus the Eleusinian and the house of Cleinomachus, which now Spintharus has bought from him for 7 minas (£140). Thus, this place was the whole of Stephanus's property at that time—he had nothing else.

He had two reasons for bringing her here : first, that he would have a handsome mistress without expense ; second, that her profession would provide him with the necessaries of life and keep the household, for he had no other source of income, except what he picked up by occasional blackmail.

When Phrynion heard that she was in Athens and living with the defendant, he took some young men with him and went to Stephanus's house to get her. Stephanus asserted her freedom, according to law, and Phrynion thereupon summoned her before the Polemarch, under surety. In proof of this I will bring before you the Polemarch of that year.

(*To the Clerk*) : Please call Aietes of Ceiriadae.

(*The witness named comes forward in support of his deposition, which is read aloud*) :

Aietes of Ceiriadae bears witness that when he was Polemarch, Neaera the defendant in this case was summoned before him under surety by Phrynion the brother of Demochares, and that the persons who went surety for Neaera were Stephanus, Glaucetes and Aristocrates.

When she had thus been bailed out by Stephanus and was living with him, she carried on the same profession no less than before, but she exacted a larger fee from those who wished to consort with her, as having now a certain position to keep up and as being a married woman. Stephanus helped her by blackmail : if he caught any rich unknown stranger making love to her, he used to lock him up in the house as an adulterer caught with his wife, and extract a large sum of money from him—naturally, because neither Stephanus nor Neaera had anything, not even enough to meet their daily expenses, but their establishment was large. There were himself and herself to keep, and three small children—the ones she had brought with her to him—and two maids and a man-servant ; and above all, she had acquired the habit of good living, as formerly it had been others who had provided her with all necessaries. And Stephanus here was not making anything worth mentioning out of politics : he was not yet a public speaker, but just a political hireling, one of those who stand by the platform and shout, who bring indictments and lay information against people for money, who lend their names to be inscribed on other men's proposals.

That was before he came under the patronage of Callistratus of Aphidna. I will later explain to you how that happened and for what reason, when I have finished with the defendant Neaera, and have shown you that she is an alien, and has committed great offences against you and has sinned against religion. I want you to realize that he himself deserves no less a punishment than Neaera, but actually a much greater, in so far as he declares himself to be an Athenian citizen and yet has shown such a deep contempt for the laws, and for yourselves, and for religion, that he has not enough restraint even to keep quiet for shame at his misdeeds, but has brought a trumped-up charge against, among others, myself, and has caused my relative here to bring him and Neaera to trial in such a way that her true status should be examined, and his criminal character should be revealed.

To continue : Phrynion began his law-suit against Stephanus, on the grounds that Stephanus had robbed him of the defendant Neaera and made a free woman of her, and that Stephanus had received the goods of which Neaera had robbed him when she left. However, their friends brought them together and persuaded them to submit the dispute to arbitration. The arbitrator who sat on Phrynion's behalf was Satyrus of Alôpecê, the brother of Lacedaemonius, and on Stephanus's behalf, Saurias of Lampra ; they chose as umpire Diogeiton of Acharnae. These three met in the temple, and after hearing the facts from both the litigants and also from the woman herself, they gave their judgment, which was accepted by the litigants : namely, that the woman should be free and her own mistress, but that the goods which Neaera had taken from Phrynion when she left should all be returned to Phrynion, except the clothes and jewellery and maid-servants which had been bought for Neaera herself; further, that she should spend the same number of days with each of them ; but that if they agreed to any other arrangement, this same arrangement should hold good ; that the woman's upkeep should be provided by the person with whom she was living at the time; and that for the future the litigants should be friends and should bear no malice. Such was the settlement brought about by the decision of arbitrators in the case of Phrynion and Stephanus, concerning the defendant Neaera. In proof of this, the Clerk will read you the deposition.

(*To the Clerk*): Please call Satyrus of Alôpecê, Saurias of Lampra, and Diogeiton of Acharnae.

(*The witnesses named come forward in support of their deposition, which is read aloud*):

Satyrus of Alôpecê, Saurias of Lampra and Diogeiton of Acharnae testify that they were arbitrators in the case of Stephanus and Phrynion concerning Neaera, the defendant in the present case, and that they effected a settlement; that the terms of the settlement were as Apollodorus states.

(*Terms of settlement.*) The following were the terms of settlement between Phrynion and Stephanus: that each shall keep at his house and have the enjoyment of Neaera for an equal number of days per month, unless they come to some different agreement.

When the business was over, the friends of each party, those who had assisted them at the arbitration and the rest, did as I believe is usual in such cases, especially when a mistress is in dispute : they went to dine with each of them at the times when he had Neaera with him, and she dined and drank with them as mistresses do. In proof of this, please (*to the Clerk*) call as witnesses those who were their guests—Eubulus, Diopeithes and Ctêson.

(*The witnesses named come forward, and the Clerk reads their deposition*):

Eubulus, Diopeithes and Ctêson testify that after the settlement arrived at between Phrynion and Stephanus concerning Neaera, they often dined and drank with them in company with Neaera, the defendant in the present case, both when Neaera was at Stephanus's house and when she was living with Phrynion.

I have now outlined the facts about Neaera, and have supported my statements with evidence : that she was originally a slave, was twice sold, and practised the profession of a prostitute; that she ran away from Phrynion to Megara, and on her return to Athens was summoned before the Polemarch under surety. I now desire to prove to you that Stephanus himself has given evidence against her, showing that she is an alien.

The daughter of the defendant Neaera, whom she had brought as a little girl to Stephanus's house, was in those days called Strybelê, but now has the name Phano. Stephanus gave this girl in marriage, as being his own daughter, to an Athenian citizen, Phrastor, together with a dowry of 30 minas (£600). When she went to live with Phrastor, who was a hard-working man and who had got together his means by careful living, she was unable to accommodate herself to his ways, but hankered after her mother's habits and the dissolute ways of that household, being, I suppose, brought up to a similar licence. Phrastor observed that she was not well-behaved nor willing to be guided by him, and at the same time he found out for certain that she was not the daughter of Stephanus, but only of Neaera, so that he had been deceived on the first occasion when he was betrothed to her. He had understood that she was the daughter of Stephanus and not Neaera, the child of Stephanus's marriage with a free-born Athenian lady before he began to live with Neaera. Phrastor was most indignant at all this, and considering himself to have been outrageously treated and swindled, he turned the young woman out of his house after having lived with her for a year and when she was pregnant ; and he refused to return the dowry.

Stephanus began a suit against him for alimony, lodged at the Odeon, according to the law enacting that if a man divorce his wife, he shall pay back the dowry, or else be liable to pay interest on it at the rate of eighteen per cent per annum ; and that her legal guardian is entitled to bring a law-suit for alimony at the Odeon, on the wife's behalf. Phrastor also brought an indictment against Stephanus before the Thesmothetae, that Stephanus had betrothed to him, an Athenian citizen, the daughter of an alien woman, pretending that the girl was his own daughter, contrary to the following law. (*To the Clerk*) Please read it.

(*The Clerk of the Court reads out the following law*) :

If any person give in marriage an alien woman to an Athenian citizen, pretending that she is related to him, he shall be deprived of his citizen status, and his property shall be confiscated, the third part to go to the person securing the conviction. The indictment shall be brought before the Thesmothetae, by any person so entitled, as in the case of usurpations of citizenship.

The Clerk has read out to you the law followed by Phrastor when he laid an indictment against Stephanus before the Thesmothetae. Stephanus, realizing that if convicted of having sponsored the betrothal of an alien woman he ran the risk of incurring the severest penalties, came to terms with Phrastor, giving up the claim to the dowry and withdrawing the suit for alimony; and Phrastor likewise withdrew his indictment before the Thesmothetae. In proof of this, I shall call Phrastor himself before you, and shall compel him to give evidence according to the law.

(*To the Clerk*) : Please call Phrastor of the district Aegilia.

(*Phrastor, the ex-husband of Neaera's daughter Phano, comes forward reluctantly in support of his deposition, which is read aloud*) :

Phrastor of Aegilia testifies that when he discovered that Stephanus had betrothed to him the daughter of Neaera, pretending that she was his (Stephanus's) own daughter, he laid an indictment against Stephanus before the Thesmothetae according to law, and turned the woman out of his house and ceased to live with her; and as Stephanus had begun a suit for alimony at the Odeon, I came to terms with Stephanus, the agreement being that each should withdraw his suit, Stephanus his suit for alimony and I my indictment before the Thesmothetae.

Now let me put before you another piece of evidence, derived from Phrastor and the members of his clan and family, to prove that Neaera, the defendant, is a foreigner. Not long after Phrastor had repudiated Neaera's daughter, he fell ill. His condition became serious, and his life was in grave danger. He had for a long time been at variance with his relatives, and he regarded them with resentment and dislike. Besides, he was childless. Thus he was seduced during his illness by the attentions of Neaera and her daughter, who went to him while he was ill and had no one to nurse him, bringing all the things necessary for his complaint and looking after him; and you know yourselves, of course, the value of a woman's presence during illness, as nurse to a sick man. And so he was persuaded to take back the child which Neaera's daughter had borne after being turned out of Phrastor's house during her pregnancy—which happened when he found out that she was the daughter, not of Stephanus, but of Neaera, because of his resentment at the deception—to take it back and to accept it as his legitimate son. His reasoning was human and natural : he was ill and had no great hope of recovery, and so in order to prevent his relatives from getting his property, and himself from dying childless, he adopted the child as his legitimate son and took him into his house. He would never have done this if he had been well, as I shall show you by a weighty and undeniable piece of evidence.

As soon as Phrastor got up after this illness, and recovered his health and strength, he took as wife an Athenian woman according to law, namely the legitimate daughter of Satyrus of Melitê, the sister of Diphilus. This, then, is a proof for you that his acceptance of the child was not voluntary but the result of pressure : his illness, his childlessness, their nursing and his enmity towards his relatives, whom he did not wish to be his heirs if anything happened to him. But this will be shown even more clearly by the sequel.

When Phrastor during his illness presented the child, his son by Neaera's daughter, to his clansmen, and also to the Brytidae, to which family Phrastor belongs, the members of his family, knowing, doubtless, who the woman was whom Phrastor had originally taken to wife, namely Neaera's daughter, and knowing of her divorce by him, and also that it was his illness which was the cause of his consenting to take back the child, voted against the child's acceptance and refused to register him as one of themselves. Phrastor began a law-suit against them for refusing to register his son. The members of his family then challenged him before an arbitrator to swear by the sacred victims that he did verily and truly believe the child to be his son by a free Athenian woman, legally married to him. On the issue of this challenge to Phrastor by the members of his family before the arbitrator, Phrastor defaulted and did not take the required oath. In proof of this, I shall put before you as witnesses those members of the Brytid family who are here present.

(*Six members of the Brytid family come forward in support of their deposition, which is read aloud*):

Timostratus, Xanthippus, Eualces, Anytus, Euphranor and Nicippus testify that they and Phrastor are members of the family called Brytidae; and that when Phrastor demanded the admission of his son to the family, they, knowing that the child was Phrastor's son by Neaera's daughter, refused permission to Phrastor to present his son.

I thus prove to you beyond dispute that even the nearest connections of the defendant Neaera have given evidence against her that she is a foreigner, including Stephanus here who now keeps her and lives with her, and Phrastor who married her daughter : Stephanus by refusing to continue the case on behalf of this woman's daughter when he was indicted by Phrastor before the Thesmothetae and preferring to forgo the dowry, Phrastor by turning out Neaera's daughter after marrying her, when he discovered that she was not Stephanus's daughter, and by refusing to repay the dowry ; and also by his conduct later, when he had been persuaded for the aforesaid reasons to adopt the child, yet on the refusal of the members of the family to allow the presentation, he declined to take the suggested oath, preferring not to perjure himself; and when later he married a free Athenian woman according to law. All these actions offer indisputable proof that the defendant Neaera is an alien.

Now observe the covetousness and criminal character of the defendant Stephanus ; you will see from this too that Neaera is not a free-born Athenian woman. A certain Epaenetus from Andros, an old lover of Neaera's, who had spent a good deal of money on her and who used to stay at their house whenever he visited Athens on account of his affection for Neaera, was the victim of a scheme of Stephanus's. He sent for Epaenetus to join them in the country for a celebration, and then, pretending to catch him in adultery with Neaera's daughter, extorted by intimidation the sum of 30 minas (£600), accepting as sureties Aristomachus who then held office as one of the Thesmothetae, and Nausiphilus the son of the Chief Magistrate Nausinicus, and letting him go on condition that he would pay this amount. Epaenetus, when he got away and was again master of his own actions, brought an indictment against Stephanus before the Thesmothetae, alleging illegal detention, according to the law which directs that if any person illegally detain another as an adulterer, he shall be indicted before the Thesmothetae on a charge of illegal imprisonment ; and if the prosecutor win his case and be proved to have been the victim of an illegal plot, he and his sureties shall be released from their engagement; but if he be proved an adulterer, he shall be handed over by his sureties to his captor, who may in the law-court inflict on him any punishment he pleases, provided that no stabbing weapon be used, on the ground that the man who was detained was an adulterer.

Epaenetus therefore indicted Stephanus according to this law, and admitted to having had intercourse with the woman, but denied that he was an adulterer, since she was not the daughter of Stephanus but of Neaera, and that the mother knew of his relationship with her daughter. He declared that he had spent a great deal of money on both women, and that whenever he came to Athens, he kept the whole establishment. He produced the law which forbids the seizure of any man as an adulterer when he is with a woman who is of the class that are stationed in a brothel or are openly for hire, alleging that Stephanus's house was a brothel—that this was their profession and their chief source of income.

On this declaration by Epaenetus and the bringing of the indictment, Stephanus realized that he would be exposed as a brothel-keeper and blackmailer; so he referred the matter to the arbitration of the very men who were sureties, suggesting that they should be released from their engagement, and Epaenetus should withdraw his indictment. Epaenetus accepted these terms, and withdrew his suit against Stephanus. A meeting was held, with the former sureties sitting as arbitrators. Stephanus had nothing to say in his own justification, but begged Epaenetus to contribute something towards the marriage-portion of Neaera's daughter, speaking of his poverty and the woman's previous bad luck with Phrastor, resulting in the loss of the dowry, so that he could no longer get her a husband. " But you," he said, " have been her lover, so you ought to do her a good turn," and he added further persuasion, employing such language as is usual when a man in a weak position begs a favour.

The arbitrators, after hearing both sides, arranged a settlement between them, and persuaded Epaenetus to contribute 1,000 drachmas (£200) towards the marriage-portion of Neaera's daughter. In support of this, I shall call before you as witnesses the men who acted as sureties and arbitrators on that occasion.

*(The witnesses named come forward, in support of their testimony and of the document recording the terms of settlement.)*

Nausiphilus and Aristomachus testify that they acted as sureties for Epaenetus of Andros, when Stephanus alleged that he had caught Epaenetus in adultery; and that when Epaenetus got away from Stephanus and was master of his actions again, he brought an indictment against Stephanus before the Thesmothetae, alleging illegal detention; and that later, themselves being constituted arbitrators, they arranged a settlement between Epaenetus and Stephanus, the terms of which were as stated by Apollodorus (the present speaker):

*(Terms of Settlement.)* The following are the terms arranged by the arbitrators between Stephanus and Epaenetus, that the matter of the illegal detention shall be forgiven and forgotten, and that Epaenetus shall give Phano 1,000 drachmas (£200) towards her marriage-portion, since he has often had enjoyment of her; and Stephanus shall hand over Phano to Epaenetus whenever he comes to Athens and wishes to consort with her.

Thus the young woman was openly adjudged to be an alien, although Stephanus had dared to pretend to have caught a man in adultery with her.

Yet the defendants Stephanus and Neaera had reached such a pitch of impudence that they were not content with merely declaring her to be a free-born Athenian woman. They noticed that Theogenes of Cothocidae had been chosen by the lot as King-Archon, a man of good family, but poor and without business experience; so Stephanus supported him at his examination, and helped him out with his expenses. When he entered upon office, Stephanus wormed his way in, and having bought from him the office of assessor, he gave him this woman, Neaera's daughter, as wife, guaranteeing her to be his own daughter: such was his contempt for you and for the laws! So this woman Phano performed for you the secret sacrifice for the safety of the State; she looked upon mysteries which she, as an alien, had no right to behold. This was the sort of woman who entered into the holy place where no other of all the great Athenian people can enter except only the wife of the King-Archon. She administered the oath to the reverend priestesses who officiate at the sacrifices;

she went through the ceremony of the Bride of Dionysus, and carried out the ancestral religious duties of the State, fulfilling numerous sacred and mysterious functions. How can it be in accord with piety that things which the rest of the community are not allowed even to hear spoken of should actually be done by any woman chosen by chance, especially such a woman as this, and one who is guilty of such actions?

I should like to go back historically and give you a more detailed account of these matters, so that you will give more careful consideration to the penalty, and realize that you will be giving your verdict not only in defence of yourselves and the laws, but also of the service due to the gods, if you penalize sacrilege and punish the offenders. In ancient times, gentlemen, there was a hereditary monarchy in this State, and the King performed all sacrifices. The most holy and mysterious of these were performed by his wife, as was right, since she was Queen. When Theseus united this people and created a democracy, and the population increased, the people went on electing a King from among the foremost men, choosing him for excellence of character; and they passed a law that his wife must be a free-born Athenian woman and have had no intercourse with any other man than her husband: that is to say, he must marry a virgin, in order that the mysterious sacrifices for the safety of the State should be carried out according to ancestral tradition, and the customary rites be performed in a pious manner, nothing being lost or altered. They inscribed this law on a stone pillar and set it up in the temple of Dionysus in the Marshes, alongside the altar. This pillar stands there to this day, exhibiting its message in worn Attic lettering. In this way the people testified to their piety towards the god, and left it as a trust to posterity, that they required the woman who would be offered as a bride to the god and who would perform the sacred rites, to be of this character. This was why they placed it in the most ancient and most holy temple of Dionysus—so that not many people should see the inscription: for the temple is opened once a year only, on the twelfth day of the month Anthesterion (February).

Therefore, gentlemen, where holy and revered rites are concerned, rites which your ancestors cared for so nobly and magnificently, it is right that you too should show concern; it is right that those who recklessly despise your laws, and shamelessly sin against religion, should meet with chastisement, for two reasons : first, that they may suffer punishment for their crimes ; second, that other people may have a care, and may fear to offend against the gods and against the State.

I should like to call before you the sacred Herald, who attends upon the wife of the King-Archon when she administers the oath to the reverend priestesses when they are carrying their baskets at the altar, before they touch the sacred victims. This is in order that you may hear the oath and the words spoken, in so far as it is permitted to hear these, and may know how holy and ancient is the customary rite.

*(The sacred Herald comes forward, and reads the oath administered to the priestesses by the wife of the King-Archon, before they are permitted to officiate at the sacrifices.)*

### Oath of the Reverend Priestesses

I practise chastity, and am pure and undefiled of all things which bring impurity, including intercourse with man. I perform the sacrament of the wine-festival and the holy Bacchic rites according to the ancestral usage and at the appointed times.

You have now heard the oath and the ancestral usage, in so far as it is permitted to hear them ; and how the woman whom Stephanus betrothed to Theogenes the King-Archon as his own daughter performed these sacrifices and administered the oath to the reverend priestesses, when it is forbidden even to the women who look on at them to repeat these mysteries to any other person. I will now put before you evidence which has been given in secret, but which I shall show to be indisputably true.

When these ceremonies had been performed and the Nine Magistrates had gone up to the Areopagus on the appointed days, immediately the Council of the Areopagus, as always a valuable instrument to the State for preserving religion, began inquiring into the identity of Theogenes's wife, and discovered the truth, and in their concern for religion, proposed to fine Theogenes the highest sum legally in their power. They acted in secret and with restraint, for they have no absolute power to punish any Athenian as they please. A hearing was arranged, at which the Council of the Areopagus expressed indignation and proposed to fine Theogenes for having married such a woman and allowed her to perform the sacred and mysterious rites for the safety of the State. Theogenes, however, besought them with prayer and entreaty, saying that he had not known that she was the daughter of Neaera, but had been deceived by Stephanus; he had taken her legally to wife as being Stephanus's legitimate daughter, and because of his lack of practical experience and his own guileless nature had adopted Stephanus as his assessor so that he himself could carry out the duties of his office; he had thought that Stephanus was friendly towards him, and that was the reason why he had become Stephanus's son-in-law.

"To show you," he said, "that I am not lying, I will give you weighty and indisputable proof: I will divorce the woman, since she is not Stephanus's daughter but Neaera's. If I do this, let my plea be accepted by you that I was deceived. If I do not, then punish me as a criminal who has offended against the gods."

When he made this promise and entreaty, the Council of the Areopagus, pitying him because of his innocent nature, and believing him really to have been deceived by Stephanus, suspended judgment. Theogenes, having come down from the meeting of the Council, immediately turned Neaera's daughter out of his house, and dismissed Stephanus, who had deceived him, from the Board of Magistrates. Hence the members of the Council of the Areopagus remitted their action against Theogenes and dropped their indignation, pardoning him because he had been duped. In proof of this I shall call as witness Theogenes himself, and shall compel him to give evidence.

(*Theogenes is called, and comes forward in support of his deposition, exacted under compulsion, which is read aloud and is as follows*):

Theogenes testifies that when he held office as King-Archon, he married Phano as being the daughter of Stephanus; and when he discovered that he had been deceived, he divorced the woman and ceased to live with her, and dismissed Stephanus from his assessorship and refused permission to him to act any longer as his assessor.

(*To the Clerk*): Now please take the law I have here, which deals with these matters, and read it. (*To the jury*): You will see from this that it was proper for her, as a woman of such a character and such activities, not only to keep away from all these rites, from seeing, from sacrificing, from performing any of the ceremonies laid down by ancestral usage for the safety of the State : she should have been debarred from all public occasions at Athens. The law decrees that where a woman is found with an adulterer, she is forbidden to attend any of the public sacrifices, even those which the laws permit an alien woman or slave to attend for the purpose of worship and prayer. The only class of woman forbidden by law to attend the public sacrifices is the woman caught in adultery ; if she attends and breaks the law, the law allows any person who wishes to inflict upon her with impunity any punishment short of death, the right of punishment being legally granted to any chance person. The reason why the law permitted the infliction with impunity of any ill-treatment upon her except death, was to avoid any pollution or sacrilege in the temple ; it holds out for women a threat terrifying enough to deter them from unrestraint or any sort of misbehaviour, and compel them to carry out their duties at home, teaching them that if anyone misbehaves in this fashion, she will be banished not only from her husband's house but from the public places of worship. That this is so will be clear to you when you hear the law itself read out.

(*To the Clerk*) : Please take the law.

### Law on Adultery

If the husband catch the adulterer in the act, he (the husband) shall not be permitted to continue cohabitation with the wife. If he continues cohabitation, he shall be disfranchised. It shall not be lawful for the woman to be admitted to the public sacrifices, if she has been caught with an adulterer. If she gains entrance, she shall be liable to suffer any ill-treatment whatsoever, short of death, with impunity.

I now wish, gentlemen, to put before you evidence derived from the Athenian people itself, to show how much it cares about these religious ceremonies and how great is the concern for them. The Assembly of the Athenian People, the supreme ruling body in this State, which has power to do whatever it will, has counted it so noble and lofty a gift to grant anyone Athenian nationality that it has made laws for itself, in accordance with which the creation of any given person an Athenian citizen must be carried out. These are the laws which are now trampled underfoot by Stephanus the defendant and those who have contracted similar marriages. You will be the better for hearing them, and will learn how the noblest and highest gifts granted to our city's benefactors have been insulted.

First of all, there is a law enacted by the Assembly that it shall not be lawful to bestow Athenian nationality on any person except such as have earned the citizenship by meritorious conduct towards the Athenian people. Next, when the Assembly has agreed to bestow this privilege, the grant does not become valid unless, by a vote taken at the next meeting of the Assembly, more than six thousand Athenians confirm it, the ballot being secret. The law enacts that the Presidents shall place the balloting-urns in position and shall give the voting-pebbles to the people as they walk up, before the barricades are moved, so that each Athenian may come to an independent decision concerning the merits of those whom he wishes to see granted the citizenship. Next, after that, the law has established the indictment for illegality, open to any Athenian, to be brought against any person considered unworthy of the privilege. Indeed, some who have been granted the citizenship by the Assembly, which had been misled by the arguments of their sponsors, have later been the objects of an indictment for illegality, and when the case has come into court, it has been proved that the recipient was unworthy, and the jury has annulled the grant. It would be tedious to enumerate them from past history; but to quote cases you all remember, there were Peitholas the Thessalian and Apollonidas of Olynthus, who were created citizens by the Assembly and deprived of the grant by the law-court. These cases are not lost in the mists of antiquity.

Such are the excellent and cogent laws relating to the procedure of creating an Athenian citizen. There is yet another, the most authoritative of them all—such is the concern felt by the people for itself and for the gods, that the sacrifices for the safety of the State shall be performed with all reverence. The law expressly decrees that all those whom the Assembly has created citizens shall be debarred from holding office as one of the Nine Magistrates, and from holding any priesthood. To their issue, however, the Assembly grants the right to share in all such privileges, provided that the said issue are begotten in legal wedlock with a free Athenian woman. In proof of this I shall put before you weighty and unmistakable evidence; but I wish first to trace for you the origin of the law, how it came to be enacted, and to whom its provisions referred,—that it was intended to benefit honourable men who had proved themselves firm friends towards the Athenian people. All these details will show you how the people's gift, reserved for benefactors, has been trampled upon, and how great are the privileges which Stephanus and all who marry in this fashion and beget children interfere with your sole right to dispense.

### STORY OF THE AWARD OF ATHENIAN CITIZENSHIP TO THE CITIZENS OF PLATAEA

The men of Plataea, gentlemen, were the only ones of all the Greeks who came to your help at Marathon, when Datis, general to King Dareius, after leaving Eretria and conquering Euboea, landed on the coast with a huge force and was about to ravage the country. Even today there exists a memorial to their valour: the picture in the Painted Portico. Here they are represented as figures wearing the Boeotian cap, each man hastening to your aid with all possible speed. Then again, when Xerxes invaded Greece, the Thebans went over to the Persians, but the men of Plataea refused to desert from your side. They alone of all the Boeotians assisted, and half of them, posted in the Pass of Thermopylae with Leonidas and the Spartans, withstood the barbarian onset and perished there; the rest helped to man your warships, as they had no vessels of their own, and fought in the naval battles at Artemisium and Salamis. In the final battle at Plataea against Mardonius the Persian king's general, they fought side by side with you and with those who were helping to free Hellas, thus bestowing the prize of liberty to be shared by all the rest of Greece. Again, when Pausanias King of Sparta attempted to insult you and was not content with the leadership granted to the Spartans by the rest of the Greeks, this city was in reality the leader of Greek freedom, but would not oppose Spartan ambition, in order to avoid the envy of the allies. This caused Pausanias King of Sparta to be so puffed up with vanity that on the tripod set up at Delphi as a joint offering—the pick of the Spartan booty—to Apollo from all the Greeks who had fought at Plataea and Salamis, he caused the following couplet to be inscribed:

He who led the host of Hellas, and destroyed the Persian host,
Pausanias to Apollo this memorial dedicates,

as if he were solely responsible for the victory and the offering,
and it were not the joint work of the allies. The Greeks were
indignant; and the Plataeans instituted proceedings against the
Spartans before the Court of the Amphictyonic League, suing on
behalf of the allies for damages of a thousand talents (£1,200,000).
They compelled the Spartans to erase the couplet and inscribe instead
the States that had shared in the enterprise.

The speaker continues the narrate the history of the Plataean acts
of friendship towards Athens, and the consequent award of the Athenian
citizenship. The decree concerning the grant of citizenship is read and
commented on; and the speaker proceeds to draw the moral therefrom:

### THE ARGUMENT

It would be monstrous if, when you have so excellently and
minutely defined every detail concerning the grant of citizenship
to those who are your neighbours and admittedly your greatest
benefactors, you intend so ignobly and carelessly to admit this
woman, one who has practised the profession of a prostitute in
every part of Greece, and allow her to insult the city and flout
religion with impunity, though she neither inherits Athenian
status by birth nor has been granted it by popular decision. Where
has she not plied her trade? Where has she not gone for daily hire?
Has she not travelled all over the Peloponnese, and in Thessaly
and Magnesia with Simos of Larissa and Eurydamas the Mede,
in Chios and over most of Ionia with Sotades of Crete, let out on
hire by Nicaretê when she was Nicaretê's slave? What do you
suppose such a woman does who belongs to different men and
accompanies anyone who pays her? Do such women not minister
to all the pleasures of their masters? And will you then vote to
admit as an Athenian woman one whose character is of this kind,
who is clearly known to all as having practised her profession
all over the world? What deed of glory will you claim to have done
when people question you? What shame and sacrilege will you
yourselves not have incurred? Before she was indicted and brought

to trial, and all had learnt who she was and what were her sins, these crimes were her own affair, though the neglect would have been chargeable to the State. Some of you were aware of them, others who had heard were indignant, but did not know what could be done with her, as no one was bringing her to trial or giving occasion for passing a verdict on her. But now that you all do know, and you have her in your power and have authority to punish her, the crime against the gods becomes yours from now on, if you fail to chastise her.

What would any one of you say if, having acquitted her, you went home to your wife, or daughter, or mother, and she asked you, " Where have you been ? " You would answer, " We have been trying a case." She will then ask, " Whose ? " and you of course will answer, " Neaera's. She was accused of living with an Athenian citizen as his wife, although she herself is an alien, and this is illegal ; she was also accused of giving her daughter, a prostitute, in marriage to Theogenes the King-Archon, so that this girl performed the secret sacrifices for the safety of the State and went through the ceremony of being given as bride to Dionysus " ; and you will enumerate the rest of the charges against Neaera, saying how well, accurately and carefully they were stated by the prosecution. Your women-folk, hearing this, will say, " Well, what did you do ? " and you will reply, " We acquitted her." Then will not the indignation of all the most decent women be excited against you, because you have judged Neaera no less deserving than themselves of a share in public life and public worship ? And the foolish women will have received a clear mandate from you to do as they like, since you and the laws have granted them impunity ; for you will have shown by your lax and easy-going attitude that you yourselves are in sympathy with this woman's way of life.

It would therefore be much better that this trial had never been held than that you should vote for acquittal, for there will then be complete liberty to prostitutes to live as wives with whom they please, and to claim as the father of their children the man they happen to be with. Your laws will lose their force, and the ways of harlots will be supreme. You should therefore also look to the interests of the women of this City-State, and see to it that the daughters of the poor are not deprived of the chance to marry. At present, even if a man is in straitened circumstances, the law

decrees a suitable marriage-endowment for his daughter, if nature
has given her looks which are at all tolerable. But if this law is
trampled upon by your acquittal of this woman, and its force is
annulled, then the profession of the prostitutes will spread to all
daughters of citizens whose poverty prevents their being given in
marriage; and the prestige of free-born women will pass to the
prostitutes, if they are granted impunity and licence to produce
children as they please, and to take part in religious worship and
the secular privileges of the State.

Each one of you must believe, therefore, that he is giving his
vote in defence of his wife, or his daughter, or his mother, or on
behalf of the State, the laws, and religion—to prevent respectable
women from acquiring the same standing as the prostitute, and
to protect those who have been reared by their families in every
propriety and with every care, and given in marriage according
to law, from having no better position than this woman, who
with every sort of licentious behaviour surrendered herself dozens
of times a day to dozens of men, whenever anyone asked her.
You must not think of me, the speaker, merely as Apollodorus,
nor of those who will speak on the side of the defence as merely
your fellow-citizens: you must regard this law-suit as being
fought by Neaera against the laws, over the actions done by her.
So that while you are considering the case for the prosecution,
you must listen to the laws themselves, by which this City-State
is governed and in accordance with which you have sworn to give
your verdict: you must ask what the laws ordain, and how my
opponents have transgressed them. But while you are hearing
the defence, bear in mind the accusation put forward by the laws
and the proof offered by the prosecution; take a look at the
woman's appearance, and ask yourselves one thing only: if she,
Neaera, has done the things of which she is accused.

It is worth your while, gentlemen, to consider the case of
Archias the Chief Priest, who was punished by you when convicted in the law-court of sacrilege and of performing sacrifices
contrary to ancient usage. Other charges against him were that
when Sinopê the courtesan brought a victim to the altar in the
courtyard at Eleusis, during the harvest festival, he sacrificed it,
though that was a day on which sacrifice was unlawful, and although
the right to perform it belonged not to him but to the priestess.
This man was of the priestly family of the Eumolpidae; his

ancestors were men of honour and he was a citizen of this State. Yet you punished him for his transgression, and neither the intercession of his family and friends availed him anything, nor the services he and his ancestors had performed for the State, nor the fact that he was Chief Priest : you nevertheless punished him for his offence. Will it not be shameful therefore if this woman Neaera, who has sinned against this same deity and against the laws—if both she and her daughter are going to escape chastisement from you ?

I wonder what on earth my opponents will say to you in their defence! Will they say that Neaera is an Athenian and has a legal right to live with Stephanus as his wife ? But the evidence has proved her to be a prostitute and the slave of Nicaretê. Will they say that he keeps her not as his wife but as his concubine ? But the presentation of Neaera's children to the clansmen of Stephanus, and the giving in marriage of. Neaera's daughter to an Athenian citizen, clearly prove that he makes her out to be his wife. Neither Stephanus nor anyone else on his behalf, I imagine, will prove that the evidence and the accusations are untrue, and show Neaera to be a free-born Athenian woman.

I hear, however, that he intends to put forward some such defence as this : that he keeps Neaera not as a wife but as a mistress, and that the children are not hers, but his by another woman, who was his wife and an Athenian, he having formerly married a kinswoman. As a counter-measure, therefore, to the impudence of the plea itself and the trickery of the defence and of those suborned by him to give evidence, I issued to him a challenge which was both fair and exact, and which would have enabled you to find out the whole truth. I challenged him to hand over for examination the maid-servants who continued in Neaera's service when she came to Stephanus from Megara, to wit, Thratta and Coccalina, and also those whom she later acquired when living with him, to wit, Xennis and Drosis. They know definitely about the children, namely Proxenus who has died, Ariston who is still alive, Antidorides the runner in the foot-races, and Phano who used to be called Strybele and who was married to Theogenes the King-Archon of the year. And if it should appear from the examination by torture that Stephanus here has married an Athenian lady and not Neaera, I was willing to withdraw from the case and proceed no further with this indictment. The state of matrimony exists when a man begets children and presents his sons to his clansmen and fellow-members of his district, and gives his daughters, as being his own, in marriage to their husbands. Mistresses we keep for pleasure, concubines for daily attendance upon our person, but wives for the procreation of legitimate children and to be our faithful housekeepers. So that if he had formerly married an Athenian lady, and these children are hers and not Neaera's, he could have proved it by the most accurate testimony : that of the maid-servants handed over for examination by torture.

In proof that I issued this challenge, the Clerk shall read you the deposition and the challenge.

(*To the Clerk*) : Please read first the deposition, then the challenge.

### Deposition

Hippocrates son of Hippocrates of Probalinthus, Demosthenes son of Demosthenes of Paeania, Diophanes son of Diophanes of Alopecê, *et ceteri*, testify that they were present in the market-place when Apollodorus challenged Stephanus, calling on him to hand over for examination by torture the maid-servants, on the matters concerning Neaera with which Apollodorus was charging Stephanus, and that Stephanus refused to hand over the maid-servants ; and that the challenge was such as Apollodorus puts forward.

(*To the Clerk*.) Please read now the challenge which I issued to the defendant Stephanus.

### Challenge

Apollodorus issues the following challenge to Stephanus on the matters connected with the indictment which he (Apollodorus) is bringing against Neaera, namely that Neaera, an alien, is living with Stephanus as his wife :

Apollodorus declares himself ready to receive the maid-servants of Neaera, whom she brought with her from Megara, to wit, Thratta and Coccalina, and also those whom she acquired later when living with Stephanus, to wit, Xennis and Drosis, as these have accurate knowledge about Neaera's children, that they are not the children of Stephanus, namely, Proxenus now deceased, Ariston still living, Antidorides the runner in the foot-races, and Phano ; that he is ready to receive these maid-servants for examination by torture. If they agree that these children are Neaera's, Neaera shall be sold into slavery and also her children, as being aliens. If they deny that these children are hers, and declare their mother to be another woman, a free-born Athenian legally married, Apollodorus offers to withdraw from his case against Neaera, and if the female slaves have suffered any damage from the torture, to pay corresponding compensation.

This was the challenge I issued to Stephanus, gentlemen of the jury; but Stephanus declined it. Do you not therefore think that Stephanus himself has already condemned Neaera, gentlemen, of the charges brought against her by me, and that I have told you the truth and supported my case with truthful evidence, whereas his story will be completely false, and his words will be condemned of utter unsoundness by his own action in refusing to hand over for examination by torture the maid-servants for whom I asked her?

### THE EPILOGUE

And so I, gentlemen of the jury, in defence of religion, which the defendants have insulted, and of myself, have brought these people into court and submitted them to your jurisdiction. You too must remember that the gods against whom they have sinned will not fail to see which way each one of you gives his vote. Vote therefore for justice, and avenge the wrongs done above all to the gods, but also to yourselves. If you do this, all will acclaim as honourable and just the verdict you have given in this case which I have brought against Neaera on the grounds that she, an alien, lives with an Athenian citizen as his wife.

·　　　·　　　·　　　·　　　·

This speech, delivered about two years before the extinction of Athenian independence at the battle of Chaeronea (338 B.C.) and the consequent ending of the distinctive Greek civilization known as "classical", is remarkable for its long and detailed narrative, and the light it throws on the Athenian attitude towards law, religion, marriage and social conditions generally. The speaker Apollodorus, who is the real prosecutor, has gone to great trouble in trying to find out the details of Neaera's career, tracing it back some fifty years or more to her childhood in Corinth, and collecting evidence from many witnesses, voluntary and otherwise. But although the narrative is so circumstantial, the argumentation is weak, and it is improbable that the case succeeded. The defendant Stephanus evidently was able to contend, and therefore to bring witnesses in support of his contention, that his actions had not been contrary to law, in that he did not claim Neaera to be his legal wife, and that the children he had given in marriage were his own by a legal marriage.

Apollodorus, an experienced litigant, states frankly that his reason for supporting the indictment is personal hostility to Stephanus and a desire for revenge. Reprisal for acts of enmity was considered normal: the accepted code was " to benefit one's friends, to injure one's enemies ". Only the best of the ethical thinkers, like Plato, said that to injure one's enemy meant injuring oneself; and to refrain from retaliation would have seemed not only foolish but cowardly to the average Athenian, one of whose strongest motives for action was that expressed by Medea in Euripides' play: " Do I wish to incur the laughter of my enemies by letting them go unpunished? " The declaration of Apollodorus would not prejudice his case at all in the eyes of the Athenian jury.

The religious festivals mentioned in the speech were the chief events of the Athenian year. The Mysteries, celebrated at Eleusis (on the coast of Attica, fourteen miles west of Athens) were secret: initiation into them was accompanied by some sort of revelation, probably about the next world. Preparation for initiation took eighteen months: the candidate had to have instruction, and to pass through two lesser ceremonies, held in February and September of the same year, and then wait a year before the final event. This began in Athens, with a purification in the form of bathing in the sea, and sacrifice. Then there was a procession from Athens to Eleusis along the Sacred Road (still so called). On arrival, the candidates fasted and carried out other exercises on the sacred site at Eleusis, including meditation on the story of Demeter and her sorrow at the loss of her daughter to Hades of the underworld. The final revelation was made in the Great Hall: its exact nature is unknown, but its effect was profound, even on well-instructed and well-disciplined minds; and the religion itself was for a time a rival to Christianity, as the strictures of early Christian writers show.

The ceremony of the " bride of Dionysus " was also a Mystery. It took place in February (Anthesterion, the month of flowers) as part of the three-days' festival in honour of Dionysus. The first day was dedicated to the Opening of the Wine-Casks, when the previous autumn's wine was broached. Early in the morning, a torch-procession went to the Potters' Quarter (Cerameicus) where was the great cemetery;

the torch-bearers escorted Dionysus, the god of wine and of the new life of spring, from outside the city through the Dipylon Gate to the ancient temple in the Inner Cerameicus where the god was to meet his bride. This part was played by the wife of the King-Archon; she as chief priestess administered the vow to the other priestesses and offered a sacrifice; then she retired to the inner sanctuary, where she spent the following night. The second day was the day of Libations, devoted to drinking and feasting, when wine was poured out to Bacchus God of Revelry, and to Hermes of the Underworld, Conductor of Souls. There was dancing and singing, a banquet in the Theatre, and great spending of money, for all wages had been paid; prizes were offered for the man who could drink off a pot of wine first at one draught. The ghosts of the dead were supposed to have left the neighbourhood of their tombs and to be visiting the houses of their relatives and taking part in the celebrations. The third day—the thirteenth of the month— was called the Day of Vessels, when the citizens took offerings of food to the cemetery for the ghosts of their ancestors. The final ceremony, presided over by the King-Archon, was an offering to the souls who had perished in the Flood: a pit was dug, and into it the King-Archon threw grain, corn and honey mixed together. Lastly, at sundown, a Herald proclaimed: "Forth from our gates, ye spirits! The Festival is ended!"

These two festivals were primarily religious, and show the great respect felt by the Athenians for the deities connected with the under-world, and for the sacred rites and ritual purity in connection with them. This speech shows that it was ceremonial correctness rather than the moral aspect which concerned the average citizen, because he felt that the safety of the State depended on not offending these deities.

The Panathenaic Festival, celebrated every four years, was concerned still more with the State than with religion: it was held with great pomp and magnificence in honour of Athena, the patron goddess of the city. Athletic and musical competitions were held, as well as a torch-race and a regatta at the Peiraeus. The main event was the great procession to the temple of Athena on the Acropolis, when the women offered to the goddess a splendidly-embroidered robe. The whole celebration was dedicated to the glory of the Athenian City-State, and was designed to impress foreigners as well as to evoke national pride in the citizens themselves.

Various legal matters of interest are touched upon. The speaker Apollodorus displays an exact knowledge of the law. The challenge to hand over slaves for examination was put to the defendants and rejected; this is used by Apollodorus in the conventional way against the defendants. The evidentiary oath—a challenge to declare on oath that certain facts are or are not true—was also declined by Stephanus, because, so the prosecution maintains, he dared not risk the charge of perjury. A witness was compelled to give evidence, or else take an oath denying knowledge of the facts, under pain of certain penalties; a number of Apollodorus's witnesses gave their evidence under this compulsion. The conduct of a private arbitration is also incidentally described, one member sitting for each of the litigants, and a third being impartial; a compromise agreement was arrived at. The Court of the Palladion is referred to as dealing with a case of unintentional homicide. The Odeon, built by Pericles for musical performances, was also used as a law-court and for other purposes of State: here it is mentioned as the Court where claims for alimony were lodged. The Painted Portico (*Stoa Poikilé*) was a favourite place of assembly in Athens; it was a colonnade, the walls of which were adorned with paintings; the celebrants of the Mysteries gathered here before their excursions, and in later times it became famous as the place where Zeno taught philosophy, thus giving its name to the Stoic School.

The entrance test to the Council here referred to involved a scrutiny of the person's character and general fitness to serve in a public office; it was intended as a safeguard when all appointments were made by lot. The "ninth Presidency of the Council" refers to the system by which the Council of Five Hundred sat, not as a whole, but in committees of fifty, the members from each of the ten Attic Tribes or local divisions sitting in turn for a tenth part of the year in an order decided by lot. The period of session of each committee was called its Presidency.

The Amphictyonic League (League of Neighbours) was a body consisting of delegates from twelve City-States of Central Greece, including Athens, who met twice a year at Thermopylae and Delphi to deal with disputes arising between members and to try to prevent aggression. By this time, however, it was a battleground for various rivalries, and in 340 B.C. it gave an opening to the aggressor Philip of Macedon, by inviting him to intervene in a dispute between two member-States. The reference here is to an episode in the past history of the League; probably the invitation to Philip had not yet occurred. This event was the direct cause of the loss of Athenian and Greek independence to the dictator-king.

The two speakers for the prosecution are entirely on the side of resistance to Philip, that is, for the policy advocated by Demosthenes. Theomnestus the first speaker describes the "time of crisis" in 349 B.C. when Philip was threatening Athenian possessions in the northern Aegean, and refers to a resolution proposed by Apollodorus that the budget surplus should be devoted to military purposes. Demosthenes at the same time was urging the Athenians to do the same with the Festival Fund, and to despatch Athenian forces to withstand the aggressor. The proposal of Apollodorus was rejected as illegal. Demosthenes himself could not persuade the Athenians to appropriate the Festival Fund for military needs until nine years later, in 340 B.C., when it was too late. Probably the speech of Theomnestus was made before Demosthenes had succeeded in this matter, otherwise he (Theomnestus) would have referred to it in his remarks on the wisdom of Apollodorus's proposal.

The connection between Apollodorus and Demosthenes is interesting. Demosthenes wrote a speech for Phormio the banker, Apollodorus's step-father, in 350 B.C., and other speeches later for Apollodorus, including one against another Stephanus, not the protector of Neaera, in 349 B.C. Demosthenes' enemies blamed him for this conduct; his political enemy-in-chief Aeschines accused Demosthenes of writing the speech for Phormio, taking money for it and then revealing the contents to Apollodorus who was fighting Phormio on another charge. Another writer (Plutarch) says that Demosthenes was justly blamed for writing speeches for Apollodorus against Phormio, Stephanus and the general Timotheus, and against Apollodorus for Phormio, exactly as though he had sold daggers out of his cutler's shop to two contestants to use against each other. All this is mere spiteful gossip.

Demosthenes was entitled to write speeches for and against the same litigant at different times and for different causes, and there is no proof that he was guilty of any breach of confidence. The speech ascribed to Demosthenes against the general Timotheus on a charge of debt is generally thought, like the present speech against Neaera, not to be his; it has been suggested that Apollodorus wrote them both himself.

Apollodorus was a powerful member of the anti-Macedonian party led by Demosthenes. In the last analysis, the real reason for the action against Neaera was not concern for morality or the purity of the race, nor for the privilege of Athenian citizenship, nor even Apollodorus's personal desire for retaliation against Stephanus, but the determination to eliminate a political opponent, a member of the pro-Macedonian party that favoured friendship with Philip. If this action succeeded, Stephanus would lose his citizen-rights, and could take no further part in public life. We do not know what happened; but we do know that two years later Philip was master of Greece, and therefore, even if Stephanus was condemned on the present charge, he must then have been restored. The days of Athenian greatness were ended, and for ever.

# *A*

# *COMPLAINT*

# *OF*

# *SLANDER*

# XVIII

## *ADDRESS TO A GATHERING OF FRIENDS*

Speech for the complainant, written by LYSIAS. Date unknown: between 400 and 380 B.C.

This speech was not written for delivery in the law-court, but before a gathering of friends, perhaps a club or society. A tale-bearer has brought to the speaker a report of unkind things that are being said of him by some of the members present, and he takes the opportunity of putting all his complaints before them as a prelude to his resignation.

.     .     .     .     .

THIS is a suitable opportunity, I think, which I have taken to put before you matters of which I have long wished to speak. There are present here the men against whom my complaint is directed; there are also present those before whom I wish to utter my reproof against the men who are wronging me. One puts more earnestness into speaking to people face to face; and though, I suppose, my detractors will not mind in the least being shown up as unfriendly to their friends—if they had, they would never have even started to offend against me—yet I should like to show the rest of you that it was they who began harming me, though I never harmed them. It is painful to be compelled to speak about these matters, but impossible to refrain from speaking, when contrary to my expectation I am badly treated and discover that those who I thought were my friends are doing me wrong.

First of all, in case any one of you, perhaps, in defence of what that person has done to offend me, may put forward an excuse for the harm done, I ask you : if any one of you has been badly treated by me whether in word or deed, let him speak up ; or if anyone has asked for and been refused anything which it was in my power to give as he suggested. (*To his opponents*) : Why, actually, do you try to injure me by word and deed ? Why do you try to run me down to these men, whom you formerly ran down to me ? You made so much mischief that one man preferred to be thought to care for my interests rather than let someone else bring me the report.

I could not tell you all that he said. I was deeply hurt by it when I heard it, and not even as part of my reproaches to you would I repeat that you said this against me. I should be absolving you from blame if I should say about myself the same things as you did. I will repeat merely those offensive things you said, thinking to make fun of me—and thereby making yourselves ridiculous instead. You said that I forced my company and conversation on you, and that, do what you would, you could not get rid of me ; and finally that I went with you in the procession to Eleusis, against your will. By these remarks you think you are blackening me— whereas you are revealing your own ill-breeding : what else is it, to wish to run a man down behind his back while treating him like a friend to his face ? You should have either not said things against me, or refrained from mixing with me, and have openly renounced your association with me. If you were ashamed to do this, why were you ashamed of my company, when you did not consider it decent to give me my *congé* ?

And yet I fail to see what reason you could have found for despising my company. I was not aware of any vast wisdom in you as contrasted with extreme ignorance in myself ; nor that you were blessed with countless friends while I was destitute of them ; nor that you were rich while I was poor ; nor that you were held in the highest esteem and I was of low repute ; nor that my position was shaky while yours was secure. How then could I suspect that you found my company such a bore ?— especially as you told it to the last people who you thought would repeat it to me. How could I suspect that you would have the bright idea of running round accusing yourselves of mixing with your inferiors of your own free will ?

You will never succeed in finding out who it was that told me. To begin with, you know the man you are going to inquire about —for I suppose you know to whom you told your story! Secondly, I should be a cad if I treated him as he treated you. His passing on the information is not on a par with your gossiping to him, for *he* passed on the remarks to my relatives as a kindness to *me*, but you told them to him with a view to doing me harm.

If I disbelieved his statements, I would have tried to test them. As it is, I do not, because this disparagement of me fits in well with what has gone before, and to me the one is a sufficient proof of the other, and *vice versa*. First there was all that I did, through your agency, about the deposit for the horse. The man brought me the horse, which was worn out with having been used in war. I wished to withdraw; but Diodorus here attempted to dissuade me, saying that Polycles would not dispute at all over the 12 minas (£240), but would pay them back. Yet although he said this at the time, later, after the horse had died, he joined the other side in a suit against me, saying that it was not right that I should get my money back.

I thought that they were arguing against me in the suit for purely intellectual reasons; but they went beyond words—they opposed me in deed. The reason why they thus worked against me was in order that Polycles might discover what my case was. This has all come out since. In the presence of the arbitrators, Polycles said in a rage that even my friends thought I was in the wrong— they had told him so. Does that not agree with the other declarations? My informant declared that you had said you could dissuade those who were intending to speak for me, and that you had already stopped some of them . . .

Now at last I understand how for a long time you were looking for an occasion, when you alleged that Thrasymachus had slandered you through me. I asked him if he had spoken ill of Diodorus on my account. He completely disclaimed my suggestion that it was on my account, declaring that nothing would induce him to slander Diodorus on *anybody's* account. Further, when I took him with me to see Diodorus, he was ready to submit to examination in what he had said. But Diodorus took all measures to prevent this. After that, Autocrates in my presence said to Thrasymachus that Euryptolemus had complained of him on the grounds that he had been slandered by him; his informant, he said, was Menophilus. Immediately Thrasymachus went with me to Menophilus— who said that he had never heard of it, and had not been Euryptolemus's informant; more than this, he had not even had a conversation with Euryptolemus for a long time.

Such were the occasions you manufactured out of the friendship of Thrasymachus and myself. Now that no such chances are left, you revile me more freely and omit nothing. I ought to have realized then that I was bound to suffer the same when you ran one another down to *me*. I have spoken to you about Polycles whom you are now supporting. Why on earth was I not on my guard against all this ? Because I was fool enough to think that I, being your friend, was immune from any hostile gossip, for the very reason that you all gossiped to me about the others : I thought that I held as a pledge from each of you his spiteful talk about the rest.

I therefore gladly withdraw from friendship with you. Really, I cannot see what I stand to lose by ceasing to associate with you. Shall I feel the loss, when I have some litigation in hand, of someone to support me with a speech, or of people who will give evidence for me ? Hardly! At the moment, instead of speaking in my support, you try to prevent the man who is going to do so, and instead of standing by me and giving evidence in a just cause, you associate with my adversaries and give evidence for them. Perhaps I shall miss you as wellwishers who are going to praise me ? Why, even now you are the only people who run me down!

Well, for my part I shall not stand in your way. I can see now what will happen to you among yourselves, since it is your custom to abuse one of your companions by word and deed. When I am no longer with you, you will turn against one another; next, you will conceive a hatred of one another, each and all, one by one. Lastly, there will be one single member left—and he will run *himself* down! I shall at least gain this much, that being now the first to sever my connection with you, I shall suffer the least from you. You abuse in speech and in act the people who have dealings with you, but to those who avoid your company, you can never do any harm.

·　　·　　·　　·　　·

This speech has difficulties and obscurities, and it is the present fashion to label it as "almost certainly not by Lysias". It has, however, at least one Lysian feature: it is in character. Certainly it is not the essence of fatuity that Jebb thought it; nor does it look like a student's exercise. The subject is not a conventional thesis, such as were set in the schools of rhetoric; it is a genuine grievance, with details and names. The writers of exercises went in for large generalities. Moreover, however trivial it may seem to a reader two thousand three hundred years later when he compares it with great speeches of historical moment, it must be remembered that the back-biting and disloyalty of friends is not trivial at the time, to the person concerned. In a narrow society like that of the wealthy young Athenian intellectuals, such an experience could be not merely galling but almost intolerable, especially for some-one as sensitive and as blind as the speaker. There is no reason why he should not have chosen to call together the members of his set, or club, and openly make his complaint and his gesture of withdrawal; there is no reason why Lysias should not have written such an address, provided that the young man paid him for his services. Whether it might not have been wiser to refrain is a matter that we cannot decide without further knowledge of the circumstances.

Actually the speech is moving, and in places forceful. The character is that of an impulsive, very proud, rather too trusting and surely very young man, who belongs to the upper class. He has plenty of money—note the high price paid for the horse—and had thought that because of his advantages of birth and position, his company was bound to be acceptable. He thought that he was being treated with confidence, whereas he was being laughed at, made use of, and betrayed. Finally, over the purchase of the horse, his cronies first led him on and then openly let him down. A " kind friend" lets him know what they are saying about him. He is deeply hurt; but he can afford to repudiate them: " I gladly withdraw from friendship with you." He prophesies for them a future of internecine strife, and the gradual dissolution of the club until one member is left, to rend himself with spiteful gossip. The humour is not unworthy of Lysias.

One little touch gives the picture of this " young intellectual " society: he thought that they were taking sides against him in a *law-suit* for purely theoretical reasons!

# XIX

## *EPILOGUE*

OUR survey of trials from the Athenian law-courts is now ended. They are a selection from many other surviving speeches; but they clearly show, as no other source of information we possess can do, what life was like in the city from which emanated the most astonishing products of the human intellect, at a time when its streets were being trodden by men like Pericles and Euripides, Socrates and Aristophanes, Aristotle and Demosthenes, and many more who have contributed to the world's heritage of art and thought. These speeches show the market-place, the shops, the interior of the home; they show men and women at work and at play, on the farm, at the religious festival; in all their relationships, in marriage and kinship, in enmity and friendship; buying and selling, mourning and rejoicing, sailing the sea, fighting in the streets, going off to the wars. They exhibit, not the great passions of the theatre, but the intense preoccupation of the ordinary man with his own affairs. These are the people who sat in the theatre and watched the tragedies of Sophocles and Euripides; this is the audience for which these supreme poets wrote. We can appreciate their genius all the better if we realize that the Athenian dramatist did not write his plays to be read by a select group of cultivated people—though doubtless his finer points were meant for them—but for a particular place and a particular occasion, and for an audience consisting of the whole adult population of the City-State—thousands of men who on other days were sitting as jurors in the law-courts, perhaps, or figuring there as litigants themselves.

Again, the trials show the working of an extremely complicated legal system, the basic principles of which were equal justice for all, trial by one's peers, and complete publicity. Only a small part of the system has been covered by the preceding trials; but nevertheless they reveal something of the nature of the rules of procedure—for instance, the summoning and examination of witnesses, the use of the evidentiary oath, regulations governing arrest, bail and imprisonment; the use of arbitration, one of the most valuable features of the system, and its worst feature, the extraction of evidence by torture from slaves; the manner of conducting cases when they came before a jury, and the general outlook of these juries themselves. This is not the place to set out the details of the system, nor to discuss more minutely its merits and demerits as an instrument of justice. The important thing is that the system existed, and with all its faults, was a tremendous advance in principle on anything known previously or elsewhere. It was designed to serve, not any particular class or interest, not even the State, but the individual citizen, whatever his status. It looked not to the caprice of a ruler or an official, but to the Law, and its working was never secret, but open to all to see, to share in and to criticize.

SOLON, founder of the Athenian legal code, wrote of his own work in the early sixth century B.C. :

> " These things I achieved by main strength, fashioning that blend of force and justice which is Law. Ordinances for noble and commoner alike I wrote, fitting a rule of jurisdiction straight and true to every man."

He wrote his views in verse, in order to instruct his fellow-countrymen on the importance of his work ; and though he was not by nature a poet, he rose to heights of eloquence in his verses on his great ideal of the Law :

> " These are the lessons which my heart bids me teach the Athenians, how lawlessness brings innumerable ills to the State, but obedience to the Law show forth all things in harmony and order, and at the same time sets shackles on the unjust. It smooths what is rough, checks greed, dims arrogance, withers the opening blooms of ruinous madness, makes straight the crooked judgment, tames the deeds of insolence, puts a stop to the work of civil dissension, and ends the wrath of bitter strife. Under its rule all things among mankind are sane and wide."

LYSIAS, speaking two centuries later on the founders of democracy, said :

" They believed that it was the way of wild beasts to be forcibly ruled by one another, but that the proper way for men was to define justice by law, to convince by reason, and to serve both by their actions; acknowledging as their master the Law, and as their teacher the voice of Reason."

ARISTOTLE, writing fifty years later, could still proudly proclaim :

" We do not accept as our ruler a man, but only the Law ; for a man rules in his own interest, and becomes a tyrant. But the Ruler must be a guardian of justice, that is, of what is fair."

When these words were written, the civilization which had produced that ideal was already ending ; but the principle that in all human relationships, and in government, Law, that is, Reason, and not passion or self-interest, must rule, did not die and is still one of the greatest gifts of Greece to mankind. It still needs to be defended, especially by democracies, for it is the first to be swept away in totalitarian *régimes*. It still needs to be preached, until its scope includes the whole world, if mankind is not to return to the jungle. To conclude with the words of PLUTARCH, a Greek living under Roman rule in the late first and early second centuries A.D. :

" Who then shall rule the Ruler ? The 'Law, King of all, both mortals and immortals ', as Pindar says : not just the laws written in books and on tablets, but the living Reason within him, which ever dwells with him and guards him and never leaves his soul bereft of its guidance."

*LIST*

*OF*

*SPEECHES*

# LIST OF SPEECHES GIVEN WHOLLY OR IN PART
# AND TRANSLATED BY DR. KATHLEEN FREEMAN